THE McGRAW-HILL INTERNATIONAL SERIES IN SOFTWARE ENGINEERING

Consulting Editor

Professor D. Ince
The Open University

Titles in this Series

Further titles in this Series are listed at the back of the book

SYSTEM REQUIREMENTS ENGINEERING

Pericles Loucopoulos
Vassilios Karakostas

McGRAW-HILL BOOK COMPANY

London · New York · St. Louis · San Francisco · Auckland
Bogotá · Caracas · Lisbon · Madrid · Mexico · Milan
Montreal · New Delhi · Panama · Paris · San Juan · São Paulo
Singapore · Sydney · Tokyo · Toronto

Published by
McGraw-Hill Book Company Europe
SHOPPENHANGERS ROAD, MAIDENHEAD, BERKSHIRE, SL6 2QL
Telephone 01628 23432
Fax 01628 770224

British Library Cataloguing in Publication Data

Loucopoulos, P.
   System Requirements Engineering. –
(McGraw-Hill International Series in
Software Engineering)
I. Title   II. Karakostas, Vassilios
III. Series
005.1

   ISBN 0-07-707843-8

Library of Congress Cataloging-in-Publication Data

Loucopoulos, P. (Pericles)
   System requirements engineering/Pericles Loucopoulos,
Vassilios Karakostas.
      p. cm. – (McGraw-Hill international series in software engineering)
   Includes bibliographical references (p.) and index.
   ISBN 0-07-707843-8
   1. Software engineering.   I. Karakostas, Vassilios
II. Title.   III. Series.
QA76.758.L68 1995
005. 1'2–dc20   94–39117
                                   CIP

McGraw-Hill

*A Division of The **McGraw·Hill** Companies*

2345BL99876

Typeset by TecSet Ltd, Wallington, Surrey
and printed and bound in Great Britain by Biddles Ltd, Guildford and King's Lynn

Printed on permanent paper in compliance with ISO Standard 9706

CONTENTS

PREFACE

While a commonly accepted concise definition of the term 'requirements engineering' is yet to be defined, it is widely agreed that

- Requirements engineering deals with activities which attempt to understand the exact needs of the users of a software intensive system and to translate such needs into precise and unambiguous statements which will subsequently be used in the development of the system.

Requirements engineering is becoming the key issue for the development of software systems that meet the expectations of their customers and users, are delivered on time, and are developed within budget.

Since the mid-1970s when requirements engineering was established as a distinct field of investigation and practice, a great deal of progress has been made in the methods, techniques, and tools used within this important phase of system development. Despite this, however, a significant gap exists in terms of theories and technology between on the one hand the activities pertaining to the specification of requirements, and on the other hand those activities concerned with the design and implementation of software systems. Today, requirements are still, in many cases, collected, analysed, and translated to system components thanks to excessive informal interaction between users and developers, trial and error, and the ingenuity of a few individuals — often with failures which are more spectacular than the success stories!

In contrast to other areas of system development, research and practice in requirements engineering are fragmented. Although there is a vast literature covering individual facets of the area, such as descriptions of tools, methods, or techniques, each contribution falls into one of two categories: either it represents a prescriptive approach to requirements, normally as part of a development method of a wider scope than just requirements, or it deals with a narrow set of issues from a particular philosophical or technological viewpoint. Furthermore, the coverage of the area tends to pay more attention to specification languages issues, while issues such as, for example, understanding organizational aspects and their influence on system requirements, or understanding requirements in terms of system properties, are virtually ignored.

This book is our response to these shortcomings. In our involvement in the field of requirements engineering as teachers, researchers, and practitioners, we have very often felt the need for a broad-based book with the aim of:

- Providing a discussion of the issues, models, techniques, and tools applicable to the field of requirements engineering within a general framework applicable to many different viewpoints.
- Covering both practical experience as well as research efforts in the area.
- Avoiding 'cookbook' solutions which so often describe the style adopted by many methods or tools.

We believe that the book that has emerged addresses all these objectives. Since the book appears in a 'software engineering' series, the discussion of the various topics in the book is influenced by the target of requirements engineering in the form of software systems. An attempt, however, is made to relate requirements for such systems to the organizational and social settings within which they are intended to operate. The book is intended to serve the needs of different audiences in a balanced way by:

- Presenting teachers and students of information systems/software engineering with material which can provide the basis for a stand-alone course on requirements engineering or as part of a more broad systems analysis/software engineering course.
- Providing practitioners and researchers with state-of-the-art material on techniques, methods, and tools for the elicitation, representation, and validation of requirements.

Despite our research involvement in the field, we have opted for a rather detached stance on the issue called best practices in software requirements engineering. Without any intention of nominating the 'best' requirements engineering method, technique, or tool, we attempted to make an uncompromising statement of facts based on the latest and most authoritative views on the subject as they appear in textbooks, journals, reports on standards, and conference proceedings, and which are of concern to the community of practitioners and researchers working in this area. We deliberately avoided including cookbook recommendations of requirements 'solutions', preferring instead an integrated treatment of the requirements *issues*, to avoid disorienting the reader with a maze of sometimes misleading, often contradicting, approaches. We believe that practitioners of such a complicated task as requirements engineering should first equip themselves with a thorough understanding of the best concepts and theories, then become exposed to a number of tools and techniques, and finally formulate their own opinion about what works and what does not in the areas they practice. Also, for those who seek to advance requirements engineering beyond the current state-of-the-art, we hope that this book gives insights into the most important and fruitful paths to the unparalleled challenge posed by software requirements.

Establishing requirements for a software-intensive system involves, among others, two intellectual activities, analysis and specification. The former requires conceptual analysis of the needs of customer and user needs, their goals and assumptions whereas the latter is concerned with descriptions of the system behaviour and constraints placed on the system and its development by its environment. These activities are carried out in a social setting involving the requirements engineer, the builder of the system, the customer who commissions the system, the user who will eventually interact with the system, and the personnel who will finally introduce the system in the enterprise.

The material in this book is presented from a system engineering perspective while recognizing that the contextual setting of requirements engineering is a social one.

The book is organized around a framework which captures the pivotal aspects of requirements engineering, i.e. processes, models, and tools that address analysis and specification issues.

Chapter 1 provides all the essential background and terminological knowledge required for the understanding of the material in succeeding chapters. Requirements engineering is viewed from different perspectives, i.e. business, software engineering, and even from an experiential perspective which describes the behaviour of requirements analysts.

Chapter 2 seeks to shed light on the confusion caused by different (and sometimes contradicting) terminology used for describing the same concepts within requirements engineering, by suggesting a framework for requirements engineering activities. The framework views requirements engineering as a combination of three concurrent interacting processes which correspond to the three major concerns of eliciting knowledge related to a problem domain, ensuring the validity of such knowledge, and specifying the problem in a formal way. The three succeeding chapters are devoted to these three topics.

In Chapter 3 the first of the requirements engineering processes, namely requirements elicitation, is examined from the perspectives of concepts methods and tools. First the conceptual foundations of elicitation as a process in its own right are established, followed by a detailed discussion of approaches to elicitation, which range from traditional systems analysis techniques such as user interviews, to the latest methods employed in disciplines such as ethnomethodology and knowledge engineering.

Chapter 4 deals with another concern of requirements engineering, namely the development of conceptual models which specify the desired behaviour of the software system and the properties that the system must exhibit. Modelling principles and techniques are introduced which ensure that all the relevant information and concerns can be captured in a conceptual model. A requirements specification is viewed as a composite of three components: enterprise requirements, functional requirements, and non-functional requirements. In this sense this chapter takes a wider and, in our opinion, a more appropriate view of requirements specifications than the traditional view of concentrating almost exclusively on functional requirements.

The threefold view of requirements engineering as elicitation, specification, and validation is completed in Chapter 5, where the process of requirements validation is covered. In a similar manner to preceding chapters, this chapter discusses the difficulties inherent in obtaining the users' agreement on what constitutes a valid description of their problem, and presents methods, techniques, and tools which attempt to overcome such difficulties. Following a discussion on the importance of validation within requirements engineering, this chapter introduces validation techniques such as prototyping, animation, and expert system approaches.

Chapter 6 focuses on the 'tools' aspect of the 'concept–method–tool' view of requirements engineering. This chapter gives a historical overview of the role of computer-aided software engineering (CASE) in requirements engineering. The multiple classifications of CASE technologies in this chapter aim to guide the reader into establishing criteria for selecting, integrating, and using CASE tools for requirements engineering.

Requirements engineering is a discipline which addresses issues within both spheres of 'business' and 'software systems' and importantly it is concerned with the relationship between the two. The need for rapid response to changing business environments, the employment of new approaches to organizational restructuring and the enabling influence of computers and communications lead us to believe that requirements engineering is an essential discipline of study and enquiry which brings systems engineering concerns closer to problems experienced in organizational settings. Requirements engineering is about addressing the problems associated with *business* goals, plans, process, etc., and *systems* to be developed or to be evolved to achieve organizational objectives.

In this book we have striven to cover in a non-prescriptive manner a range of issues of importance to requirements analysis and specification. To this end we have opted for a wide coverage of the subject concentrating on a discussion of the issues and current approaches to the problems being experienced in requirements engineering.

The book is aimed at students of undergraduate and postgraduate programmes with a substantial component of system development subject matter. The book assumes that the reader has already knowledge of system development techniques for either data-intensive or real-time systems.

ACKNOWLEDGEMENTS

We wish to express our thanks to our colleagues who worked with us in exploring the exciting field of requirements engineering. In particular we wish to thank Janis Bubenko, Matthias Jarke, John Mylopoulos, Barbara Pernici, Colette Rolland, Colin Potts, Arne Sølvberg, Alistair Sutcliffe, Linda Macaulay, and Babis Theodoulidis with whom we had many informative and stimulating discussions in project and workshop settings.

We would also like to thank Vangelio Kavakli, Vana Konsta, Nikos Loucopoulos, and Roger Smith for their help with case studies material. As always, Janet Houshmand has provided much appreciated administrative support. Finally, we would like to thank Rupert Knight and his colleagues at McGraw-Hill for their help and collaboration in the production of this book.

Pericles Loucopoulos
Vassilios Karakostas

1

INTRODUCTION

1.1 INTRODUCTION

Information systems are increasingly becoming an integral part of our everyday lives to the extent that the welfare of individuals, the competitiveness of business concerns, and the effectiveness of public institutions often depend upon the correct and efficient functioning of these systems. The success of these systems, often referred to as socio-technical systems (i.e. systems that involve computer-based components interacting with people and other technical system components in an organizational setting), depends to a large extent on their ability to meet the needs and expectations of their *customer* (i.e. the individual, group, or organization that commissions the development of the system) as well as their *user* (i.e. the individual, group, or organization that will work with the system itself). It is therefore the task of the *supplier* of the system (i.e. the system developer, or service provider) to deliver a solution that meets the expected level of functionality and ensures successful 'integration' of the technical system in the organizational setting.

It has long been established that the effectiveness and flexibility of a system are inextricably related to the correct understanding of the needs of the system's customers or users. There is a key component, therefore, of any development process, which plays a central role in this process namely the *requirements specification*. The process of developing a requirements specification has been called *requirements engineering* (Computer, 1985; TSE, 1977).

As a discipline requirements engineering is still evolving with a diversity of approaches being proposed and a lively debate going on. Therefore, it is neither possible nor appropriate to be prescriptive about *the* approach that one might adopt in developing a requirements specification. It is, however, important to discuss some of the concerns underpinning the field of requirements engineering and highlight some of the major issues

1

of current investigation and practice before proceeding with a discussion on approaches to eliciting, representing, and validating requirements.

To this end, this chapter first examines the term 'requirements' from two relevant perspectives: the organizational perspective and the software perspective. Section 1.2 briefly discusses the issue of requirements from an organizational perspective, and in particular from the need of organizations to transform their functioning by using an information system as a facilitator to such a transformation. Furthermore, understanding the organizational setting is crucial to developing a more complete understanding of requirements for information systems. Information systems and their formal descriptions exist for some reason—they serve some strategic, tactical, and operational objectives of the enterprise. Indeed the development of an information system impacts on the functioning and social organization of the enterprise itself, and therefore it is important to establish at the outset the significance that requirements have in an organizational context.

Section 1.3 considers requirements from a software engineering perspective and highlights the place of requirements in the software development lifecycle. This is the traditional view of examining requirements, assuming that the task of developing a requirements specification precedes other development activities such as design and implementation.

To complete the discussion on requirements, Section 1.4 examines the characteristics of the requirements engineering process itself. The processes involved in requirements engineering, as observed in controlled experiments and by analysis of industrial practices, are discussed in this section. This gives an insight into the nature of problems that are specific to the task of requirements specification and analysis.

1.2 REQUIREMENTS

A definition of requirements in IEEE-Std.'610' (1990) is given as follows:

1. A condition or capacity needed by a user to solve a problem or achieve an objective.
2. A condition or capability that must be met or possessed by a system or system component to satisfy a contract, standard, specification, or other formally imposed documents.
3. A documented representation of a condition or capability as in 1 or 2.

Although this definition has been given with software systems in mind, it is general enough to apply to non-software-specific situations.

In general, requirements fall into two broad categories: *market driven* and *customer specific*. These two broad categories of requirements have different characteristics and are often treated differently within a development process. Some of the key differences reported in an extensive study of requirements engineering projects (Lubars *et al.*, 1993) are shown in Fig. 1.1.

The primary concern of this book is with 'customer-specific' requirements, i.e. requirements for systems that will need to operate within a well identifiable organizational context, although it should be stressed that some of the issues discussed in the book are equally applicable to 'market-driven' requirements, e.g. specification of the functionality

Market-driven projects	Customer-specific projects
• Requirements are sketchy and informal • Use of techniques from manufacturers rather than software engineering, e.g. QFD • Specification is in the form of a marketing presentation • No readily identifiable 'customer'. Developers tend to have less experience in application domain • Projects rely on consultants for advice on desirable features • Less structured approaches adopted. Task force used in 'brainstorming' sessions	• Requirements are voluminous and more 'formal' • Use techniques from software engineering • Specification may be in hundreds of pages of documentation • Make use of domain expertise. Developers have in-depth knowledge of domain (even sometimes surpassing that of the customer) • Projects rely on in-house personnel • Structured approach following a particular approach

Figure 1.1 Comparisons between market-driven and customer-specific projects.

of the intended product or identifying the enterprise objectives that motivate the development of a 'product'.

1.2.1 Requirements—an organizational perspective

The use of information systems has evolved from the automation of structured processes to applications that introduce change into fundamental business procedures. In increasing orders of sophistication, the contribution of information systems to organizations can be examined in the following terms:

• *Automating* production by reducing the cost of the processes that make up production.
• *Informing* decision makers through the exploitation of automated processes.
• *Transforming* the organization in such a way that management and business processes make the best use of information technology by strategically aligning the information systems to the objectives of the organization and its personnel.

In order for organizations to meet the challenges and opportunities presented by information systems in the automating, informing, and in particular in the transforming stages, the following are regarded as a general set of prerequisites (Morton, 1991):

• Clear definition of business purpose and vision of what the organization should become. This vision should be visible and understood by the organization itself.
• Alignment of corporate strategy and information systems development.

In other words, the development of information systems is not simply about designing database structures and algorithms but also about understanding the needs of individuals and other stakeholders within the enterprise, and ensuring that the system meets user requirements and business strategy. There is, therefore, a natural relationship between the 'enterprise' domain and the 'system' and 'system user' domains as shown in Fig. 1.2.

For example, by examining the objectives of the organization, a rationale is established not only about the organization itself but also about the infrastructure that supports or

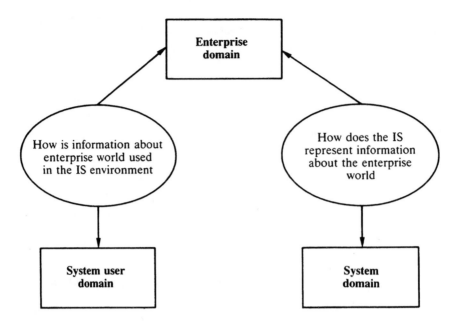

Figure 1.2 Relating information systems to organizations.

will support in the future the enterprise, and the way that the system will fit the organization and be used by different end-user communities (Bubenko and Wangler, 1993). From an organizational perspective, therefore, determination of requirements involves a number of interrelated tasks, shown in Fig. 1.3, that address management, social, and information system concerns which need to be considered in a co-operative way in order to develop systems that fit their intended purpose.

Information systems are entering a new phase, moving beyond the traditional automation of routine organizational processes and towards the assisting of critical tactical and strategic enterprise processes. Development of such systems needs to concentrate on organizational aspects, delivering systems that are closer to the culture of organizations and the wishes of individuals. Specifying requirements in this context directly addresses issues such as the following:

- *Improving change management* by explicitly identifying and specifying those aspects of enterprises that are liable to change and by developing information systems that go beyond the automation of existing processes.
- *Providing integration of views within an enterprise* by adopting an approach which encourages a co-operative generation and assessment of requirements.
- *Relating information systems to business strategy* by facilitating the modelling of business goals and their realization in information systems structure.

Many organizations perceive that a major challenge in the future will be to make the transformations necessary for a sustainable growth in a globally competitive environment. Competitiveness means increased quality, innovation, and responsiveness to change. Business success is today critically dependent on the ability of enterprises to link their

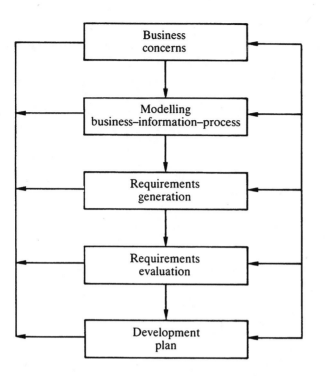

Figure 1.3 Requirements specification from an enterprise perspective.

information systems—their development and use—more closely to the business development process, and such a success can only be achieved if infrastructure systems truly meet the needs and expectations as articulated within an organizational framework.

Crucially therefore, requirements engineering is about establishing the 'connection' between the need for some change within an organizational framework and the technology that could bring about such a change. In other words, requirements engineering can be considered as a way of managing change. This involves:

- An understanding at a conceptual level of the current status.
- A definition of the change in terms of the transition from the 'old' conceptual situation to a 'new' target conceptual situation.
- The implementation of the change in terms of the new components of the system.
- The integration of this new implementation in the environment which contained some legacy system.

1.2.2 Requirements—a software perspective

Interest about the role of requirements for software systems development can be traced to the early days of software engineering with the realization that errors in the requirements definition stage resulted in costly maintenance of software systems at best and total rejection at worst (Bell and Thayer, 1976). As a consequence, requirements engineering was established as a sub-field of software engineering with the task of developing models, techniques, and tools that addressed this particular area. Since these early days the field has expanded in scope and point of view, and there are many strands of investigation and practice nowadays that go beyond the strict confines of software construction.

Historically, the term 'software engineering' was introduced when it became apparent that an engineering approach to software construction was needed. It was subsequently thought that if software development is to be approached in an engineering manner, then the same should apply to individual stages within it. As a result the term 'requirements engineering' was adopted to describe an engineering approach to the early stages of software construction.

The *IEEE Glossary of Software Engineering Terms* gives the following definition of software engineering:

- Software engineering is a systematic approach to the development, operation, maintenance, and retirement of software.

The above term implies the existence of a *lifecycle* view of software. According to this view, software generally undergoes the phases of development, operation, maintenance, and retirement. Each of these phases can be seen from a dynamic viewpoint as a *process*. The term 'process' which will be used throughout this book, is defined according to the International Standards Organization (ISO) as follows:

- A unique, finite course of events defined by its purpose or by its effect, achieved under given conditions.

Software development, therefore, is a process which has as a purpose the development of a complete software system. Within software development there are events which correspond to the start of individual (sub)processes. Thus, requirements determination is a sub-process within software development. Other processes within software development include design, coding, and testing. Each of these processes has a unique purpose which, however, contributes to the overall purpose of developing the software. The purpose of design, for example, is, according to IEEE-Std.'729' (1983):

- Defining the software architecture (structure), components, modules, interfaces, test approach, and data for a software system to satisfy specified requirements.

The view of software development as a sequence of processes is not dissimilar to other areas of engineering endeavour, e.g. manufacturing. Manufacturing of a product involves a number of stages with processes such as product design, production planning, production monitoring, and so on. Each manufacturing process has a purpose which contributes to the overall purpose, i.e. the manufacturing of a complete product.

Manufacturing, however, is done in a systematic way. More specifically, there are three key elements—*methods, tools*, and *procedures*—that enable the control of the manufacturing process and the development of a quality product.

- A *method* is a prescription of steps that need to be employed in order to achieve a specified result.
- A *procedure* is a sequence of *actions* that must be performed.

- A *tool* is the machinery used to perform some action as part of a procedure.

It is not difficult to draw analogies between software engineering and other engineering activities such as manufacturing. Similar to any other engineering discipline, software engineering uses methods, tools, and procedures in a systematic way in order to arrive at the desired result—the development of a complete software product.

Models for software development have been and are still being developed. With particular reference to the processes involved in requirements engineering, Chapter 2 discusses a number of such process models.

There are many different models of software development. However, the majority of these different process models recognize the existence of components shown in Fig. 1.4 (note that no process model is shown in Fig. 1.4 but rather a set of deliverables—their derivation depends on the process model advocated by a particular method):

- The *requirements specification* details the concerns of customers and users of the system, including the functionality of the system and the constraints that must be satisfied (both system and organizational constraints).
- The *system specification* is concerned with the definition of the system boundary and the information used in the interaction of the system and its environment. This specification represents a 'black box' view.
- The *architectural design* represents a high-level view of the system's internal design.
- The *detailed design* represents a decomposition of the system and concentrates on the details of individual components.
- The *implementation* is concerned with the software components that finally realize the original user requirements.

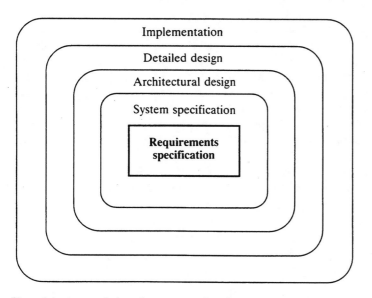

Figure 1.4 A general view of components in software development.

The model shown in Fig. 1.4 recognizes that a software development process consists of a number of distinct activities, with each activity yielding a particular category of 'product'.

Developing a system constitutes a *design* activity. A design process typically involves the following aspects (Dasgupta, 1991) : (a) a set of requirements to be met by some artefact, (b) the output of the process is some design specification document, (c) the goal of the designer is to produce a design such that if an implementation of this design were to materialize, then the artefact would satisfy the requirements, and (d) the designer has no knowledge of any design that satisfies the requirements. These properties of the design process are common to all information systems development approaches, although the degree to which different methods adhere to these four aspects may vary considerably.

The following characteristics are generally recognized in the software development process:

- The software development process involves the generation of a number of different models.
- The software development process can be viewed as a series of steps.
- These steps are goal driven and can be regarded as *transitions between representations*, preserving the semantic content, as refinements on these representations are applied.

The exact nature of the activities, the products, and the transformations depends on the chosen process model.

Software is not different from other human artefacts in the sense that it is made in order to fulfil a perceived need or to solve a specific problem. If one considers some typical areas of today's world where software is being used, it becomes obvious that software is not an ultimate end *per se*, but rather a means to an end. Software is the *enabling* technology, i.e. the technology which helps people in their problem-solving tasks, tasks which can be as straightforward as writing a letter on a wordprocessor or as complicated as flying the Space Shuttle. Since software is being used in all sorts of conceivable applications by all kinds of people, more often than not the need for a software solution is experienced by people who are not software expert themselves. Naturally, non-software experts cannot build the software they want themselves, at least in the vast majority of cases, and therefore their need for a software solution must be catered for by the experts, the software developers. It is this seemingly straightforward situation, but in fact laden with many problems and difficulties, where a software user requires the services of a software provider, which gave birth to terms like 'software crisis' and to the emergence of requirements engineering as a discipline.

At first, having a non-expert requiring the services of an expert seems like a totally natural situation which is often encountered in everyday life. To those who have been involved with software either as users or as builders, the situation regarding the provision of software that satisfies some requirement, where this requirement is part of a larger set of organizational needs and expectations, would be recognized as sufficiently different to everyday needs for a number of reasons:

- Because software is not made of any physical substance it cannot be described in standard physical descriptions such as material, colour, dimensions, etc.; it is rather described in terms of the often intangible characteristics of the situations, tasks, and environments in which people use it.

- Software users best understand and describe their own work; software experts are more familiar with their domain-software.

It becomes apparent now that the seemingly straightforward task of understanding one's requirements and translating them into a software solution is in fact a far cry from being straightforward. The requirements part of software development is what is termed a *hard* problem, and yet one which we can ill-afford to leave unsolved. One obvious reason why requirements are important is because they set the criteria for the acceptance, success, and usefulness of the software that is to be built. As discussed already, software on its own has no particular value; it is only when used as an enabler to other activities that it acquires a value. The best-engineered piece of software is therefore worthless to someone if the software cannot be utilized to address their problem-solving needs.

In addition, developing software is an activity which taxes a scarce resource, namely human software developers. Statistics during the 1980s show (DOD, 1982; Charette, 1986) that while our ability to produce software was increasing at a rate of 4 per cent a year, this was outstripped by the demand for new software, which is currently increasing at an annual rate of 12 per cent. In contrast, the rate of increase in the number of qualified software developers is only 4 per cent a year. It is obvious that we cannot afford the development of useless software and the waste of scarce resources such as time, people, and money. A systematic approach to software requirements is needed, which will ensure the understanding of the user requirements and the production of useful software in a cost-effective way. Such an approach has to follow an *engineering* discipline, i.e. to apply proven methods, techniques, and tools in a well-described fashion.

1.3 REQUIREMENTS SPECIFICATION

Documenting requirements for software construction is an activity which results in what has been traditionally termed *requirements specification*. According to Rzepka and Ohno (1985), a requirements specification represents both a model of what is needed and a statement of the problem under consideration. There is a wide variety of ways of expressing a requirements specification, ranging from informal natural language text to more formal graphical and mathematical notations. The structure of the specification itself varies according to different standards and practices (DOD-STD-2167A, 1988; IEEE-Std.'830', 1984; NCC, 1987).

At this point it is important to address the question 'what is the purpose of a requirements specification?'. There are a number of reasons for striving to develop a requirements specification. First, it provides a focal point for the process of communicating one's understanding about the domain, the business and the intended system. In other words it is the target of a systematic approach with the specification itself relying on the use of some 'language' for representing the contents of the specification. Second, the specification may be part of contractual arrangements, a situation that may become especially relevant when an organization wishes to procure a system from some vendor rather than develop it 'in house'. Third, the specification can be used for evaluating the final product and could play a leading role in any acceptance tests agreed between system consumer and supplier. Irrespective of its intended use the need for developing a requirements specification which at the very least expresses the problem in hand is well accepted by practitioners.

The traditional view of a requirements specification is that of a *functional* specification, i.e. a definition of the desired service of the intended system. For example, requirements for a system that handles a customer transaction in an airline ticket reservation system would need to address issues such as 'what is the information required by the system in order to issue a ticket and what results will the transaction processing function yield?' This view of specification is indeed prominent in many contemporary information systems methods. (For a discussion on functional requirements models as found in contemporary methods, the interested reader may refer to Computer, 1985; Olle *et al.*, 1983, 1984, 1986.)

A functional requirements specification is concerned, as the name implies, with the description of the fundamental functions of the software components that make up the system. One is interested in defining the transformations which the system components should perform on inputs in order to produce some output. Functions are, therefore, specified in terms of *inputs*, *processing*, and *outputs*. A dynamic view of a system's functionality would need to consider aspects such as *control* (e.g. sequencing and parallelism), *timing* of functions (e.g. starting and finishing), as well as the behaviour of the system in terms of *exceptional* situations. Inevitably, since functions deal with a variety of data formats, data will also need to be defined and form part of the functional specification. Data can correspond to inputs and outputs to functions, stored data, and transient data. The specification of 'real-world' *entities* and their *relationships*, particularly for data-centred systems, need to be defined at appropriate levels of abstraction and related to descriptions of system functions.

The emergence of software development methods during the late 1970s and 1980s gave prominence to the importance of functional specifications. A variety of specification languages—there exist, for example, a number of formalisms that are ideally suited to this task—have been developed and extensively used for industrial and commercial projects. However, this over-reliance on functional specifications has been criticized as having a number of undesirable side-effects. One concern is the amount of detail with which both requirements holders and requirements analysts have to deal. It has been argued (cf. McDermid, 1994) that when a functional specification becomes the focal point of requirements analysis, then one makes a decision on the boundary of the system before any understanding is gained of the real needs of the requirements holders. In other words, functional specifications tend to deflect attention from other important aspects. For example, it is at least as important as defining a functional specification to consider issues such as the objectives of the system itself and the relationship of these to organizational objectives, or, specify to other desirable properties of the system (performance, security, usability, etc.) and constraints on its development (use of a particular toolset, economic constraints, etc.). It is only then that one can adequately understand the reasoning behind the needs and aspirations of requirements holders. Furthermore, such a wider view of a requirements specification could accommodate situations requiring resolution of conflict of requirements at an organizational level, deciding to give priorities to the stated requirements, or evaluating alternative scenarios for the satisfying of the stated requirements.

Another area of concern is the relationship between a requirements specification and a system architecture. It has long been accepted that a requirements specification should define the 'what', i.e. a description of the problem in hand, and not the 'how', i.e. the way that the problem is to be solved. It has been argued in the past that a requirements specification should just say enough about the problem and nothing else. In this sense the requirements engineering process is a front-end to a series of other activities within the domain of software development. There are a number of factors, however, that make a distinction between the 'what' and the 'how' difficult to achieve and in many situations possibly even inappropriate. There is much anecdotal evidence that in practice there are many projects in which some understanding of the system architecture is required in order to be able to articulate, represent, and evaluate requirements that by their very nature address the solution space, albeit at an architectural rather than a detailed design or software implementation level. For example, a requirement on some system characteristic (e.g. 'the display screen of an air traffic control system should be capable of handling up to 100 tracks') or a requirement on some general architectural consideration (e.g. 'the system must conform with existing practice for client–server organization' or 'the system must conform to some communication standard') are all important requirements that cannot be ignored until the detailed design stage since by their very nature they impose constraints on the design itself. Furthermore, many intended systems have to be considered in the framework of other legacy systems and developers very frequently have little choice on infrastructure components. Legacy systems are existing computer systems which are often costly to maintain but nevertheless they represent the backbone of the organization's infrastructure and therefore difficult to replace.

The example statements above can be thought as architectural requirements, i.e. requirements which inevitably are imposed on the solution by the customer or user of the system. These statements may be considered as qualifiers on some 'real' organizational problem (e.g. 'the need for air traffic controllers to visualize air traffic scenarios') but there would be little justification in this example to exclude this type of requirement from the specification. In the context of requirements engineering, the relationship between the 'what' and the 'how' is nowadays not as clear-cut as traditionally thought. A number of authors advocate that a requirements specification needs to go beyond the description of functionality and performance issues, and that by including architectural issues during requirements provides an early opportunity to consider important parameters, tangible ones such as cost, as well as intangible ones such as acceptability of the system, in the introduction or evolution of a system (Garlan, 1994; Jackson, 1994; McDermid, 1994; Mead, 1994; Reubenstein, 1994; Shekaran, 1994).

The purpose of building a software system is to be found outside the system itself, in the *enterprise* (synonyms of this are the terms 'application domain' and 'environment'), i.e. the context in which the system will function. The requirements of customers need to be represented in a specification in terms of the explicitly stated (in the specification) observed phenomena about the enterprise itself (Bubenko and Wangler, 1993; Bubenko *et al.*, 1994; Greenspan, *et al.*, 1994; Jackson, 1994; Jackson and Zave, 1993; Loucopoulos and Katsouli, 1992; Loucopoulos, *et al.*, 1991; Nellborn *et al.*, 1992; Yu, 1993; Yu and Mylopoulos, 1994).

A broader view, therefore, of requirements specification is one that goes beyond the description of system functionalities. A functional specification should be one view supplemented, or even motivated, by two other perspectives. First, an understanding should be gained of the domain within which the intended system will be firmly embedded. An explicit definition of the enterprise within which the system will eventually operate is a fundamental prerequisite to the development of a common understanding of the requirements holders, system customers, system users, and system developers about the problem in hand. The emerging consensus within the requirements engineering community is that a requirements specification should include not only software specifications but also any kind of information describing 'real world' phenomena. Second, an understanding should be gained of the constraints that can be placed on the system, its environment, or its development, known as *non-functional* requirements (NFRs — security, availability, portability, usability, performance, etc.). For example the requirement that the 'airline booking system must respond within 15 seconds' would be a non-functional requirement that needs to be considered by the system designer who would have to make a number of design choices in order to meet this constraint. (The distinction between functional and non-functional requirements often is not clear and some authors prefer to avoid this distinction. It has been rightly argued that some requirements, after originally being classified as non-functional, become, in due course, functional requirements themselves. For example, in an air traffic control system, the need to be able to handle some upper limit of aircraft tracks would be originally expressed as a NFR but this eventually will have to be handled by a system function. However, from a methodological perspective the distinction is useful in delineating different areas of concern during requirements analysis, and therefore NFRs are considered from a distinct viewpoint in this book.)

The term 'requirements specification' is used throughout this book from the broader perspective to refer to a description of requirements in the enterprise expressed in terms of the phenomena that are common to the enterprise and system domains. Descriptions of the enterprise are independent of any behaviour of any system, whereas descriptions of the system refer to properties that the system must provide. This view is depicted in Fig. 1.5,

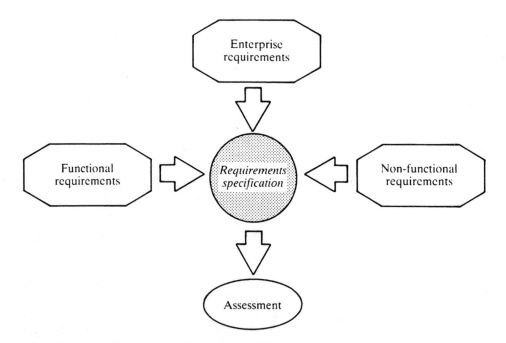

Figure 1.5   Conceptual framework for requirements specifications.

where a requirements specification is shown to constitute an interrelated set of descriptions in three domains, namely the enterprise, functional, and non-functional domains.

1.4 REQUIREMENTS ENGINEERING

Requirements engineering (RE) can be defined as

- the systematic process of developing requirements through an iterative co-operative process of analysing the problem, documenting the resulting observations in a variety of representation formats, and checking the accuracy of the understanding gained.

This definition reflects the view that requirements specification involves an interplay of concerns between representation, social and cognitive aspects (Pohl, 1993). Issues of representation range from informal descriptions such as natural language expressions and hypertext to formal conceptual modelling languages. In the social domain, consideration is given to the complex social process in which the communication and co-operative interaction between the stakeholders of the requirements determines the quality of the final product. Issues in the cognitive domain concern different orientations of models in terms of understanding the process itself and validating the requirements.

The success of the requirements engineering process often depends on the ability *to proceed from informal, fuzzy individual statements of requirements to a formal specification that is understood and agreed by all stakeholders.* However, the process is far from deterministic and straightforward. A requirements specification cannot be developed in a simple, linear fashion; a cyclic approach which gradually yields an involving specification seems to be more appropriate.

The transition from informal to formal requirements constitutes a conceptualization activity within which a developer might make use of domain knowledge partly expressed in descriptions of the enterprise, and partly in existing requirements specifications. Reflecting back from formal to informal requirements is a process of validation which may take a number of different forms including prototyping, and explanation as to the decisions made in producing a requirements specification.

It is a truism that there is no unique or standard way for specifying requirements and although a number of authors have argued that specifications need to conform to certain characteristics such as completeness, correctness, unambiguity, understandability, modifiability, and consistency (Dorfman and Thayer, 1990), many of these qualities are hard to achieve. For example, it is very hard to test for completeness since there is no other 'model' against which the specification can be tested; it is only through repeated validation cycles that one can gain some confidence of completeness. The process is typically situation, context, and issue dependent, i.e. the kind of specification that is being developed during a development step depends on the development issues and questions experienced in previous steps.

While most of the skills required to develop software are primarily technical in nature, this is not sufficient for the task of eliciting, specifying, and validating requirements. The need to understand the underlying skills for the task of systems requirements analysis and their relationship to successful job performance has involved the use of other disciplines, apart from computer science, in attempting to define the way that systems analysts perform certain tasks. For example, the task of systems requirements analysis can be viewed as a type of *problem solving* (Newel and Simon, 1972). Under this perspective, requirements analysis is the reasoning process which attempts to understand the requirements of a problem domain in order to synthesize a solution for a system which will satisfy the needs of its users. During this thought process, an analyst may use clues, goals, strategies, heuristics, hypotheses, information, and knowledge which has been acquired from different sources, i.e. the problem domain as well as from the analyst's own experience.

Examination of various requirements engineering projects has provided insights into the problem itself. For example, the following observations have been made about requirements and requirements analysis (Vitalari and Dickson, 1983; Button and Sharrock, 1994):

- Analysis problems, at their inception, have ill-defined boundaries, structure, and a sufficient degree of uncertainty about the nature and make-up of the solution.
- Requirements are found in organizational contexts, with associated conflicts on expectations and demands about some intentional system.
- The solutions to analysis problems are artificial. That is, they are designed and hence many potential solutions exist for any one problem. Ending the process of requirements specification is a matter of practical necessity.
- Analysis problems are dynamic. That is, they change while they are being solved because of their organizational context and the multiple participants involved in the definition and specification process.
- Solutions to analysis problems require interdisciplinary knowledge and skill.
- The knowledge base of the systems analyst is continually evolving and the analyst must be ready to incorporate changes in the technology and to participate with users in different ways.
- The process of analysis itself is primarily cognitive in nature, requiring the analyst to structure an abstract problem, process diverse information, and develop a logical and internally consistent set of specifications. All the other skills, such as interpersonal interaction and organizational skill, facilitate this cognitive process.

A number of empirical studies have also examined the way that the requirements engineering process is carried out within the software engineering domain. A study of software engineering practices, in many different application areas, reports that 'accurate problem domain knowledge is critical to the success of a project' and 'requirements volatility causes major difficulties during development' (Curtis et al., 1988).

The uncertainty inherent in trying to 'discover' and document requirements is also problematic. A review of the state of practice in requirements engineering (Lubars et al., 1993) revealed that 'although most informants were able to describe the nature of requirements specification that they produced, they were unable to describe the *process* by which they arrived at these specifications'. Also, 'in customer-specific projects, changes to the requirements occurred due to changes in the environment whereas in market-driven projects competing products and insights to the market affected requirements. The importance of tracking the effects of changes to requirements through designs and implementation was recognised by most organizations'.

By observing the way that requirements analysts carry out their work, and by comparing experienced analysts to novices, the following characteristics emerged (Curtis *et al.*, 1988; Fickas, 1987; Sutcliffe, 1990; Sutcliffe and Maiden, 1992, 1990; Vitalari and Dickson, 1983):

- Analysts use information from the environment to classify problems and relate them to previous experience. Experienced analysts begin by establishing a set of context questions and then proceed by considering alternatives. Much of the contextual information depends on previous knowledge about the application domain and the analogies that an analyst will establish are based on such knowledge.
- Expert analysts tend to start solving a problem by forming a mental model of the problem at an abstract level. This model is then refined, by a progression of transformations, into a concrete model, as further information is obtained.
- Hypotheses are developed as to the nature of a solution, as information is collected. Experienced analysts use hypothetical examples to capture more facts from a requirements holder. Such examples are also used to clarify some previously acquired information about the object system.
- Developers almost always summarize in order to verify their findings. It has been observed that during a typical user–analyst session, the analyst will summarize two or three times and each time the summarization will trigger a new set of questions.

A requirements specification is likely to change many times before proceeding to design, and as discussed already, a specification needs to be subjected to evaluation in order to gain confidence as to its validity. This cyclic approach of acquisition–representation–evaluation involves a succession of propositions which are increasingly closer to end users' perceptions about the target system.

A requirement for an improved system begins with an initial hypothesis which is vague and requires further elaboration in order to produce the desired result. In this sense, requirements analysis involves the generation of hypotheses, and subjecting these hypotheses to a process of disconfirmation (Aguero and Dasgupta, 1987; Hooton *et al.*, 1988). These hypotheses are generated and evaluated against anticipated properties of the intended system. Hypothesis formulation is based on the vision or belief that the participants in the analysis process may hold about the intended system, its role in the enterprise, its effects on organization practices, its effects on personal and group status, and so on. In short, the participants define a set of system characteristics which in their opinion will lead to an improved situation. Hypothesis evaluation is based on the idea that every hypothesis undergoes criticism and is thoroughly examined for its validity, i.e. one looks for evidence to disconfirm the hypothesis. This implies that a specification describing objects, processes, business rules, agents, information system components, and so on represents a set of propositions that are considered to be true until proven otherwise.

1.5 SUMMARY

Requirements engineering is the activity that transforms the needs and wishes of customers and potential users of computerized systems, usually incomplete, and expressed in informal terms, into complete, precise, and consistent specifications, preferably written in formal notations.

This activity is arguably the most crucial activity in system development, if only because errors made in the early requirements specification phases are the most costly to repair once the system has been implemented. It is also a most delicate social activity, as it requires heavy involvement of requirements stakeholders, and a consensus between them, as well as between requirements stakeholders and system designers, who have quite different backgrounds and concerns.

Requirements engineering is a systematic process, normally carried out within a broader spectrum of development activities, that attempts to discover, capture, and document the requirements of many different stakeholders—those that commission the project as well as those that will eventually use the product. The input to this process is usually an informal, ill-defined 'wish-list', whereas the output should be a specification which is formal enough to be analysed and agreed upon by requirements stakeholders and developers alike. Such a specification should have three orientations:

- A view of key aspects of the enterprise defining the objectives for the target system.
- A view of the required functionality of the system.
- A view of the properties that must be exhibited by the system and its environment for it to meet the enterprise objectives.

The above issues have been examined from a number of different disciplines and indeed different 'philosophical' standpoints.

Areas of concern, which ultimately influence the approach adopted in deriving a requirements specification, fall into two broad categories:

- Issues of functionality and service to be provided by the intended system.
- Issues of suitability of the intended system in an organizational context.

Traditionally, these two classes of concern have given rise to two broad classes of approaches, the so-called 'hard' and 'soft' methods. This rather unhelpful distinction has tended to polarize the way that one considers requirements determination with the effect that important facets of requirements go missing from specifications. However, recent realization that requirements for socio-technical systems span the areas of concern of both 'hard' and 'soft' methods has resulted in the investigation of techniques that go beyond the traditional divide (cf. Jirotka and Goguen, 1994; Petrie, 1992). Emerging techniques within the field of requirements engineering advocate a balanced view between technical and organizational considerations.

REFERENCES

Aguero U. and Dasgupta S. (1987) A plausibility-driven approach to computer architecture design. *Communications of the ACM*, **30**(11), 922–931.

Bell T. E. and Thayer T. A. (1976) Software requirements: are they really a problem? *Second International Conference on Software Engineering*, pp. 61–68.

Bubenko J. A. and Wangler B. (1993) Objectives driven capture of business rules and information systems requirements. *IEEE Conference on Systems, Man and Cybernetics*.

Bubenko J., Rolland C., Loucopoulos P. and de Antonellis V. (1994) Facilitating 'fuzzy to formal' requirements modelling. *IEEE International Conference on Requirements Engineering*.

Button G. and Sharrock W. (1994) Occasioned practices in the work of software engineers. In Jirotka M. and Goguen J. A. (Eds) *Requirements Engineering: Social and Technical Issues*. Academic Press, London, pp. 217–240.

Charette R. (1986) *Software Engineering Environments*. McGraw-Hill, New York.

Computer (1985) Special issue on requirements engineering. *IEEE Computer*.

Curtis B., Krasner H. and Iscoe N. (1988) A field study of the software design process for large systems. *Communications of the ACM*, **31**(11), 1268 ff.

Dasgupta S. (1991) *Design Theory and Computer Science*. Cambridge University Press, Cambridge.

DOD (1982) *Strategy for a DOD Software Initiative*. US Department of Defense, Washington, DC.

DOD-STD-2167A (1988) *Defense System Software Development*. US Department of Defense, February.

Dorfman M. and Thayer R. H. (Eds) (1990) *Standards, Guidelines, and Examples on System and Software Requirements Engineering*. IEEE Computer Society Press, Los Alamitos, CA.

Fickas S. (1987) Automating the analysis process: an example. *Fourth International Workshop on Software Specification and Design*. Monterey.

Garlan D. (1994) The role of software architecture in requirements engineering—position statement. *First International Conference on Requirements Engineering*. IEEE Computer Society Press, Colorado Springs, CO.

Greenspan S., Mylopoulos J. and Borgida A. (1994) On formal requirements modeling languages: RML revisited. *Sixteenth International Conference on Software Engineering* (ICSE-94). IEEE Computer Society Press, New York, pp. 135–148.

Hooton A., Aguero U. and Dasgupta S. (1988) An exercise in plausibility-driven design. *IEEE Computer*, **27**(7), 21–33.

IEEE-Std.'610' (1990) *IEEE Standard Glossary of Software Engineering Terminology*. Institute of Electrical and Electronics Engineers, New York.

IEEE-Std.'729' (1983) *IEEE Standard 729. Glossary of Software Engineering Terminology*. Institute of Electrical and Electronics Engineers, New York.

IEEE-Std.'830' (1984) *IEEE Guide to Software Requirements Specifications*. Institute of Electrical and Electronics Engineers, New York.

Jackson M. (1994) The role of software architecture in requirements engineering—position statement. *First International Conference on Requirements Engineering*. IEEE Computer Society Press, Colorado Springs, CO.

Jackson M. and Zave P. (1993) Domain descriptions. *IEEE International Symposium on Requirements Engineering*. IEEE Computer Society Press, San Diego, CA, pp. 56–64.

Jirotka M. and Goguen J. (Eds) (1994) *Requirements Engineering: Social and Technical Issues*. Gaines B. R. and Monk A. (Eds). Computers and People Series. Academic Press, London.

Loucopoulos P. and Katsouli E. (1992) Modelling business rules in an office environment. *ACM SIGOIS*, August.

Loucopoulos P., McBrien P., Schumacker F., Theodoulidis B., Kopanas V. and Wangler B. (1991) Integrating database technology, rule-based systems and temporal reasoning for effective information systems: the TEMPORA paradigm. *Journal of Information Systems*, **1**(2), 129–152.

Lubars M., Potts C. and Richter C. (1993) A review of the state of the practice in requirements modelling. *IEEE International Symposium on Requirements Engineering*. IEEE Computer Society Press, San Diego, CA, pp. 2–14.

McDermid J. A. (1994) Requirements analysis: orthodoxy, fundamentalism and heresy. In Jirotka M. and Goguen J. A. (Eds) *Requirements Engineering: Social and Technical Issues*. Academic Press, London, pp. 17–40.

Mead N. R. (1994) The role of software architecture in requirements engineering—position statement. *First International Conference on Requirements Engineering*. IEEE Computer Society Press, Colorado Springs, CO.

Morton M. S. (1991) *The Corporation of the 1990s: Information Technology and Organisational Transformation*. Oxford University Press, Oxford.

NCC (1987) *The STARTS Guide: A Guide to Methods and Software Tools for the Construction of Large Real-time Systems*. National Computing Centre, Manchester.

Nellborn C., Bubenko J. and Gustafsson M. (1992) Enterprise modelling—the key to capturing requirements for information systems. SISU, F3 Project Internal Report.

Newel R. and Simon H. (1972) *Human Problem Solving*. Prentice Hall, Englewood Cliffs, NJ.

Olle T. W., Sol H. G. and Tully C. J. (Eds) (1983) *Information Systems Design Methodologies: A Feature Analysis*. North Holland, Amsterdam.

Olle T. W., Sol H. G. and Verrijn-Stuart A. A. (Eds) (1984) *Information System Design Methodologies: A Comparative Review*. North Holland, Amsterdam.

Olle T. W., Sol H. G. and Verrijn-Stuart A. A. (Eds) (1986) *Information Systems Design Methodologies: Improving the Practice*. Elsevier/North Holland, Amsterdam.

Petrie C. J. (Ed) (1992) *Proc. 1st Conference on Enterprise Integration Modeling*. Scientific and Engineering Computation Series. MIT Press, Cambridge, MA.

Pohl K. (1993) The three dimensions of requirements engineering. In Rolland C., Bodart F. and Cauvet C. (Eds) *Fifth International Conference on Advanced Information Systems Engineering (CAiSE'93)*. Springer-Verlag, Paris, pp. 275–292.

Reubenstein H. B. (1994) The role of software architecture in requirements engineering—position statement. *First International Conference on Requirements Engineering*. IEEE Computer Society Press, Colorado Springs, CO.

Rzepka W. and Ohno Y. (1985) Requirements engineering environments: software tools for modelling user needs. *IEEE Computer*, April.

Shekaran M. C. (1994) The role of software architecture in requirements engineering—position statement. *First International Conference on Requirements Engineering*. IEEE Computer Society Press, Colorado Springs, CO.

Sutcliffe A. (1990) Human factors in information systems: a research agenda and some experience. In Finkelstein A., Tauber M. J. and Traunmuller R. (Eds) *Human Factors in Information Systems Analysis and Design*. North Holland, Scherding, Austria, pp. 5–23.

Sutcliffe A. G. and Maiden N. A. M. (1992) Analysing the Analyst: Cognitive Models in Software Engineering. *International Journal of Man-Machine Studies*, **36**, 719–740.

Sutcliffe A. and Maiden N. (1990) Analysing the analyst: requirements for the next generation of CASE tools. In Brinkemper S. and Wijers G. (Eds), *The Next Generation of CASE-tools*. SERC, Noordwijkerhout, The Netherlands, pp. C2-1–9.

TSE (1977) Special issue on requirements engineering. *IEEE Transactions on Software Engineering*.

Vitalari N. P. and Dickson G. W. (1983) Problem solving for effective systems analysis: an experimental exploration. *Communications of the ACM*, **26(11)**.

Yu E. S. K. (1993) Modelling organizations for information systems requirements engineering. *IEEE International Symposium on Requirements Engineering*. IEEE Computer Society Press, San Diego, CA, pp. 34–41.

Yu E. and Mylopoulos J. (1994) Understanding 'why' in software process modeling, analysis and design. *Sixteenth International Conference on Software Engineering*, Sorrento.

2

PROCESSES IN REQUIREMENTS ENGINEERING

2.1 INTRODUCTION

Chapter 1 introduced the major deliverables of the requirements engineering process as being the *problem domain* model, the *functional* requirements model, and the *non-functional* requirements model. However, what has not been mentioned so far is *how* requirements engineering derives the above deliverables. This chapter introduces a *framework* for describing the dynamics ('how') as opposed to the deliverables ('what') of requirements engineering. By integrating current proposals for requirements engineering processes, this chapter arrives at a description of the process in terms of three major interacting, concurrent (sub)processes, namely *requirements elicitation, requirements specification*, and *requirements validation* (Sections 2.3–2.4). These processes are discussed with respect to their place in the requirements engineering lifecycle, their products, and the ways of interacting with each other. The requirements process model presented in this chapter is compared with other models found in the literature. Additionally, this chapter discusses the relative roles and importance of the elicitation, specification, and validation processes in the context of major software development paradigms such as the waterfall model, prototyping, and others.

2.2 A FRAMEWORK FOR DESCRIBING REQUIREMENTS ENGINEERING PROCESSES

Contemporary software methods do not prescribe a formal requirements engineering process. The majority of them (with a few exceptions, e.g. the framework for software specification described in Rombach, 1990) focus on the deliverables of the process rather than on the process itself. Such apparent inability or unwillingness to provide a formal description of requirements engineering probably explains the proliferation of requirements models.

Requirements engineering is easier described by its products than its processes. However, there is a need for a point of reference, as a basis for understanding, evaluating, and comparing different requirements engineering proposals.

A framework for describing requirements engineering processes can be constructed by considering three fundamental concerns of requirements engineering:

- The concern of *understanding* a problem ('what the problem is').
- The concern of formally *describing* a problem.
- The concern of attaining an *agreement* on the nature of the problem.

Each of the above concerns implies that some activities must take place in order to provide answers, and in doing this some resources must be used. For example, in order to understand a problem, relevant information about it (a resource) must be available to the problem solver. If that information is not already available to the problem solver, then it must be obtained (an activity). In the same way, the relevant information must be validated in order to ensure its accuracy, consistency, and relevance (another activity).

The current literature on software requirements classifies activities such as the above under various terms — 'acquisition', 'elicitation', 'analysis', 'specification', 'validation', etc.

However, such terms have multiple interpretations in software development methods with regard to their scopes, objectives, inputs, and deliverables. In order to avoid adding to the existing confusion, this chapter uses the minimum amount of terminology to describe requirements engineering processes. The processes proposed here (namely elicitation, specification, and validation) correspond to the three fundamental concerns of requirements engineering, namely understanding, describing, and agreeing on a problem.

Sections 2.3–2.5 discuss further the fundamental requirements engineering processes. Each process is described in terms of the following:

- The *purpose* of the process.
- The *input* to the process and its origins.
- The *activities* which take place during the process and the techniques used.
- The *final* and *intermediate* deliverables.
- The *interaction* with other requirements engineering processes.

In Section 2.6, existing models for requirements processes are classified and comparisons between them and the framework are made. The purpose of introducing this framework is to provide the reader with an integrated (but not simplistic) view of the requirements engineering process. Such view is not readily available in the relevant literature.

Figure 2.1 shows a schematic representation of the framework.

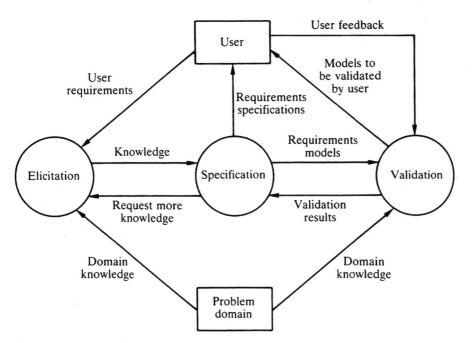

Figure 2.1 A framework for requirements engineering processes.

2.3 REQUIREMENTS ELICITATION

The importance of requirements elicitation cannot easily be overestimated. Even within methods which do not consider it as a separate process (i.e. by placing it under the name of 'analysis'), elicitation is the first activity that takes place and continues through the requirements engineering lifecycle. There are many reasons for this, with the most obvious one being that *when you have to solve somebody else's problem the first thing you have to do is to find out more about it.*

2.3.1 Purpose of requirements elicitation

In the majority of cases, at the start of a software project, an analyst knows very little about the software problem to be solved. The only way to reverse this is by delving into *everything* that is relevant to the problem and, in a sense, becoming a problem owner. Software-related problems, however, are usually complex enough to have the relevant knowledge about them distributed among many people, places, and sources. Moreover, the knowledge is usually available in a variety of notations which range from sketches, through natural language prose to formal models (e.g. mathematical models), to, even worse, some mental model in people's minds!

The purpose of requirements elicitation, therefore, is to gain knowledge relevant to the problem, which can be used to produce a formal specification of the software needed to solve the problem. It is not an exaggeration to say that at the end of the requirements engineering phase the analyst should become an expert on the problem domain. If this does not happen, it will most likely mean that some important parameters of the problem were not considered (or not considered in the right way) and the software will not provide the best solutions to the users' problem (or even worse it will provide no solution at all).

2.3.2 Input to requirements elicitation

While some approaches restrict the source of elicitation to be humans (the users), the approach taken in this book does not restrict the possible sources of domain knowledge. In reality, all of the following can be sources of domain knowledge:

- Domain experts
- Literature about the domain
- Existing software systems in that domain
- Similar software applications in other domains
- National and international standards, which constrain the development of software in that domain
- Other stakeholders in the larger system (e.g. an organization) which will host the software system

2.3.3 Activities and techniques of requirements elicitation

In requirements elicitation, the analyst is presented with the following tasks:

- Identifying all the sources of requirements knowledge.
- Acquiring the knowledge.
- Deciding on the relevance of the knowledge to the problem in hand.
- Understanding the significance of the elicited knowledge and its impact on the software requirements.

A variety of techniques for requirements elicitation exist today and a number of them are examined thoroughly in Chapter 3. Each technique has unique strengths and weaknesses and is more applicable to some types of problem than others. The most typically used techniques elicit the requirements from users through interviews, and through the creation of mock-up (prototype) software. More recent elicitation techniques attempt to *reuse* knowledge acquired in similar problem domains.

Elicitation is a labour-intensive process, taking a large share of time and resources for software development. This is partly due to the fact that knowledge elicitation (particularly from humans) is inherently a difficult task.

2.3.4 Deliverables of requirements elicitation

The majority of the practised methods do not prescribe a formal outcome (model) for the elicitation process, as it is traditionally believed that the only formal outcome of requirements engineering should be the requirements specification model.

Experience, however, shows that a better view of requirements engineering is as a *model creation* process. According to this view a succession of models is created throughout requirements engineering, starting with *conceptual* models and ending with the requirements specification model. The analyst starts formulating models of the problem

Figure 2.2   A succession of models is created in requirements engineering.

domain in the early stages of requirements engineering (elicitation). Such mental models, which contain domain-dependent knowledge such as environmental factors, domain goals, policies, constraints, etc., are usually formulated and exist in the analyst's head. As the analyst's understanding of the problem domain grows, these models become more refined and elaborated. Moreover, as the requirements engineering process progresses, the conceptual models become more software oriented than problem domain oriented (Fig. 2.2). It is therefore safe to say that although elicitation does not (always) produce any formal models, it produces a succession of mental models of the problem domain which become more elaborate as the analyst's understanding of the domain increases.

2.3.5 Interactions between elicitation and other processes

Elicitation can be considered as an ongoing process of requirements engineering. It can be viewed as providing the 'raw material' to other processes, such as specification, needed for the production of a formal model. In this respect, elicitation occurs in parallel with specification and validation processes.

2.4 REQUIREMENTS SPECIFICATION

A specification can be viewed as a contract between users and software developers which defines the desired functional behaviour of the software artefact (and other properties of it such as performance, reliability, etc.) without showing how such functionality is going to be achieved.

In arriving at such a 'blueprint' there is a need, as discussed in Chapter 1, to include other types of description such as application domain (enterprise models) and non-functional models.

2.4.1 Purpose of requirements specification

The requirements specification process derives formal software requirements models to be used in subsequent stages of development. The purpose of producing a formal specification model is twofold:

- The specification model is used as an agreement between the software developers and the users on what constitutes the problem which must be solved by the software system.
- The specification model is also a blueprint for the development of the software system.

2.4.2 Input to requirements specification

The process of specification requires knowledge about the problem domain as input. This knowledge is supplied by the elicitation process (Section 2.2). In most cases the input knowledge comes in a 'raw' format which must be converted into meaningful information in order to produce a formal specification model. Knowledge about an organization's general policies, for example, must be interpreted with respect to how they affect the requirements for software systems. Other types of knowledge produced by the validation process are also employed in specification. Such knowledge states what is valid and what is not in the formal specification, and as such it acts as a force for changing the formal requirements model.

2.4.3 Activities and techniques in requirements specification

It is important to see specification as a complex process which requires feedback from the analyst to the user and vice versa. The process uses and produces a variety of models including the final formal requirements specification. The process is *analytical* because all different kinds of knowledge that the analyst elicits from the problem domain must be examined and cross-related. Specification is also *synthetic* because the heterogeneous knowledge must be combined to produce a logical and coherent whole which is the requirements specification.

Requirements specification is therefore described by the following major activities:

- Analysis and assimilation of requirements knowledge.
- Synthesis and organization of the knowledge into a coherent and logical requirements model.

2.4.4 Deliverables of requirements specification process

The majority of requirements engineering approaches assume that the outcome of this process is the requirements specification model. It is more appropriate, however, to view the specification process as producing a variety of models which correspond to different views of the problem. In this respect, requirements specification produces the following:

- User-oriented models specifying the behaviour, non-functional characteristics, etc., of the software which serve as a point of understanding between the analyst, the customer and the user.
- Developer-oriented models specifying functional and non-functional properties of the software system as well as constraints on resources, design constraints, etc., which act as blueprints for further development stages.

All the above models correspond to what was termed in Chapter 1, as enterprise models, functional requirements models, and non-functional requirements models. However, some requirements methods do not distinguish between different models for reasons of simplicity and effort. Such methods, for example, use the same functional specification model for all classes of requirements stakeholders. Nevertheless, this is not always appropriate since a specification notation which is perfectly clear for developers can be difficult for users to comprehend.

2.4.5 Interactions between requirements specification and other processes

Requirements specification is the central process of requirements engineering. Specification controls both the elicitation and validation processes as follows. During specification it may become apparent that more information about the problem is required. This will trigger the process of elicitation, which will in turn supply the information needed. On the other hand, some change in the problem domain (e.g. a change in some assumption, made about the domain) can trigger a change in the specification model. Thus elicitation can take place during the specification process. Similar interactions appear between specification and validation. Completion of some part of the specification model can cause the need for validation. For example, completing the specification of the user interface may necessitate validating the results in co-operation with the user. If the validation has negative results (i.e. the user is not satisfied with the proposed interface), then more analysis and specification must take place.

2.5 REQUIREMENTS VALIDATION

Requirements validation is an ongoing process of requirements engineering which aims to ensure that the right problem is being tackled at any time. In many requirements engineering methods, validation is not considered as a separate activity but instead is taken as a part of requirements specification. Nevertheless, it is important, for conceptual as well as practical reasons, to make the distinction between validation and other processes and activities of requirements engineering as is shown in the rest of this section and again in Chapter 5.

2.5.1 Purpose of requirements validation

Requirements validation is defined as the process which certifies that the requirements model is consistent with customers' and users' intentions. This view of validation is more general than those found in the literature because it treats validation as an ongoing process which proceeds in parallel with elicitation and specification. The need for validation appears at the moment a new piece of information is assimilated in the current requirements model (i.e. when the relevance, validity, consistency, etc., of the new information must be examined) and also when different pieces of information are integrated into a coherent whole. Validation, therefore is not applied only on the final formal requirements model, but also on all intermediate models produced, including the raw information received by the elicitation process. In this respect, validation encompasses activities such as *requirements communication*.

2.5.2 Input to requirements validation

Any requirements model (formal or informal) is subject to validation and thus provides an input to the process. Knowledge about the problem domain, for example, must be validated, i.e. checked for accuracy, consistency, relevance to the project, etc. In a similar way, some part of the formal requirements model must be validated in parts and as a whole. For example, the specification of a mathematical routine must be checked for correctness. At the same time, the routine must be tested against the rest of the specification model, in order to make sure that it provides the results required by other parts of the specification.

2.5.3 Activities and techniques used in requirements validation

Validation is a process which requires interactions between analysts, customers of the intended system, and users in the problem domain. This is similar to the scientific process of formulating a new theory (specification) and subsequently testing it by performing experiments (validation). In some occasions, however, the analyst can test the validity of the requirements model without resorting to experimentation, e.g. by using common sense. In a scientific sense, validation is therefore characterized by two principal types of activities:

- Preparing the settings for an experiment.
- Performing the experiment and analysing its results.

Chapter 5 contains an extensive discussion of techniques used for requirements validation. Some of the techniques require some preparation before the actual validation of the requirements, e.g. the development of a mock-up software system. This corresponds to the 'preparation for experiment' activities above. Other validation techniques involve extensive interaction between the analyst and the user through imaginary scenarios about the use of the software system. These techniques correspond to the 'experiment and result analysis' type of activities mentioned above.

2.5.4 Deliverables of requirements validation

Validation delivers a requirements model which is consistent and in accordance with the users' expectations. This does not mean that the model is in any sense correct. In the majority of the cases, validation yields a compromise between what was desired by the users and what is possible and feasible under the project constraints.

2.5.5 Interaction between validation and other requirements engineering processes

Validation is ever present in all stages of requirements engineering. The need for validation is triggered by the acquisition of new knowledge about the problem domain (elicitation), or by the formulation (even in part) of a requirements model (specification). Validation is also needed during the analysis and synthesis phases of requirements specification, since information analysed must be checked for correctness, and synthesized requirements must be checked for logical consistency and coherence.

2.6 OTHER REQUIREMENTS PROCESS MODELS AND TERMINOLOGY USED IN THE LITERATURE

Despite existing attempts for its standardization (e.g. IEEE, 1984) a consensus on requirements engineering terminology has not yet been achieved. There are specific reasons for the proliferation of concepts and terminology used in requirements engineering, including the following:

- The field of requirements engineering is relatively young.
- Proprietary requirements engineering methods employ their own terminology which leads to a fragmentation.
- Requirements engineering consists of ill-structured, ill-defined processes which are hard to define formally.

This section compares other suggested requirements process models to the framework introduced in this chapter.

The definition of *elicitation* according to the framework is slightly more general than others appearing in the literature (e.g. IEEE, 1984) which define the deliverable of the elicitation process to be software requirements only. According to the framework, the elicitation process produces not just software requirements but also all other kinds of domain knowledge which can be directly employed in analysing and specifying the software requirements. The framework makes a distinction between requirements elicitation and other activities known as *context analysis*, *business analysis*, etc., which attempt to establish the technical, economic, and operational boundary conditions for the software development process. Also, according to the framework, requirements elicitation commences after all the boundaries and development conditions have been established for the software project.

The framework's definition of requirements elicitation partially overlaps with what is termed in the literature as *requirements identification* (Davis, 1982; Martin, 1988; Powers *et al.*, 1984), *requirements determination* (Yadav *et al.*, 1988), and *requirements acquisition*. Requirements identification and determination also partially overlap with the analytical phase of requirements specification.

In a similar manner, the analytic phase of requirements specification according to the framework encompasses activities which the literature places under the headings of *software requirements analysis* (Department of Defense, 1988), *requirements analysis* (Wasserman *et al.*, 1986; Pressman, 1987), *problem analysis* (Davis, 1990), *problem definition* (Roman *et al.*, 1984), *requirements definition* (Berzins and Gray, 1985).

The analysis phase can also contain activities such as assessment of potential problems, classification of requirements, and evaluation of feasibility and risks. The synthesis phase of specification contains activities such as the following:

- *External product description* (Davis, 1990) which corresponds to the specification of the functionality (behaviour) of software.
- *Requirements presentation* (IEEE, 1984) in which the results of requirements identification are portrayed.
- *Software requirements specification* which includes complete documentation of what the software does externally (without regard to *how* it works internally) (Davis, 1990).

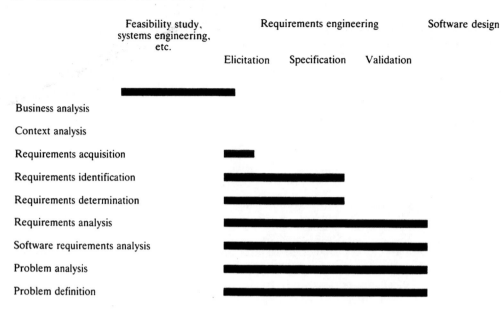

Figure 2.3 Coverage of requirements engineering activities by different approaches.

Also, terms such as *system design* (Roman *et al.*, 1984) and *external design* (Wasserman *et al.*, 1986) are (confusingly) used to describe the functional requirements specification.

Finally, validation according to the framework encompasses activities such as *requirements communication* (IEEE, 1990), which is defined as the activity in which 'results of requirements definition are presented to diverse audiences for review and approval'.

Figure 2.3 shows the scope of the above process/activity requirements approaches with respect to processes of the framework.

2.7 PROCESSES OF REQUIREMENTS ENGINEERING IN THE CONTEXT OF SOFTWARE DEVELOPMENT MODELS

This section discusses the processes of requirements engineering, in the context of the following software development models:

- The *waterfall* model
- The *spiral* model
- The *prototyping* model
- The *operational* model
- The *transformational* model
- The *knowledge-based* model
- The *domain analysis* model

At the end of this section, a comparison of the various software development models is made.

2.7.1 Requirements engineering in the waterfall model

The philosophy which describes the 'waterfall model' (Royce, 1970) is that software development consists of a stepwise transformation from the problem domain to the solution through a number of phases which are wholly satisfied before their successors begin. According to this philosophy, requirements engineering is the phase in which the software requirements are acquired, analysed, validated, and a formal specification of them is produced. This phase is usually preceded by another one known as *market analysis* (also as *business analysis/planning* or, in cases where software is part of a larger hybrid system, as *systems engineering*) which defines the context for the requirements engineering phase. Finally, requirements engineering is succeeded by the design phase which is concerned with specifying the software solution to the requirements specification. The popularity of the waterfall model lies in its principle that each of the phases are autonomous and can produce their deliverables using only the deliverables of their immediate predecessors, which guarantees that each phase can be completed and yield a specific outcome.

The waterfall model views requirements engineering as a *comprehension* phase which is succeeded by the *invention* (design) and *realization* (coding) phases. Variations of the waterfall model adopt slightly different organizations of the requirements engineering process. Also, the formality of the produced requirements model and the extent of tool-support varies with different waterfall-based approaches. All the variations, however, suffer (to different extents) the consequences of the assumptions made by the waterfall model. More specifically, the assumption the waterfall model makes, namely that a phase only relies on the results of its previous one, is simplistic. In real-life situations it is common that changes or new discoveries in a late phase of development (i.e. coding) can affect many earlier ones, including requirements engineering. In addition, changes in a phase after it has been completed can have a ripple effect on changes in subsequent phases. For example, changes in some business plan can have effect on the software requirements, on the design, on the code, etc. In this respect, the waterfall model, which is designed to resist change, becomes impractical in many situations. In the literature, the waterfall approach has been criticized for a variety of reasons, including the following:

- Lack of user involvement in the development after requirements specification has ended (McCracken and Jackson, 1982).
- Inflexibility to accommodate prototypes (Alavi, 1984).
- Unrealistic separation of specification from design (Jackson, 1982).
- Inability to accommodate reused software (Castano and De Antonellis, 1993; Fugini and Pernici, 1992).
- Maintainability problems (Balzer *et al.*, 1983).
- Complicated systems integration (Yeh and Ng, 1990).

In conclusion, the waterfall model takes a static viewpoint of requirements engineering by ignoring issues such as the inherently dynamic nature (volatility) of requirements and its impact on earlier and later phases of development.

2.7.2 Requirements engineering in the spiral model of software development

The spiral model of software development (Boehm, 1988) recognizes the iterative nature of development and the need to plan and assess risks at each iteration. According to this model, in each of the software development phases, the following activities must be performed:

- Plan next phases
- Determine objectives, alternatives, constraints
- Evaluate alternatives, identify and resolve risks
- Develop, verify next level product

The spiral model introduces the additional sub-processes of requirements engineering, known as *requirements risk analysis*, using techniques such as *simulation* and *prototyping* (both are discussed in Chapter 5) and *planning for design*. Such additions aim at reducing the risk of change at some subsequent stage. By evaluating the feasibility of the proposed requirements, for example, the approach reduces the risk of having to repeat requirements engineering once it has reached a stage (e.g. design) where it might be discovered that it is not feasible to produce the required software system. The spiral model cannot, however, cope with unforeseen changes during some stage of development and their impact on other phases. If, for example, a new business objective occurs while the development has reached the coding stage, then requirements engineering and design has unavoidably to be repeated.

2.7.3 Requirements engineering in the prototyping model

In the context of software development, *prototyping* (Floyd, 1984) is a technique which constructs and experiments with a mock-up version of the software system, in order to gain some understanding of the functionality and behaviour required from it.

It must be emphasised that prototyping is now a widely accepted technique which can be used in the context of any software development model. The *spiral* model of software development, for example, uses prototypes of the final software system in order to assess various risks associated with its development. Prototyping as a requirements validation technique is extensively discussed in Chapter 5. In the context of this section, however, prototyping is viewed as the core activity in a software development methodology.

According to the prototyping model of development, processes of requirements engineering such as elicitation, analysis, and specification are concerned with the planning, development, and testing of a prototype. After an initial (and possibly incorrect and/or incomplete) understanding of users' needs, the prototype developers determine the objectives and scope of the prototype. It may be decided that a prototype has to be constructed for one (or more) of the following reasons:

- To understand the requirements for the user interface (such requirements are, in fact, difficult to specify using conventional means).
- To examine the feasibility of a proposed design approach.
- To understand system performance issues.

After a number of necessary revisions the developers will usually feel that the prototype is satisfying all the objectives. At this point there are two options available to developers:

- Refine the prototype into a complete system.
- Begin a conventional development process having benefited from developing the prototype.

If the first option is chosen, then it can be said that the prototype *is* the requirements specification of the system. If the developers prefer the second option, then a formal requirements specification must be developed based on the enhanced understanding of the requirements that was gained in the prototyping process. The choice between the first and second option must be made based on a number of key factors, namely:

- The level of functionality already present in the prototype.
- How robust, flexible, and maintainable the prototype-based production system will be.

In conclusion, the prototyping development model views processes of requirements engineering such as elicitation, specification, and validation as occurring in the context of developing a prototyping system. More specifically:

- Elicitation of requirements is achieved by involving the user in experimental use of the prototype.
- Analysis of requirements is done by analysing the structure and behaviour of the prototype.
- Formal specification coincides with prototype development (in case the prototype becomes the final system).
- Validation is achieved by validating the prototype against the users' intentions.

The prototyping model has been criticized for hampering subsequent development stages when it is treated by the users as *the* solution, instead of what it actually is (i.e. a mock-up of the solution). It nevertheless presents a promising alternative to the waterfall model of development. The prototyping model is shown graphically in Fig. 2.4.

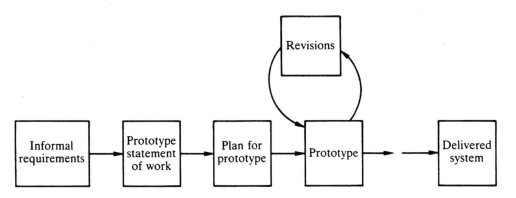

Figure 2.4 Schematic representation of the prototype model.

2.7.4 Requirements engineering in the operational specification model

The operational specification model challenges the assumption made by the waterfall model, namely that the requirements phase should be concerned with the 'how' rather than with the 'what' of development (which should be the responsibility of the design phase). More precisely, an operational specification is a system model that can be evaluated or executed in order to generate the behaviour of the software system. The operational specification is constructed early in requirements engineering and its purpose is to analyse not only the required behaviour but also the required structure of the software system. The proponents of this approach claim that it is impossible to separate structure (the 'how') from behaviour (the 'what') when analysing a system (Zave, 1984), According to them, a major inadequacy of the waterfall model is that it leaves the designer with too many things to consider, specifically:

- How to decompose the problem domain functions into a succession of lower-level functions.
- How to introduce features such as information hiding and abstraction into the design.
- How to take into account implementation issues, e.g. the feasibility of the design to be implemented in a specific software and hardware environment.

To tackle problems such as the above, the operational approach advocates that decisions about the structuring of the domain problem should be made early in the development lifecycle. Although such a suggestion may give the impression that an analyst using the operational model is forced to do design instead of analysis, this is not necessarily the case.

The behaviour of each process would be specified using an operational specification language. The main characteristics of such language are as follows:

- The language is executable (either by compilation or interpretation, similar to languages such as PASCAL, ADA, etc.).
- The data and control structures of the language are independent of specific resource configuration or resource allocation strategies.

The above characteristics imply that although the language is executable it does not refer to any particular processor, memory, or operating system organization. Such decisions, however, belong to the design rather than to the requirements engineering phase.

In conclusion, the operational approach deliberately intertwines 'what' and 'how' considerations in an executable specification model. By doing so, the approach attempts to guarantee an early validation of the (executable) requirements model by the user as well as that of the feasibility of the proposed solution. The operational approach considers requirements engineering processes such as elicitation, specification, and validation as follows:

- The process of elicitation is carried out at an initial stage, prior to the construction of the operational specification.
- The specification process coincides with the construction of an executable specification model.

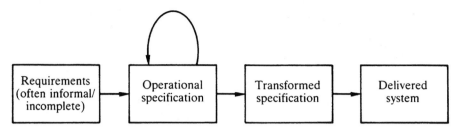

Figure 2.5 The operational paradigm.

- The validation process coincides with the exercise of the operational specification model.

The operational approach has been criticized for dealing with too many detailed technical issues too early. For example, concepts such as processes, asynchronous communication, etc., used in the operational specification are regarded as difficult concepts to be fully understood by end-users. The diagram of Fig. 2.5 shows the various stages of development using the operational model.

2.7.5 Requirements engineering in the transformational model

The transformational approach to software development (Balzer *et al.*, 1983) attempts to automate labour-intensive stages of development such as design and implementation by using the concept of a *transformation*. A transformation is defined as a mapping from a more abstract object (such as a specification) to a less abstract one (such as a design or piece of code). The transformational approach advocates the use of a series of transformations that change a specification into a concrete software system.

The transformational approach implies the need for a formal specification as the initial input, as automatic transformations can only be applied to a formal object (specification). The need for a formal specification, however, contradicts the need for specifications which are comprehensible by the users. In general, the closer the specification is to the users understanding, the harder (in time and effort) it becomes to apply the transformational process. Despite this problem, however, the transformational approach presents a promising new way of developing software for the following reasons:

- Since the transformations are *correctness preserving*, it is guaranteed that once the specifications are proved correct, the final system will also be correct. Thus the specification is the only object that needs to be validated.
- The maintenance effort is significantly reduced since maintenance is now performed on the specification which is easier to understand and modify than code.

The altered code is produced by a two-step process. First, changes are made to the series of transformations which produced the original code and which were recorded during development. Second, the modified set of transformations is 'replayed' in order to derive the new version of the software system.

The transformational systems which have so far been implemented vary as to the degree of human participation in the transformation process which ranges from completely

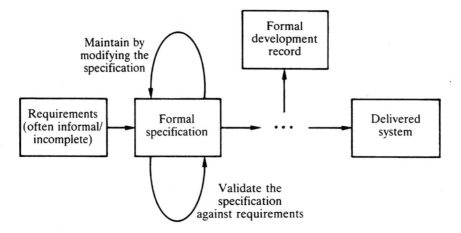

Figure 2.6 The transformational model.

automatic transformations to manual selection of the appropriate ones by the analyst. The stages of the transformational model (shown in Fig. 2.6) correspond to requirements engineering processes as follows:

- Requirements elicitation is the phase which derives an initial informal and incomplete requirements model, prior to starting transformational development.
- Requirements specification is the phase which produces the formal specification model.
- Requirements validation is the transformational phase where the formal model is validated by the user.

The transformational approach has been also criticized for its need to create and validate a formal specifications model as well as for the difficulty of automating the transformation process.

It can be seen from the above discussion that the three software development models—prototyping, operational, and transformational—are not so dissimilar in principle. All three models were proposed as a solution to the problem of inadequate end-user participation caused by the 'waterfall' mode of development. All three models, therefore, propose the creation of an object (prototype, operational specification, and formal specification, respectively) early in the development lifecycle, which can be used as a means of understanding and validating the user requirements.

2.7.6 Requirements engineering in the knowledge-based model

This section briefly describes approaches to requirements engineering which are characterized by the use of intelligent software tools to perform (or support) some activity within requirements engineering. The term 'intelligent' implies that the tools incorporate a knowledge-base consisting of the following:

- knowledge about how to perform some aspect of requirements engineering (e.g. elicitation, specification, validation); and/or

- knowledge about the characteristics of some problem domain (called *domain knowledge*) which can be employed in requirements engineering.

The knowledge-based paradigm does not necessarily imply the use of a software development model different from those discussed previously. Thus, there can be knowledge-based requirements engineering approaches which adopt any of the waterfall, prototyping, operational, etc., models. Therefore, the major differences between knowledge-based and non-knowledge-based approaches exist in the degree of intelligent tool usage in a process within requirements engineering. For instance, requirements validation is conventionally performed by letting the user inspect the requirements model (which can be a piece of text, diagrams, prototype, etc.). If, however, validation is performed by checking the requirements model for consistency against rules (which state when a model is consistent) stored in a knowledge-base, then validation becomes a knowledge-based approach.

Knowledge-based approaches to requirements validation are discussed in Chapter 5. More general knowledge-based tools which assist the process of requirements engineering are examined in Chapter 6.

2.7.7 Requirements engineering according to the domain analysis model

The domain analysis paradigm (Arango, 1988) is the only one introduced so far which departs from the assumption that requirements engineering (and software development in general) is a 'one-off' activity. More specifically, the paradigm realizes the existence of similarity between applications belonging to the same problem domain and advocates that the analysis results from one application be reapplied to the analysis of a similar one.

Domain analysis has been viewed as an activity that takes place prior to requirements engineering (Hall, 1991). While requirements engineering is concerned with analysing and specifying the problem of developing a software application, domain analysis has been concerned with identifying commonalities between different applications under the same domain. The deliverable of domain analysis is a set of objects, relations, and rules that are common in a problem domain and thus can be reused across different applications. For instance, software applications which deal with airline ticket reservations all consider a standard set of objects such as passenger, flight, reservation, ticket, etc. Domain analysis suggests that concepts such as the above can be abstracted and organized in libraries so that they can be reused 'off-the shelf' in future applications. In this respect, domain analysis radically changes our understanding of requirements engineering for the following reasons:

- Phases such as problem understanding which are traditionally considered in requirements engineering are reduced to 'selecting and retrieving the contents of the appropriate library which contains the analysis results of the domain under consideration'.
- The effort for requirements elicitation is significantly reduced since to a large extent elicitation has already be done as part of domain analysis.
- Requirements specification consists of selection of an appropriate component from the reusable analysis components library with possible adaptation if necessary.

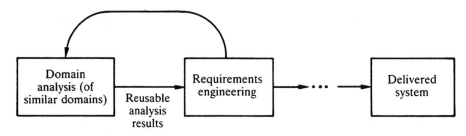

Figure 2.7 The domain analysis approach.

- Finally, the need for validation is reduced since the library components have already been validated as part of domain analysis.

Domain analysis is considered again in Chapter 3 regarding its impact on requirements elicitation. Figure 2.7 shows the impact of domain analysis on requirements engineering.

2.8 MANAGING THE REQUIREMENTS ENGINEERING PROCESSES AND THEIR DELIVERABLES

The previous sections described requirements engineering as the set of intertwined processes of elicitation, specification, and validation. It is important to emphasize that the deliverables of requirements engineering are in a state of *flux*, during this process, and may even remain so through subsequent stages of development such as design and coding. A formal software specification is the end-product of a large number of decisions, negotiations, and assumptions made throughout the requirements engineering process, and, as such, a specification is as valid as the assumptions and decisions which underlie it. It is therefore important to be able to recreate the *rationale* behind some specification item in order to question its appropriateness and validity in the light of changed circumstances. However, this is not possible without assistance from a *rationale recording* process which runs throughout requirements engineering. Such process is beneficial for the following reasons:

- In an explicit form, the rationale behind a system requirement provides a communication mechanism among the members of the development team so that during later stages of development, such as design and maintenance, it is possible to understand what critical decisions were made during requirements specification, what were the alternative options to a particular specification, and why this particular one was selected over the other alternatives.
- The effort required to produce the rationale behind a specification forces requirements engineers to deliberate more carefully about their decisions. The process of deliberation can be assisted by explicitly showing all the arguments in favour or against a particular specification decision.

There are several possible ways of capturing the rationale of specifications in a model. Among them the most widely used is based on a model called *IBIS* (Issue-Based Information System). IBIS was developed in the 1970s for representing design and

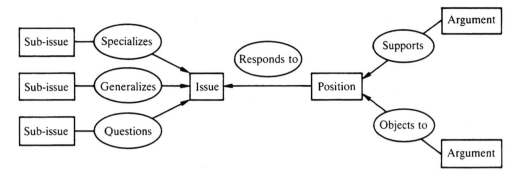

Figure 2.8 The IBIS model.

planning dialogues. Graphical versions of it such as *gIBIS* have been used for documenting the rationale behind software design decisions (Conklin and Begeman, 1989).

Figure 2.8 shows the basic concepts of the IBIS model. An *issue* is the root of the model (e.g. a user need for which a software solution is required). There are also secondary issues (*sub*-issues) which modify the root issue in some way. A *position* is put forth as a potential resolution for the issue (i.e. a *position* represents a software specification which satisifies the user need). There can be more than one alternative position (specification) associated with an issue. In turn, each position is related to arguments which support it and arguments which object to it. These might refer to technical, financial, etc., criteria and constraints, under which the merits of each alternative specification will be judged. Such repertoire of modelling constructs allows IBIS models to be used during requirements analysis and specification sessions as a means of recording the issues deliberated and the decisions made.

In conclusion, rationale capturing models such as IBIS can provide an effective answer to the problem of managing and evolving the products and by-products of the requirements engineering process.

2.9 SUMMARY

Reviewers of the current software engineering literature soon arrive at the conclusion that today no consensus exists as to what constitutes software requirements engineering—its scope, stages, aims, and deliverables. The problem is caused partially by the fact that requirements engineering has only recently been acknowledged as a discipline of software development in its own right. The lack of consensus is also caused by the varying degrees of rigour and formality with which requirements engineering is treated in various software development methods. Finally, the lack of consensus in defining requirements engineering lies in the fact that systems analysis is an inherently ill-defined and ill-structured process. For all these reasons, contemporary software development methods prefer to describe requirements engineering by its products rather by its processes, as proved by the plethora of modelling formalisms in use.

This chapter aimed to look at requirements engineering from a dynamic perspective (i.e. looking at *how* requirements engineering is done) rather than a static one (i.e. what requirements engineering *produces*). In doing so, it abstracted from current proposals for organizing requirements engineering into processes, stages, steps, and so on, to produce a framework of three fundamental processes within requirements engineering, namely elicitation, specification, and validation.

Requirements elicitation was defined as the process of acquiring all the necessary knowledge which is used in the production of the formal requirements specification model.

Requirements specification was defined as the process which receives as input the deliverables of requirements elicitation in order to create a formal model of the requirements (called the requirements specification model).

Requirements validation was defined as the process which attempts to certify that the produced formal requirements model satisfies the users' needs.

The above processes were examined in the context of different software development paradigms, since different paradigms usually put more emphasis on one or other of the processes. In general, recent software paradigms such as prototyping and operational approach pay more attention to validation of requirements by constructing a formal object (prototype, operational specification) with which the user can experiment early in the development lifecycle.

It can be said that all the software development models consider these three major processes of requirements engineering. It is also true that different approaches tend to underestimate or overemphasize one or more of these processes. Traditionally, the least emphasized and considered process of requirements engineering has been *validation*. This, however, has proved to have catastrophic consequences for software projects. It is only natural, therefore, that more recent models such as the prototype model, the operational model, etc., put more emphasis on requirements validation by the user. Furthermore the latest approaches to requirements engineering attempt to rectify the fact that the process still remains the most labour-intensive one in software development. The approaches taken towards requirements engineering automation belong to two broad categories. The first category attempts to automate fairly trivial but nonetheless labour-intensive tasks such as document preparation. The second category includes approaches which attempt to automate (fully or partially) activities in requirements engineering such as specification and validation by using support from knowledge-based software tools. This category also contains approaches which advocate the improvement of productivity in requirements engineering by reusing results from previous analysis activities. Automation of requirements engineering processes will become the key issue in software trends of the near future.

REFERENCES

Alavi M. (1984) An assessment of the prototyping approach to information systems development. *Communications of the ACM*, **27**(6).

Arango G. (1988) Domain engineering for software reuse. Ph.D. thesis, Department of Computer Science, University of California, Irvine.

Balzer R., Cheatham T. E. and Green C. (1983) Software technology in the 1990s: using a new paradigm. *IEEE Computer*, November.

Berzins V. and Gray M. (1985) Analysis and design in MSG 84: formalising functional specifications. *IEEE Transactions on Software Engineering*, **11**(8).

Boehm B. W. (1988) A spiral model of software development and enhancement. *IEEE Computer*, **21**(5).

Castano S. and De Antonellis V. (1993) Reuse of conceptual requirement specifications. *IEEE International Symposium on Requirements Engineering*. IEEE Computer Society Press, San Diego, CA, pp. 121–124.

Conklin J. and Begeman M. L. (1989), gIBIS: A tool for all reasons. *Journal of the American Society for Information Science*, March.

Davis G. B. (1982) Strategies for information requirements determination. *IBM Systems Journal*, **21**(1).

Davis A. M. (1990) *Software Requirements Analysis and Specification*. Prentice Hall, Englewood Cliffs, NJ.

Department of Defense (1988) *Military Standard: Defense System Software Development*. DOD-STD-2167A. Washington, DC, February.

Floyd C. (1984) A systematic look at prototyping. In Budde R. (Ed) *Approaches to Prototyping*. Springer-Verlag, Berlin.

Fugini M. G. and Pernici B. (1992) Specification reuse. In Loucopoulos P. and Zicari R. (Eds), *Conceptual Modelling, Databases and CASE: An Integrated View of Information Systems Development*. Wiley, New York, pp. 535–548.

Hall P. A. V. (1991) Domain analysis. *Proc. UNICOM Seminars*. London, December.

IEEE (1984) *IEEE Guide to Software Requirements Specifications*. Institute of Electrical and Electronics Engineers, New York, IEEE/ANSI Standard 830-1984.

IEEE (1990) *IEEE Standard Glossary of Software Engineering Terminology*. Institute of Electrical and Electronics Engineers, New York, Standard 610.12-1990.

Jackson M. (1982) *Systems Development*. Prentice Hall, Englewood Cliffs, NJ.

Martin C. (1988) *User-centered Requirements Analysis*. Prentice Hall, Englewood Cliffs, NJ.

McCracken D. and Jackson M. (1982) Life cycle concept considered harmful. *ACM SIGSOFT Software Engineering Notes*, **7**(2).

Powers M., Adams D. and Mills H. (1984) *Computer Information Systems Development: Analysis and Design*. South-Western, Cincinnati, OH.

Pressman R. (1987) *Software Engineering: A Practitioner's Approach*, 2nd edn. McGraw-Hill, New York.

Roman G.-C. *et al.* (1984) A total system design framework. *IEEE computer*, **17**(5).

Rombach H. D. (1990) Software specification: a framework. Curriculum Module SEI-CM-11-2.1. Software Engineering Institute, Carnegie Mellon University, Pittsburgh, PA., January.

Royce W. W. (1970) Managing the development of large software systems: concepts and techniques. In *Proc. WESCON*, August.

Wasserman A. *et al.* (1986) Developing interactive information systems with the user software engineering methodology. *IEEE Transactions on Software Engineering*, **12**(2).

Yadav S. *et al.* (1988) Comparison of analysis techniques for information requirements determination. *Communications of the ACM*, **31**(9).

Yeh R. and Ng P. A. (1990) Software requirements—a management perspective. In Thayer R. H. and Dorfman M. (Eds) *System and Software Requirements Engineering*. IEEE Computer Society Press, San Diego, CA.

Zave P. (1984) The operational versus the conventional approach to software development. *Communications of the ACM*, **27**(2).

3

REQUIREMENTS ELICITATION

3.1 INTRODUCTION

In Chapter 2 requirements engineering was said to consist of three major processes, namely requirements elicitation, requirements formalization, and requirements validation. The first of these processes, requirements elicitation, is defined as follows:

- The process of acquiring (eliciting) all the relevant knowledge needed to produce a requirements model of a problem domain.

The above definition implies that requirements elicitation is all about 'understanding' some particular problem domain. Only after understanding the nature, features, and boundaries of a problem can the analyst proceed with a formal statement of the problem (requirements specification) and subsequently with its validation by the user (requirements validation). The following example makes more apparent the need for a thorough understanding of the problem domain, before formal specification is attempted. The example is about the specification of a radar and tracker system for aviation.

The system shall accept *radar messages* from a *short-range radar*. The *scan-period* of the *radar* is 4 seconds. The *frequency* is 2.6–2.7 GHz. The *pulse-repetition interval frequency* is 1040 Hz. The *number of tracks* shall be for 200 aircraft. The *band-rate* is 2400. The *message-size* is 104 bits/message. The system shall begin tracking aircraft that are within 2 miles of the controlled area. *Track initiation* will occur after 6 seconds.

Even in such a small fraction of requirements like the above, the radar-specific terminology can be overwhelming for the analyst who is not familiar with the domain. Moreover, it is impossible for the unfamiliar analyst to test the above specification for things such as consistency and completeness. For instance, there is a possible conflict in the above requirements, between the 2 mile margin for the controlled area and the distance of 4 miles that can be covered by an aircraft travelling at 600 m.p.h. for 24 seconds (which is the initiation time of the tracker). The necessity of understanding radar technology is beyond doubt in this example. This leads, however, to a different sort of question: *where can such (domain) knowledge be found and how can it be elicited?*

In the case of the radar system above, an obvious solution is to have the knowledge supplied to the analyst by the radar (electronics) engineers who are developing the non-software components of the tracker system. They will be able to explain all the domain-specific concepts to the analyst, who will in addition be expected to have a basic understanding of radar technology, as well as mathematical skills. Indeed, as real-life shows with the all the different specializations of software engineers that exist today (commercial systems, telecommunications, real-time systems engineers, etc.), it would probably take an analyst with significant experience in the field to produce a trusted specification for the tracker system above.

Naturally, it is impossible for an analyst to acquire experience in more than a handful of different categories of applications in the span of a lifetime. Moreover, there exist software applications which are 'one of a kind', i.e. knowledge about them cannot be acquired either from other similar ones or from textbooks. Nevertheless, for common or 'one-off' applications the task of the analyst is to

- elicit the knowledge about some problem domain and to some extent become an 'expert' about the domain.

Coad and Yourdon (1991) argue, for example, that the involvement with the domain of the analyst developing a system for air traffic control must be so close as to result in nuances to be discovered which even experts in air traffic control have not yet fully considered.

This chapter is concerned with the problem of *domain knowledge transfer* from some source (i.e. human, book, or any other type of source) to the analyst. Knowledge transfer is classed as a problem for the following reasons:

- The knowledge is not always readily available in a form that can be used by the analyst.
- It is difficult for the analyst to elicit the knowledge from its source, especially when the source is a human 'expert'.

This chapter discusses methods and techniques for eliciting knowledge from some problem domain. It starts with the discussion of the most obvious source of requirements, i.e. the application domain expert. Section 3.3 discusses approaches which view the requirements model as a set of goals that must be achieved, activities that must be performed to achieve the goals, and constraints which restrict the activities that can take place. The idea is intuitive, because in a way the whole software system can be seen as serving a purpose within some larger system (office, factory, etc.). It is only natural, then, that the functioning of the software system must be guided by goals, which are set by the host system. The principle of viewing requirements as goals has many different variations and has been even used for the modelling of non-functional requirements (Chapter 4).

Another requirements elicitation technique discussed is that of *scenario-based elicitation* (Section 3.4). Again, this technique belongs to the more broad category of *prototyping* techniques which are presented in Chapter 5. Under this technique, users participate in executing scenarios that mirror problem solving in real-life situations and in such a way that their expertise (which constitutes part of the problem domain knowledge) is elicited.

Form analysis (Section 3.5) is another elicitation technique and concentrates on knowledge that can be extracted from the various documents (forms) used in the problem domain rather than from humans. This technique is effective in dealing with data-intensive software applications. In contrast, natural language-based knowledge elicitation approaches (Section 3.6) rely not on formal documentation about the problem domain, but on more easily available natural language descriptions, either in the form of text, or as direct input from the user.

Section 3.7 discusses a family of elicitation techniques which are based on the idea of reusing existing requirements specifications. This is based on the following premise:

- There are commonalities between different applications belonging to the same category. Thus eliciting requirements from scratch each time we want to analyse a new application is like reinventing the wheel. In many situations it is feasible (and very cost effective) to reuse requirements from similar old applications into new applications.

In Section 3.8 a different view of requirements elicitation as a *social* process is presented. The basic premise of these approaches is that the problems of requirements elicitation cannot be solved in a purely technological way, because the social context is crucial in this phase of the development process, much more so than subsequent phases such as design and programming.

Section 3.9 gives a comparative of two related disciplines (which have grown independently from each other), namely *requirements elicitation* and *knowledge elicitation*. Knowledge elicitation is the process of extracting knowledge from a human expert with the purpose of encoding it in a *knowledge-based expert system*. There appear to be knowledge elicitation techniques that can be applied to requirements elicitation (and vice versa) and therefore of potential benefit to a requirements analysis professional.

3.2 REQUIREMENTS ELICITATION FROM USERS

Elicitation of requirements from users working in the application domain is the most intuitive of the elicitation approaches since it is the users who should 'know what they want' from the planned software system. In practice, however, elicitation from users presents difficulties for the following reasons:

- Users may not have a clear idea of what they require from the new software system.
- Users may find it difficult to describe their knowledge (expertise) of the problem domain.
- The backgrounds and aims of the users and analysts differ; users employ their own domain-oriented terminology while analysts use a computer-oriented vocabulary.

- Users may dislike the idea of having to use a new (unknown) software system and thus be unwilling to participate in the elicitation process.

To overcome problems such as these, a number of techniques have been devised which enable communication between the analyst and the user and thus the transfer of knowledge from the latter to the former.

The easiest interaction to conceive between analyst and user is called *open-ended interview* (Graham and Jones, 1988). The analyst simply allows the user to talk about his or her task. The lack of formality in the interview makes for a relaxed atmosphere which facilitates the flow of information from the user to the analyst. Open interviews are more appropriate for obtaining a global view of the problem domain and for eliciting general requirements. However, such techniques are inadequate for eliciting detailed information requirements or for describing user tasks in detail. The reason for this is psychological since 'uncaused recall' is often incomplete and unstructured. For the elicitation of more detailed requirements, therefore, methodical approaches are used. *Structured interviewing techniques* (Edwards, 1987) direct the user to specific issues of requirements which must be elicited. In structured interviewing techniques the analyst employs *closed, open, probing*, and *leading* questions in order to overcome the elicitation problems discussed above. Using structured interviews, a great deal of information is acquired and used for the following tasks:

- To fill gaps in domain knowledge acquired so far.
- To resolve obstacles such as lack of consensus among the users.
- To achieve a better support for the environment.

Another technique used to overcome the problem of lack of consensus among the users is the *brainstorming collective decision-making approach* (BCDA) (Telem, 1988). BCDA combines brainstorming and collective decision-making in order to help the analysts understand the problem domain. Brainstorming tackles the problem discussed above, i.e. the difficulty users experience in describing their own expertise. Collective decision-making reduces the problem of lack of consensus with respect to the goals, priorities, etc., that different users set for the software system. In addition, BCDA has the positive effect that it helps users to understand information technology, and analysts to understand organizational needs.

In summary, interviewing techniques are the most straightforward techniques for software elicitation. They require, however, special skills from the analyst since these techniques are sensitive and delicate. These techniques also suffer from a number of problems such as the limited amount of time that users may be available for interviews, psychological difficulties in eliciting user expertise, etc.

3.3 OBJECTIVE AND GOAL ANALYSIS

This category of requirements elicitation approaches is concerned with questions that frequently occur at the start of a software project, such as 'Why does this organization need what its staff have expressed in their requirements statements?, or 'Do they really want what they are stating?' Questions like these reinforce what was emphasized at the beginning of this chapter: 'Only after understanding the nature, features, and boundaries of a problem can the analyst proceed with a formal statement of the problem'. The aim of the activity and goal approaches is therefore the following:

- To attempt to place the requirements (problem) in a wider context.
- To understand how the problem relates to the ultimate problems and objectives of the larger system which will be hosting the software system.
- In short, to attempt to 'get the right requirements'.

Objective and goal analysis approaches are based on a set of key concepts such as *objectives*, *goals*, and *constraints*, which will be defined below.

3.3.1 Concepts of objective and goal analysis

Fundamental to the following discussion is an understanding of the concept of the *teleological view of systems*. According to the teleological view, a system (such as an organization, machine, human, etc.) has a set of goals which it seeks to attain. Thus, the teleological view attempts to explain a system's behaviour in terms of its goals. A *goal* is defined as a defined state of the system. Since a state is described in terms of the values of a number of parameters, a goal can be alternatively defined as a set of desired values for a number of parameters. For instance, if the system is a (profit-making) organization, then one of its goals can be the following:

To make profits of $1M in the next financial year.

Here, the goal parameter is 'profits' and the desired value is '$1M'.

Goals can vary in their degree of specificity (or else abstraction). In general, the more desired values are mentioned, the more specific the goal is. Thus, the goal:

To make profits of $1M in the next financial year.

is more specific (less abstract) than the goal:

To make profits in the next financial year.

The varying degree of specificity (abstraction) in goals has a lot to do with the hierarchical way most human-purpose systems are organized. In a large organization, for example, there can be many levels of management. The job of the senior management (the executives) is to make decisions on the general strategy of the organization. This, however, makes their goals necessarily more abstract than the goals in lower levels of the decision hierarchy. If, for example, the senior management decides that 'the organization must be profitable in the next financial year', it is up to the middle management to specify how profitable the organization will have to be and how this can be achieved. At the next level of seniority (operational management) the goals will be with regard to the tactics and procedures which will ensure the profitability of the organization (Fig. 3.1).

Goals which are more abstract (vague) are sometimes called *objectives*. Objectives do not usually specify 'when', 'how much', or 'how'. An objective could, for instance, state

Figure 3.1 Levels of abstraction in an organization's goals.

'The organization must strive for profitability' without specifying how this profitability will be measured or when it must be attained. Usually, an objective is decomposed into a number of more specific ones (which are therefore goals). There are two different kinds of decomposition which can be applied to the objective. An objective Ob can be decomposed to a conjunctive set of goals $G1, G2, ..., Gn$. The meaning of the AND decomposition is that in order for objective Ob to be attained, *all* goals $G1, G2, ..., Gn$ must be attained. The other kind of objective decomposition is an OR decomposition. If objective Ob is or-decomposed into goals $G1, G2, ..., Gn$, then for objective Ob *to be attained* it is sufficient that *any* of $G1, G2, ..., Gn$ is attained.

The following example shows both AND and OR decompositions. In order for the objective:

Increase profits

to be attained, any of the following goals must be attained:

Increase sales, reduce production cost.

In order for the goal 'reduce production cost' to be attained, *all* of the following must be attained:

Reduce cost of raw material, reduce cost of machinery, increase productivity, reduce staff cost.

The above decomposition of objectives to goals can continue to many different levels of abstraction, creating a *goal hierarchy* (or according to some authors a *goal–subgoal* or *goal–means* hierarchy). Usually, the goals that appear at the lower levels of the hierarchy are called *subgoals* (or *means*) since they represent specific ways in which a goal can be attained. If, for example, the goal 'increase productivity' can be achieved by 'install automatic production system XYZ', then the latter can be called a subgoal, or means towards realizing the former.

In many situations, a subgoal may be instrumental to more than one (super)goals, thus the goal hierarchy (actually a *lattice*) looks similar to Fig. 3.2.

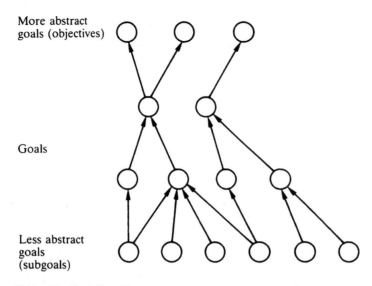

More abstract
goals (objectives)

Goals

Less abstract
goals
(subgoals)

Figure 3.2 Goal hierachies.

Apart from the goal–subgoal relation (which is inter-level), there exist intra-level relations which must be considered when modelling a goal–subgoal hierarchy. Two goals appearing in the same level of the hierarchy can be *mutually supportive* or *mutually conflicting*. Mutually supportive are those goals which affect positively the attainment of each other. Mutually conflicting goals affect negatively the attainment of each other. The goals 'increase automation' and 'reduce investment in new machinery' conflict with each other since automation implies the acquisition of new machinery.

Another concept occurring frequently in objective–goal analysis is that of a *constraint*. A constraint prohibits the full attainment of some objective/goal. Constraints may originate within the system (e.g. in an organization, physical operations, personnel structure, finance, etc., can act as constraints), from the environment (e.g. customers, competitors, laws, government regulations), and so on. When the system under discussion is software, then additional constraints to its development can be limitations of the current technology, constraints imposed by the host system, etc.

In summary, objective–goal analysis approaches view the problem domain as consisting of objectives, goals, subgoals (means), and objectives, organized into a goal–subgoal (ends–means) hierarchy. The use of the goal–subgoal hierarchy is discussed below.

3.3.2 Steps in objective–goal analysis

The purpose of constructing the goal hierarchy in the objective–goal analysis approach is first to identify the software requirements in the context of the problem domain, i.e. the larger system which will become the host of the software system, and second to map software requirements to (higher level) system objectives. Obviously, not the whole of the organization's goal hierarchy will be relevant to the requirements for the software system. The first step, therefore, is to select that portion of the goal hierarchy which is relevant to the software requirements specification. Such a portion of the goal–subgoal–constraint definitions will consist of the following:

- a hierarchy of objectives–goals–constraints which are directly relevant to the information-processing system of the organization and which will consist at the lower levels of
- means towards their realization, i.e. requirements for the software system.

For instance, if the goal 'increase productivity', is refined through many levels of goals–subgoals to 'automate task XYZ', then the latter is an expression of a software requirement. The question that arises now is whether the above requirement is a valid and justifiable one. To answer such a question, we must re-examine the goal hierarchy, paying particular emphasis to cases of conflicting goals. When cases of conflicting objectives–goals occur, some consensus must be reached about the goal structure and its refinement into subgoals (tasks). The ultimate goal of this exercise is to arrive at a consensus among the stakeholders (the parties who have an interest in the software system under development). During this process all sets of alternatives should be evaluated. If, for instance, the objective 'increase productivity' can be attained by either 'automate task XYZ' or 'automate task PQR', then the alternative which is less likely to meet the objective must be eliminated. Repetition of this exercise will arrive at a complete set of requirements which can be directly attributed to valid organizational objectives and which are also associated with organizational/environmental or technical constraints.

Further analysis of the requirement will yield all the detailed information needed for recording in the requirements specification model.

In summary, the steps of objective–goal analysis are as follows:

- Analyse organization and the external environment with which it interacts in terms of objectives, goals, constraints.
- Create goal–subgoal hierarchy consisting of organizational objectives, goals, and constraints and their interrelationships (support, conflict, constraint).
- Validate the model and achieve a consensus among the stakeholders about it.
- Identify the portion of the goal–subgoal hierarchy modelling the information-processing part of the organization.
- Eliminate cases of conflicts in the above model by negotiating/bargaining, etc., with stakeholders.
- Select tasks (requirements) by eliminating alternatives.

Objective–goal analysis approaches tackle the problem of eliciting requirements successfully for the following reasons:

- The analysts have a clear understanding of the problem domain including what belongs to the software system and what belongs to the host system.
- By placing the requirements problem in its wider context, the danger that users will be so overwhelmed by short-term problems that they loose track of the long-term objectives is reduced.
- A number of potential solutions (which otherwise would be lost) can be considered and comparatively evaluated.

Goal-oriented analysis has been used in the contexts of artificial intelligence and cognitive science. The main proposals for applying the approach to requirements modelling appear in Karakostas (1990), and also in Mittermeir *et al.* (1990) and Bubenko and Wangler (1993).

3.4 SCENARIO-BASED REQUIREMENTS ELICITATION

Approaches under this category rely on the strength of scenarios as an (almost) universal form for the organization and for dissemination of experience. In the most general sense, a *scenario* is a story that illustrates how a perceived system will satisfy a user's needs. Scenarios are important instruments for creating social meaning and a shared sense of participation (Crowley, 1982), i.e. elements needed in a process such as requirements elicitation.

More specifically, during a requirements elicitation session, a scenario represents an idealized but detailed description of a specific instance of a human–computer interaction. Scenarios can use flexible media, close to the end-user's conceptualization of the system, such as text, pictures, or diagrams. They can also be structured in various ways such as dialogues or narrative descriptions.

There is a close relation between scenarios and *prototypes*. Prototypes (which are discussed in detail in Chapter 5) are mock-up versions of the software system. The difference between scenarios and prototypes lies in the fact that the latter are more general than the former. A scenario deals with only one instance of human–computer interaction which is supposed to be typical for the expected use of the future software system. In contrast, a prototype mimics more than one instance and type of interaction between the user and the software system under development. This can be better explained in the following example concerning a university library system.

Consider a university library which has a computerized system for checking books in and out. A checkout scenario for a book is as follows. A student arrives at the assistance desk with a book to be checked out. The library assistant asks the student for his/her student card which contains the student's ID.
- The assistant enters the ID on the screen
- The assistant checks the response to see if the borrower's privileges are restricted for any reason. If not, the book's ID is entered on the screen.
- After the ID is entered, the book's title and the due date for the loan are displayed on the screen.
- The assistant enters a 'Y' at the 'OK' prompt and at that point the volume is on loan to the student.

The above scenario is supposed to represent a fictitious but realistic human–computer interaction in the library system. Because it is realistic, the scenario allows the elicitation of expertise from the user. The library assistant, for example, will be in a position to criticize the above scenario for its lack of realism, much more easily than it would have been with the case of a formal requirements model. The library assistant could for example recall that:

When I am checking-out a book for a student, I always check if that student has any overdue books, in which case I remind the student about it, by showing the book titles and due-back dates.

The analyst understands such recalled experience as a missing requirements statement. More specifically, the analyst notes the following:

- Books which are overdue (defining overdue as the due date being before 'today') must be flagged as such.
- All overdue books for a student must be displayed on the screen in a checkout session.

The analyst can proceed with other similar scenarios which will elicit more tacit knowledge from the library assistant and help towards completing and refining the requirements model. Other useful scenarios might include the following:

The student who wants to check out a book does not have his student card with him. However, the student is at the same time checking in a book he borrowed previously. Can the information from the previous checkout be used for the new checkout?

A student wants to check out a book which according to the records has already been checked out. What happens in such case?

It is obviously up to the analyst to select the most appropriate scenarios, bearing in mind that usually the user's time for participation is limited. Also, scenarios should be used to clarify issues and implications of a requirement when there is no other way to do so. If, for instance, the library procedures are clearly written down, there is no need to waste the user's time in long interaction sessions. Nevertheless, the scenarios technique is invaluable in cases where a large part of the requirements is concerned with the user interface. There is no better way of understanding the interaction requirements than giving the user hands-on experience with the software!

In summary, the scenario techniques for requirements elicitation are based on the principle that users find it easier to transfer their expertise to the analyst through an active 'story telling' session, rather than through questionnaires and interviews. Together with prototyping techniques (discussed in Chapter 5), scenario techniques present a promising solution to the difficult problem of communication and transfer of expertise between the analyst and the user. Scenario-based techniques for requirements elicitation are documented in Hooper and Hsia (1982), Holbrook (1990), Karakostas and Loucopoulos (1989) and Loucopoulos and Karakostas (1989). Today, many CASE tools (see Chapter 6) provide the ability to develop a sequence of screen layouts along with a background of narrative illustrating their use.

3.5 FORM ANALYSIS

In contrast to scenario-based requirements elicitation approaches, form analysis approaches do not regard the user as the prime source of knowledge about the problem domain. They instead rely on a communication object very widely used in organizations, namely *forms*. A form is any structured collection of variables which are appropriately formatted to support data entry and retrieval. A form is a promising source of knowledge about a domain for the following reasons:

- It is a formal model and thus less ambiguous and inconsistent than equivalent knowledge expressed in natural language.
- A form is a data model, thus it can provide the basis for developing the structural component of a functional model.
- Important information about organizations is usually available in forms.
- The acquisition of forms is easy since they are the most commonplace object in an organization.
- The instructions which normally accompany the forms provide an additional source of domain knowledge.
- Forms analysis can be automated more easily than analysis of other sources of requirements knowledge such as text, drawings, etc.

The most common use of forms is as an input to the process of constructing an entity–relationship model (Chen, 1976). An entity–relationship model consists of the following modelling constructs:

- Entities—objects of interest in the problem domain
- Relationships—meaningful associations among entities
- Attributes—properties of entities

The following example will clarify the concepts of form, entity, relationship, and attribute.

A sales order form contains information about a sales transaction. The information contained in such forms is usually about

—the sale's order number
—the date of the sale
—the number of the corresponding customer order
—the name and address of the customer that raised the order
—the name and address of the customer where the order is to be sent (billing address)
—the names, prices per unit, quantities and amounts of the products sold with the order
—the total (before tax), tax and total after tax value of the order
—the 'ID' of the salesperson that prepared the sales order

In the above description of the information appearing in a sales order a number of concepts, such as 'order number', 'date of sale', 'customer', and so on can be found. Some of these concepts can be used to model entities, relationships, or attributes in an E–R model which describes the problem domain of sales orders. Mapping the concepts 'hidden' in a form to appropriate constructs of an E–R model is actually the task of the form-analysis approaches. In general, there are no clear-cut rules which state what can correspond to an entity, relationship, etc. Different approaches therefore apply their own tactics in order to overcome the lack of formal rules:

- Some approaches apply manual methods to extract the E–R constructs from a form, i.e. they rely on the analyst's judgement and experience.
- Other approaches automate the analysis process by using heuristic rules to match forms contents with constructs.

Naturally, automated approaches to form analysis are more appealing than manual ones since they reduce the analyst's overhead as well as the number of possible errors. One of the best-known automatic form analysis approaches (Choobineh *et al.*, 1988) uses three kinds of heuristic rules, namely *entity identification rules*, *attribute attachment rules*, and *relationship identification rules*. The following are examples of such rules:

Entity identification rule
Any form field which is the source of another form field, whether of this form or another is a possible entity
Application of this rule to the sales order example will yield CUSTOMER ORDER as an entity since the value of the CUSTOMER ORDER# field comes from another form (not shown above), namely CUSTOMER ORDER

Attribute attachment rule
Any field which has a small proximity factor to a field which is 'discovered' as an entity is probably an attribute of that entity. (The proximity factor of a field is defined as the difference between the position of the field and the position of another field that has been 'discovered' as an attribute of the entity.) This rule captures the observation that the attributes of an entity appear physically close in a form.
Application of the above rule would show, for example, that TAX is an attribute of the ORDER entity, after its physically close TOTAL BEFORE TAX has been found to be an attribute of the same entity.

Relationship identification rules
Relationship identification rules are more complicated than those for entity identification and attribute attachment. Applications of such rules (which are beyond the scope of this book) would show, for example, that entity ORDER is related to entity SALESPERSON by relationship PREPARES.

Application of rules such as the above mentioned would result in the creation of an E–R model such as the one shown in Fig. 3.3 The resulting schema could be checked automatically for consistency (e.g. for things like entities having the same name). Form contents which cannot be automatically analysed must be considered by the analyst who decides about their roles in the E–R model. Finally the user would be presented with the completed E–R model in order to validate it.

In conclusion, forms are useful sources of problem domain knowledge which can be effectively used in the process of requirements elicitation. Although form analysis

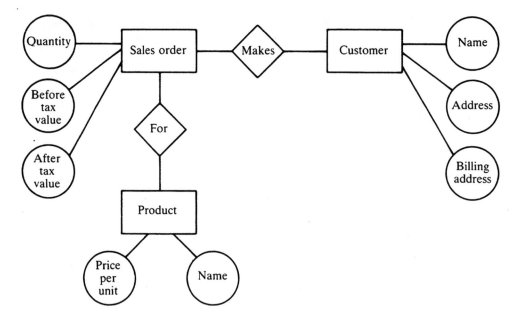

Figure 3.3 An entity–relationship model of a sales form contents.

approaches are limited to data intensive software applications, their effectiveness in eliciting domain knowledge, in particular when they are used with an expert tool, cannot be underestimated.

3.6 NATURAL LANGUAGE APPROACHES

The elicitation techniques described so far are based on a diversity of problem domain knowledge sources such as users (either as groups or as individuals) and forms. It is true, however, that for the majority of the domains the most common knowledge representation medium is natural language (NL). The attractiveness of eliciting requirements from NL descriptions lies in the fact that in most cases everything that is worth knowing about the problem domain can be stated (or is somewhere written) in NL. Thus NL elicitation approaches fall into two categories:

- Approaches which directly interact with the user in NL in order to elicit the requirements from the user.
- Approaches which elicit the requirements from NL text.

Three things make requirements statement in NL attractive: *vocabulary, informality*, and *syntax*. Indeed, the existent vocabulary of thousands of predefined words used to describe any possible concept makes NL an efficient communications medium.

Informality (i.e. the possibility that a statement is ambiguous, incomplete, contradictory, and/or inaccurate) is very important also. While informality is not a desired feature of the final requirements specifications document, it is very useful in early phases of requirements engineering as a means of dealing with complexity. As a matter of fact, in everyday situations it is the informality that comes with NL which allows us to communicate without being bogged down by detail. Syntax, finally, is a useful feature of NL because it is familiar and thus requires no time for learning it.

Features of NL such as the above have made 'programming without programmers' a dream in the first decades of computing. Soon, however, it was realized that the promising idea of automatic generation of software from user requirements is not feasible in the vast majority of situations. Today, the focus of research is on powerful formal specification languages and the use of knowledge (see knowledge-based tools for requirements engineering in Chapter 6) rather than on the pursuit of the 'NL specification' dream. However, NL descriptions of the problem domain have been proved an efficient source from which knowledge can be elicited. State-of-the-art research approaches today consider only descriptions in a subset of NL, from which they can derive a formal requirements model. Other manual approaches elicit the knowledge from NL text by applying a number of heuristics and 'rules of thumb'.

The automated approaches to NL analysis are facing the problem of the enormous richness and variety of expressions that can be stated in NL. Since unrestricted NL understanding is still an unresolved problem of artificial intelligence, such approaches necessarily restrict the acceptable input to only a small subset of NL. A NL approach called OICSI (Rolland and Proix, 1992), for example, uses so-called *cases* of NL sentences. A case is a type of relationship that groups of words have with the verb in any clause of a sentence. There are nine major cases, considered by the OICSI approach, namely OWNER, OWNED, ACTOR, TARGET, CONSTRAINED, CONSTRAINT, LOCALIZATION, ACTION, OBJECT. The meaning of these cases is exemplified by the following set of sentences.

In the sentence:

A subscriber is described by a name, an address, and a number.

'subscriber' is associated to the OWNER case, and 'name', 'address', 'number' are associated to the OWNED case.

In the sentence:

A subscriber borrows books.

'subscriber' is associated to the ACTOR case and the OWNER case, while 'books' is associated to the OWNED case. The entire clause is associated to the ACTION case.

In the sentence:

When a subscriber makes a request for a loan, the request is accepted if a copy of the request book is available, else the request is delayed.

the clause 'When a subscriber makes a request for a loan' is associated to the LOCALIZATION case. Inside this clause, the phrase 'request for a loan' is associated to an OBJECT case. The clause 'if a copy of the requested book is available' is associated to the CONSTRAINT case. The clause 'the request is accepted' is associated to the

ACTION and the CONSTRAINED case. Inside this clause, the word 'request' is associated to the TARGET case.

The above cases are mapped to the constructs of a requirements modelling formalism used by the REMORA methodology (Rolland and Richard, 1982), according to a set of mapping rules. The constructs used in REMORA are *entity*, *actions*, *events*, and *constraints*. For example, cases of type OWNER, OWNED, ACTOR, TARGET, OBJECT are mapped to entities of the requirements model, cases of type LOCALIZA-TION are mapped to events, and so on.

As a result, in the above sentences, 'subscriber' would be mapped to an entity type, the clause 'When a subscriber makes a request for a loan' would be mapped to an event, etc.

The OICSI environment also provides a facility of creating a *paraphrase* of the generated conceptual model which can be used for its validation (validation and the paraphrasing technique are thoroughly discussed in Chapter 5).

Other automated requirements elicitation approaches which use NL as input include SECSI (Bouzegoub and Gardarin, 1986) and ACME (Kersten *et al.*, 1986). However, current automated approaches have limited applicability since they can accept only a small subset of NL as input and create requirements models only in a few formalisms.

Manual approaches to NL requirements elicitation, on the other hand, are more flexible because they rely on the superior NL understanding capabilities of humans. Such approaches analyse NL descriptions in order to identify constructs (verbs, nouns, adjectives, etc.) which will map to constructs of a requirements modelling formalism, according to some rules. NL analysis is a technique favoured by a category of requirements specification approaches called *object-oriented* (Chapter 4). For the sake of this discussion it will suffice to say that object-oriented approaches consider the following constructs:

- *Objects*—entities of interest appearing in the problem domain
- *Attributes* of objects—i.e. characteristic properties of objects, and
- *Operations*—actions performed or suffered by the objects

A sample strategy for identifying objects, attributes, and operations is given below. Similar (more elaborate) strategies are proposed by authors of object-oriented analysis methods such as Booch (1986). The strategy is as follows:

- Objects are determined by looking at the NL descriptions for nouns or noun clauses.
- Attributes of objects are identified by identifying all adjectives and then associating them with their respective objects (nouns).
- Operations are determined by underlying all verbs, verb phrases, and predicates and relating each operation to the appropriate object.

To illustrate the use of the above rules, consider the NL description of the requirements for a radar and tracker system, first listed in the introduction of this chapter.

The system shall accept radar messages from a short-range radar. The scan-period of the radar is 4 seconds. The frequency is 2.6–2.7 GHz. The pulse-repetition interval frequency is 1040 Hz. The number of tracks shall be for 200 aircraft. The band-rate is 2400. The message-size is 104 bits/message. The system shall begin tracking aircraft that are within 2 miles of the controlled area. Track initiation will occur after 6 seconds.

After scanning the above description for nouns, the following objects are identified:

(tracker) system
radar
aircraft
(controlled) area

The second step identifies attributes (properties) of the above object. Most of the attributes are identified by looking at nouns and clauses that qualify the objects found above. For example, 'message' is a property of radar; 'short-range' is a qualification of radar, and is further analysed to 'range' (which is the radar's attribute) and 'short' which is the value of it. Other attribute–value pairs for the radar are:

(scan period, 4 seconds), (frequency, 2.6–2.7 GHz), (pulse repetition interval frequency, 1040 Hz),
(number of tracks, 200), (band rate, 2400) (message size 104 bits/message) (track initiation 6 seconds).

The other object with properties identified in the above text is 'aircraft' which has the property 'distance from controlled area'.

The third type of analysis of the above text attempts to identify operations suffered or performed by objects.

The operations identified by looking at action and event descriptions are 'send' performed by 'radar' and suffered by 'system'. The parameters of the operation 'send' are contained in the attribute 'message' of radar.

Similarly, the operations 'tracking' and 'track initiation' performed by 'system' are identified.

It can be seen from the above example that object-oriented analysis of NL provides the analyst with a simple mechanism for representing key concepts in the problem domain. Because the approach uses heuristic rules it relies to some extent on the ability of the analyst to apply the rules effectively, as well as on his or her familiarity with the analysed domain. Usually, a number of iterations will be required before the analyst arrives at a stable initial set of objects, attributes, and operations. Nevertheless the simplicity of the approach make its use as a first-stage requirements elicitation technique worthwhile.

In summary, requirements elicitation from NL is a promising approach (because the majority of knowledge about a domain is expressed in NL) which suffers, however, from a number of limitations, namely:

1. The complexity of NL makes the development of tools which can analyse unrestricted NL descriptions impossible; thus, today only small subsets of NL can be processed by automated tools.

2. The ambiguity of NL makes it unsuitable as a means to express a formal requirements model; therefore, all NL requirements must at some stage be translated to some formal language.

3.7 TECHNIQUES FOR REUSE OF REQUIREMENTS

Under this heading are examined approaches to requirements elicitation which are based on the following intuitively appealing idea: *requirements which have been already captured for some application can be reused in specifying another similar application.* This statement seems appealing for the following reasons:

- Since requirements elicitation is admittedly the most labour- and time-consuming part of software development, any reduction in the time and resources it uses can result in significant overall productivity improvement.
- There is a significant degree of similarity in systems which belong to the same application area. As Jones (1984) indicates, only 15 per cent of the requirements for a new system are unique to the system; the remaining 85 per cent comes from the requirements of existing similar ones.

Despite being a promising idea, requirements reusability is faced with a number of practical questions of applicability. The first question relates to the fact that requirements documents for existing systems are not easily available. This applies in particular to older systems for which the requirements were rarely recorded on any medium other than paper, or updated or revised. The second question lies in the apparent difficulty of checking the suitability (relevance, consistency, etc.) of an old requirement in the context of the specifications for the new system. It is obvious, therefore, that for the idea of requirements reusability to become reality, the following things must become possible:

- Requirements for existing systems must be easily accessible.
- There must be facilities for selecting an old requirement, testing its suitability in the context of the new requirements model and modifying it if necessary.
- All the above must cost less than simply doing requirements elicitation from scratch.

The approaches which are going to be discussed below, attempt to bring solutions to the above prerequisites to the reusability of requirements. More specifically, requirements reuse approaches tackle the problem of selecting and adopting an existing requirement for reuse.

Among the approaches falling in the category of 'requirements reuse' are the following:

- *Domain analysis.* Domain analysis has been characterized as the precursor to requirements analysis. Domain analysis identifies objects, rules, and constraints common among different (but similar) domains and formalizes them. In this way, requirements elicitation can use the results of domain analysis and save a significant amount of effort (Arango, 1959).

- *Reusable requirements libraries.* Many approaches have advocated the development and maintenance of a library of reusable requirements components. Reusable components can have a significant impact on the effectiveness of requirements elicitation.
- *Reverse engineering.* Reverse engineering is a technique of obtaining higher-level information (requirements specifications/designs) from lower-level ones such as code. The technique seems to be promising, since some part of the requirements for a new software system is usually captured in an existing older system.

The final area of techniques, *reverse engineering*, tackles the problem of acquiring the requirements for existing systems from a different angle. Reverse engineering reconstitutes the requirements model of a software system from information available in sources such as design, code, documentation, etc. The primary aim of reverse engineering is to make old applications easier maintainable by maintaining specifications instead of code. However, a by-product of reverse engineering is that it makes the requirements model available again. This model can be used either to reimplement parts of the existing system or to provide the basis for a new system. In this respect, reverse engineering facilitates the task of requirements elicitation. The above-mentioned categories of requirements reusability will now be discussed in more detail.

3.7.1 Reuse of requirements specifications

Under this heading come all the approaches which propose libraries of reusable requirements as well as techniques for reusing them. In accordance with the general trends for automation in software development, these approaches tend to automate activities such as selection and modification of a reusable requirement. It must be noticed that the approaches described below are still at an experimental stage. This does not, however, reduce the validity of the ideas which they demonstrate, i.e. that reuse of requirements is a technique which the analyst uses anyway, sometimes even subconsciously. Psychological experiments (Vitalari and Dickson, 1983) have revealed that reuse of requirements from similar systems is a common strategy employed by experienced analysts when faced with the analysis of a new system. As a matter of fact, it is exactly the ability to reuse past analysis expertise that makes the difference between an experienced analyst and an inexperienced one.

The first approach to requirements reusability comes in the context of a long-term research project known as the *Knowledge-Based Requirements Assistant* (KBRA) (Balzer *et al.*, 1988) which aims at producing an intelligent tool for requirements elicitation and analysis. The reusable requirements in the KBRA tool appear as *formulas*, which can be engineering equations of the form 'distance = rate * time', statistical tables, or simulation-generated tables. Formulas are used to capture aspects such as constraints on the non-functional requirements of the system such as accuracy, resolution, processing and response time, coverage, etc. Other uses of formulas include tracing of formula-derived requirements, critiquing requirements input, and suggesting ways for completing partial descriptions of requirements.

Another approach under the KBRA project, the *Requirements Apprentice* (Reubinstein and Waters, 1991), codifies the reusable requirements in a *cliché library*. The term cliché is used to refer to a concept which is common in a class of similar problem domains. The clichés are classified into the categories of *environment*, *needs*, and *system*.

A fragment of a cliché library contains clichés about the *information system* (which maintains a database of information) and the *tracking system* (which follows the state of something in the environment), which are both special cases of system.

In a typical session with the RA, the analyst is able to give informal definitions of requirements, which the RA matches to clichés already stored in its knowledge base. For instance, assume that the analyst wants to specify requirements for a university library system. RA has an extensive knowledge about information systems, tracking systems, and repositories, but no knowledge about libraries or library information system. The analyst can therefore define the word library in terms of a repository and specify that its state is the set of books contained in it, as follows:

```
(Define Library :Ako Repository
     :Defaults (:Collection-Type Book))
```

Because RA does not have a definition for 'books', the analyst must explain what a book is in terms of another cliché called *physical object*, while at the same time defining *title*, *author*, and *Isbn* to be properties of *book*.

```
(Define Book :Ako Physical Object
     :Member-Roles (Title Author Isbn))
```

Continuing in a similar manner, the analyst starts to define the functionality of the library system which is then checked by RA for consistency and completeness (based on expectations set up by various clichés). Obviously, in this approach RA plays an important role in requirements elicitation by allowing the analyst to speak in terms of high-level concepts which are subsequently refined into a specific and formal requirements model.

The last approach discussed under the section of 'reusable requirements' employs *analogical reasoning* as the technique for reusing a specification (Sutcliffe and Maiden, 1992). The power of analogical reasoning lies in its potential to retrieve knowledge from one domain and apply it to a different (but similar) domain. Although there are many approaches to analogical reasoning, they have as a common concept the development of an abstract knowledge structure which contains commonalities of the two domains.

For instance, consider the domains of *theatre reservation system* and *university course administration system*. Although belonging to different areas, the two domains share a significant number of features (e.g. reservations, waiting lists, places). It is therefore possible to abstract from the two domains a *resource allocation system* involving a *resource* (seats, places) and *clients* (theatre-goers, students).

Analogical reuse of requirements involves three processes, namely *categorization* of a new problem, *selection* of a candidate requirements model belonging to the same category, and *customization* of the selected analogous requirements to the new domain.

Requirements reuse by analogy is a frequently (albeit informally and sometimes subconsciously) employed technique. When supported by a tool, the technique can help to overcome the inherent difficulties encountered by inexperienced analysts. Similar to other tool-supported reuse techniques, analogical reuse is hindered by the excessive resources that the construction of a reusable requirements knowledge base takes.

3.7.2 Domain analysis for requirements elicitation

Most of the reuse approaches are silent as to how the mass of reusable requirements will be initially acquired. Domain analysis, in contrast, aims at creating the infrastructure needed for reuse of requirements, via the following processes:

- Identifying categories of problem domains, i.e. of similar applications.
- Identifying and formalizing the concepts which are common among the different applications in the domain.
- Organizing the concepts in libraries of reusable components and providing facilities for accessing them.

Domain analysis is a term used to describe the systematic activity of identifying, formalizing and classifying the knowledge in a problem domain. Jim Neighbors, one of the pioneers in the area, defined domain analysis as the activity of identifying objects and operations of a class of similar systems in a particular problem domain as well as of needs and requirements for a collection of systems which seem 'similar' (Neighbors, 1984).

It can be deduced from the above definition that the objectives of domain analysis and requirements analysis are the same, the difference being that domain analysis considers the requirements of more than one application. As mentioned in the introduction to this chapter, what makes requirements elicitation difficult is the lack of understanding of the problem domain. In this respect, domain analysis comes as an aide to requirements elicitation in the sense that it provides all the knowledge required by the latter in a reusable format. Thus, under the domain analysis paradigm, requirements elicitation becomes a sequence of selection of reusable requirement, followed by possible adaptation of requirement for incorporation in the new requirements model.

It must be noted that domain analysis caters for all the phases of software development instead of just for requirements analysis. As suggested in Prieto-Diaz and Arango (1991) for example, 'Domain Analysis is the process of identification, acquisition, and evolution of reusable information on a problem domain'.

Domain analysis needs a representation vehicle in order to convey the reusable knowledge from a domain. Requirements modelling formalisms (the most important of which being the object-oriented model) such as those discussed in Chapter 4 are usually adequate for more of the domain analysis. Domain analysis requires, in addition, a set of methods and tools for its application. As various researchers have noted, domain analysis is a difficult process, requiring usually four months of an expert's time to complete a first attempt at a domain. The cost of this initial investigation can be quickly amortized as the results of domain analysis increase the productivity and quality of the software projects on which they are applied. Major inputs to the domain analysis process are technical literature, existing system implementations, expert advice, etc. Major outputs of domain analysis include a taxonomy of domain concepts, standards (e.g. for user interfaces), generic architectures of systems, and domain-specific languages. A plethora of experts is also required to participate in domain analysis such as domain experts, analysts, librarians (who classify, update, and distribute the reusable components), etc.

Domain analysis is a young discipline, which nevertheless is capable of changing the conventional ways of developing software. So far it has been applied only to a small number of large-scale projects, such as CAMP (common software components in a missile system) with considerable success (Hall, 1991).

3.7.3 Reverse engineering

Reverse engineering (Chickofsky and Cross, 1990) is the process of analysing a software system in order to do the following:

- Identify its components and their interrelationships.
- Create representations of the system in another form or at a higher level of abstraction.

In the context of this chapter only the type of reverse engineering which reconstructs the system requirements specifications from lower-level information is considered. From this perspective, therefore, the outcome of reverse engineering is a requirements model which can be directly used in the elicitation of the requirements for the new system. Despite the preferred treatment of software development as an activity that starts from scratch, this is rarely the case. In the majority of cases, a new system is built as an 'extension', 'enhancement', etc., of an existing one, and in some cases the new system is only a sub-system of the older one. The importance of reverse engineering in obtaining the requirements of the original system cannot therefore be underestimated.

In many situations, the task of reverse engineering is hindered by the loss of information which was originally created during software development. Information such as the justification for a particular specification, the rationale behind a design decision, the link between a requirement and the corresponding design, etc., is rarely recorded during software development. Also subsequent (maintenance) changes to code are not reflected on the requirements document which thus becomes inconsistent with the actual running system. For all these reasons, reverse engineering a system to its requirements is a difficult, or sometimes impossible task.

Most existing automated approaches to reverse engineering rely on low-level documentation (i.e. code) in order to re-create higher level documents such as designs. Moving from design to requirements, however, remains an insurmountable obstacle in many situations, unless some necessary information about the software system becomes available. Recent experimental techniques (e.g. Biggerstaff, 1988; Karakostas, 1992) have succeeded in re-creating the requirements model of a system by relying more on knowledge that can be found in the program code alone. Central to the success of these approaches is the concept of the problem domain model. A domain model contains representations of the major concepts that appear in the problem domain modelled by the software system. In addition to that, a domain model contains *development-specific* knowledge, i.e. patterns which show how the concepts are *typically* transformed to design and coding constructs.

In the experimental system IRENE (an acronym for Intelligent Reverse Engineering Environment) described in Karakostas (1992), the domain knowledge base consists of the following:

- Concepts typically appearing in the domain. For instance, in a payroll application typical concepts include *tax, taxable-salary, tax-rate*, etc.
- Knowledge about relations between the concepts, e.g. that the *taxable-salary* and the *tax-rate* determine the payable *tax*.

- Implementation knowledge, such as the knowledge that *tax* is implemented in COBOL as a *small integer* (between 0 and 100).

Based on the above types of knowledge, IRENE searches the program code in order to match portions of code with domain concepts. IRENE can, for example, verify that a domain concept is mentioned in the original requirements (e.g. that *tax-rate* is defined in the requirements for calculating *tax payable*). The system can also identify possible definitions of concepts which are 'hidden' in the code but not mentioned in the requirements document. For instance, the system can come across the data name TX-RELF used in the calculation of *tax payable*. By looking at the library of domain concepts, IRENE 'suspects' that TX-RELF corresponds to concept *tax-relief* even though this was not mentioned in the requirements document! In this respect, IRENE not only reconstructs the true requirements for the software, but also corrects inconsistencies, outdated definitions, etc., that might appear in the existing requirements document.

Knowledge-based systems like the above have the potential to provide a truly automated solution to the reverse engineering of requirements. Since, however, reconstructing the original requirements is paramount to the elicitation of new requirements, the analyst must use any existing documentation that can lead to (even a partial) reconstruction of the old requirements. Care must be taken, however, that the analyst is not relying too much ('anchoring' his or her analysis) on the old requirements since they might describe things which are of no use to (or even not true about) the new system.

Despite its pitfalls, retrieving and reusing existing requirements for requirements elicitation is a pragmatic technique with real importance. The degree of successful application of requirements reusability is determined by factors such as the following:

- The availability, accessibility, testability, and modifiability of the existing requirements.
- The extent to which the new software system is similar to existing one(s).

As automation of activities like requirements analysis and specification becomes more widespread, and more software development related information is captured and stored in repositories (Chapter 6), we can expect in the near future a large increase in the popularity of requirements reusability techniques.

3.8 TASK ANALYSIS FOR REQUIREMENTS ELICITATION

Task analysis is an effective method for eliciting user requirements, in particular those requirements concerned with human–computer interaction issues. The term 'task analysis' refers to a set of methods and techniques which analyse and describe the way users do their jobs in terms of:

- Activities they perform and how such activities are structured.
- What knowledge is required for the performance of the activities.

Historically, task analysis has focused in describing in a very detailed manner the order with which people perform their activities, starting with *plans*, down to the level of basic

```
0 in order to check out a book
1 get the borrower's library card
    1.1 check to see if the card is valid
    1.2 check the borrower's record to see if the number of
        borrowed books allowed at any time has been exceeded
    1.3 get the borrower's name from the card
    1.4 get the card's number

2 get the book from the borrower

3 get a new (unused) check-out card
    3.1 enter the current date on the check-out card
    3.2 enter the borrower's name on the check-out card
    3.3 enter the book's catalogue number on the record
    3.4 enter the due back date on the record
        3.4.1 calculate the date the book is due back
        3.4.2 write the due back date on the check-out card
4 stamp the book with the due back date
5 hand the book back to the borrower
```

Figure 3.4 A plan for checking out a book.

tasks which cannot be further analysed (Diaper, 1989a). Hierarchical task analysis is a method which builds a hierarchy of tasks and sub-tasks and also plans describing in what order and under what conditions sub-tasks are performed. Figure 3.4 uses the library case study first discussed in Section 3.3 of this chapter to show the decomposition of the task *check-out book*.

In the plan shown in Fig. 3.4 not all the sub-tasks need to be performed, nor necessarily in the order presented. For example, Task 2 ('get the book from the borrower') can be performed before Task 1 ('get the borrower's library card'). In addition, there are no clear cut rules as to the level where the decomposition of tasks into sub-tasks must terminate.

Guidelines suggest, however, that the attempt further to analyse tasks which contain complex motor responses (physical actions) or internal decision-making may result in incorrect identification of sub-tasks.

The use of methods and techniques in order to describe the knowledge required to perform a task is called *Knowledge-based analysis* (Diaper, 1989b) and is complimentary to hierarchical task analysis. *Knowledge-based analysis* creates models of objects, relations and events in the task domain and in this respect it is similar to functional modelling approaches (see Chapter 4). However, the aim of knowledge-based analysis differs from that of modelling of functional requirements, in the sense that the former does not attempt to model entities which will be represented in the information system but considers instead physical entities. The example of Fig. 3.5 shows a hierarchy of real people who use the library facilities. Note that this hierarchy may differ from the one that will be eventually modeled inside the library's computerized information system.

Task analysis can provide a valuable input to the requirements elicitation process. However, such input is principally one of clarifying and organizing the knowledge about the problem domain. Task analysis cannot yield requirements for the new system since it refers to the existing system, not the planned system, and in addition it includes many elements which will not be part of the future software system. Nevertheless, task analysis can provide the basis for specifying the requirements for the new systems based on

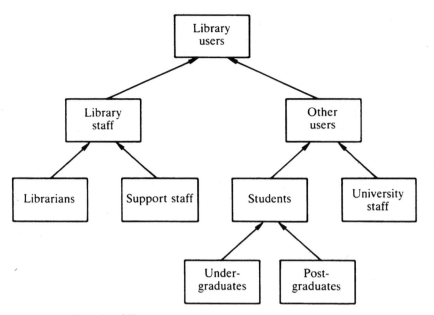

Figure 3.5   Hierarchy of library users.

modifications, extensions and novel features which must be incorporated in the current system. Going back to the example of Fig. 3.4, many of the listed tasks will continue to be performed in the new system, albeit in a new computerized form, some may disappear and others may need to be re-taught completely.

3.9 REQUIREMENTS ELICITATION AS A SOCIAL PROCESS

There is a body of work in requirement engineering which is based on the premise that requirements elicitation is not primarily a technical problem, but a process that should be carried out within a social context. Some researchers claim that the lack of proper consideration of the social context in which the software will be used accounts for the majority of failures, i.e. for projects in which either no system can be built that satisfies the user requirements, or in which the developed system does not support the real user needs.

Socio-technical approaches to requirements elicitation are based on the premise that the social issues of the system (organization) which will host the software system are as important as the technical ones and that the two are inevitably interdependent. According to these approaches 'elicitation' is probably not an appropriate term since it assumes that requirements are 'out there' to be elicited. In reality, however, a user requirement is more an outcome of the interaction between the users and the requirements engineer, rather than some pre-existing concept in the users' minds.

Elicitation, according to the socio-technical approaches, cannot be practised at the level of individual users, in isolation from their environments and from their interactions with each other. As a consequence, requirements have meaning only within the context (time, place, and situation) in which they were observed. This, of course, renders the classic requirements analysis techniques, which attempt to isolate the requirements from their context, inadequate.

The argument in favour of adopting different techniques to those advocated by traditional systems analysis methods is that in traditional methods the user plays a passive role. A user is simply considered as the provider of information pertinent to the requirements elicitation process in hand. However, socio-technical approaches suggest that system design should be considered in a social and organizational context (Mumford and Weir, (1979), that a more active participation of users is required, and that much thought must be given to the constitution of the development team. The construction of the development team is guided by the realization that technical experts and users provide different expertise and knowledge to the task of requirements elicitation and that ultimately they have vested interests in the solutions proposed. Three options are proposed in Eason (1987) for the structure of a development team:

- *Technical-centred design.* Customers are informed and consulted by technical experts throughout the development process.
- *Joint customer–specialist design.* User representatives are involved in all stages of the development process.
- *User-centred design.* Technical experts provide a technical service to users and all users contribute to the design process.

It has been shown that each approach has its advantages and disadvantages. For example, while the technical centred design approach provides the basis for appropriate use of technical skills and is acceptable to the commissioning organization, it fails to take into consideration the need for involving users in the construction of a system that ultimately will change the working practices of the users themselves. The user-centred design approach seems to answer this criticism but, is regarded as being too inefficient on resources.

According to the socio-technical approach therefore, an important consideration for the successful interpretation of user needs is the optimum involvement of all stakeholders, i.e. all those that have an interest in the change being considered, those that stand to gain from it, and those that stand to lose (Mitroff, 1980). There are typically the following kinds of stakeholders in the requirements definition process (Macaulay, 1993):

- Those that have a financial interest in the system to be developed. Typically, these may be customers procuring the system or system component or marketeers concerned with some future product or the evolution of an existing product.
- Those that are responsible for the design and implementation of the system to be developed. These may be project managers, software engineers, telecommunication experts, etc.
- Those responsible for the introduction of the system once the system has been developed, for example training personnel, user managers, etc.
- Those that have an interest in the use of the system. These could be frequent users, occasional users or even users affected by the system without necessarily being involved with its use.

These four classes of stakeholders provide the basis for organizing a series of workshops during which requirements are explored in a co-operative fashion with the help of a facilitator (Macaulay, 1994). The benefits of these workshops lie very much in the face-to-face exploration of current situations and future needs with the aim of developing a shared understanding of the issues involved. To develop this shared understanding one needs to use some 'language' for communicating individual views and for documenting agreed positions. There is a variety of such languages from natural language and informal definition of basic concepts, e.g. Macaulay (1994), to more formal specification approaches, e.g. Bubenko, *et al.* (1994), Loucopoulos, (1994), Nellborn *et al.* (1992).

In conjunction with paying attention to the concerns of development team organization, the socio-technical approach has encouraged the move away from conventional requirement elicitation techniques such as interviews and questionnaires in favour of techniques which originate in social sciences and linguistics. Social science methods such as *ethnography* are also suggested as promising techniques for understanding and eliciting the true user requirements (Goguen and Linde, 1993; Sommerville *et al.*, 1993). Ethnography is a method developed and used by anthropologists for understanding social mechanisms in 'primitive' societies (e.g. tribes). The same method, however, can be applied to the analysis of the work practices within organizations.

Ethnography is a branch of sociology which questions the validity of conventional sociological methods such as questionnaires and statistics, preferring instead methods based on the behaviour of the members of the user group. Through these observations, ethnomethodologists aim to understand the categories and methods used by the users for rendering their actions intelligible to others, instead of trying to impose their own methods and categories onto the users. Ethnography, therefore, seems to provide an alternative to classical requirements elicitation, and promises to yield higher-quality requirements than would have been the case when using traditional techniques.

The application of ethnography to the study of organizations entails the analyst spending a long period of time with the organization and making detailed observations about its work practices. Subsequent analysis of the observations can reveal vital information about the organization, which usually differs markedly from the one recorded in formal documents (manuals, handbooks) of the organization. The advantage of the ethnography approach over conventional systems analysis lies in the fact that analysts are passive observers and do not try to impose their judgements on the practices which are observed.

In contrast to task analysis, ethnography is based on the premise that there is no such thing as a context-free user task. Ethnography questions the validity of task analysis as a mechanism for analysing user activities because of the reliance of task analysis to concentrate on individual tasks and the imposition of a kind of structuring that does not take into consideration the co-operative and interactive nature of activities in organizational settings. Ethnography is also different to traditional systems analysis methods in that there are no pre-conceptions about the application being studied and there is no judgement offered on the practices being observed.

The usefulness of ethnography to requirements engineering is yet to be clearly defined. Results from empirical studies however, tend to support the notion that a social science perspective can be relevant, particularly in settings involving interaction and co-operation (Sommerville, *et al.*, 1994). Practical experience has also shown that the use of ethnography in requirements elicitation needs further elaboration and structuring; it is sometimes difficult to understand and time consuming to practise (Sommerville *et al.*, 1994; Goguen, 1994).

Moreover, there are no clear guidelines as to which of the results are useful in eliciting software requirements. Other approaches which have grown out of ethnomethodology such as 'conversation analysis' (which focuses on aspects of ordinary conversation such as timing, overlap, response, etc.) and interaction analysis (which uses videos of user activities) might also prove a useful addition to the repertoire of requirements elicitation techniques.

In summary, socio-technical approaches to requirements analysis can prove to be an important supplement to more technically oriented requirements analysis techniques, since they provide valuable information about the users' environment, i.e. activities, concepts, and patterns of interactions.

3.10 REQUIREMENTS ELICITATION VS. KNOWLEDGE ELICITATION

This section argues that the requirements engineer can no longer afford to be unaware of the developments in a field very much related to requirements engineering, namely knowledge engineering.

It has been proposed (Byrd *et al.*, 1992) that a merged awareness of both requirements engineering and knowledge engineering research must take place, resulting in an exchange of ideas, techniques, and methods between the two disciplines.

In the expert systems literature knowledge elicitation (acquisition) has been described as the transfer and transformation of problem-solving expertise from some knowledge source to a computer program (Hayes-Roth, 1984). The knowledge acquired from the user comes usually in two forms, namely a declarative form (which consists of facts about concepts, their classifications and relationships) and a procedural form which contains information about where and how to apply the declarative knowledge.

During knowledge elicitation the practitioner is faced with similar problems to those we discussed earlier in this chapter regarding the elicitation of software requirements. The major difficulty in both requirements engineering and knowledge engineering is obtaining a good understanding of the problem domain. In both cases, understanding the domain is a problem because the major source of domain knowledge is the user. The problem of extracting knowledge from the user has been coined 'the knowledge acquisition bottleneck' in the expert systems literature. The following are some of the obstacles to extracting knowledge from the user:

- The limitations of humans as information processors and problem solvers account to an extent for the knowledge engineering problems. Users find it, in general, difficult to recall and explain their actions and decisions when solving a problem.
- Communication problems stemming from the fact that users and knowledge engineers use different languages. The user's language is specialized terminology about the problem domain, while the knowledge engineer uses technical jargon related to the design aspects of the expert system.
- Problems stemming from the need to deal with a number of users with sometimes conflicting experiences and needs.

In order to tackle the above problems, knowledge engineering research has developed a number of techniques which fall into five broad categories. It must be noted that some of these techniques have close counterparts in requirements engineering, while others have not, but are nevertheless very applicable themselves. The categories of knowledge elicitation techniques are as follows:

- *Observation techniques* (the user is observed while doing a specific task). Well-known examples of observation techniques are *behaviour analysis* and *protocol analysis*.
- *Unstructured elicitation* techniques in which the user(s) participates in interviews, brainstorming sessions, etc. Typical examples of this category are *teachback interview* and *open interview*.
- *Mapping techniques* are psychological techniques used to acquire conceptual knowledge from the user; *multidimensional scaling* and *variance analysis* are examples of this category.
- *Formal analysis techniques* are automated techniques which induce rules from data, analyse text, etc. *Machine rule induction* is a typical example of this category.
- *Structured elicitation techniques* in which the users are participating in a series of structured experiments from which knowledge is elicited. *Card sort* is a typical example of this category.

Many requirements elicitation techniques discussed in this chapter can be considered as belonging to one of the above categories. *Objective/goal analysis* (Section 3.2.1), for example, is a type of unstructured elicitation technique. Natural language techniques can be considered as belonging to the *formal analysis* category. *Scenario-based elicitation* (Section 3.2.2) falls in the structured elicitation techniques category. Prototyping (discussed in Chapter 5) can be considered as another unstructured elicitation technique because of its user-participation nature.

The value of the comparison between requirements elicitation and knowledge elicitation lies in the fact that techniques from one category can be applied to the other and vice versa. Depending on the type of the problem domain and the nature of the communication problem (user limitations, language problem, etc.), analysts can improve their repertoire of techniques by selecting and applying a suitable knowledge elicitation technique.

3.11 SUMMARY

This chapter was concerned with the phase of requirements engineering known as requirements elicitation. The essence of requirements elicitation, as the process of 'understanding of the problem domain' was highlighted throughout the chapter.

There are different types of problems which make requirements elicitation a difficult task, not dissimilar to the 'knowledge acquisition bottleneck' which hinders its sister discipline 'knowledge elicitation'. The major problem of knowledge elicitation is the difficulty analysts have acquiring knowledge from the users or other sources and thus becoming experts in that domain.

The various types of elicitation techniques presented in this chapter have different strong and weak points when dealing with the above problem.

- User interviews are straightforward to use but usually require careful preparation of the questionnaire if they are to be effective.
- Objectives/goal analysis techniques succeed in achieving a consensus among the different users on explicitly defining the primary problems (goals, objectives).
- Scenario-based techniques tackle the problem of limited memory and recall of expertise of the user by making users participate in various scenarios regarding their interaction with the software system.
- Form-based analysis techniques bypass the user as a source of domain knowledge and focus instead on a rather plentiful source of knowledge in organizational environments, namely forms.
- Natural language analysis approaches tackle the problem of language differences between user and analyst by carrying out the elicitation process in the most convenient medium for the user: natural language.
- Reuse-based approaches attempt to dispense with the necessity of doing elicitation from scratch, by providing a set of reusable requirements as a starting point. Tool-supported reuse approaches store the reusable requirements in repositories and provide assistance with regard to their retrieval and adaptation. Domain analysis aims at producing formal reusable models of requirements by capturing commonalities between domains. Reverse engineering reconstructs the requirements of existing system with the purpose of partially reusing them for the new system.
- Social science approaches take into account the social rules and practices in the organization, both at the personal and group level, in order to obtain insights about their real working practices and produce a definition of their real requirements.

REFERENCES

Arango G. (1989) Domain analysis from art to engineering discipline. *Proc. 5th International Workshop on Software Specification and Design.* IEEE Computer Society Press, San Diego, CA.

Balzer R. *et al.,* (1988) RADC system/software requirements engineering testbed research and development program. Report TR-88-75, Rome Air Development Center, Griffiths Air Force Base, NY, June.

Biggerstaff T. J. (1988) Design recovery for reuse and maintenance. MCC Technical Report STP-378-88.

Booch G. (1986) Object-oriented development. *IEEE Transactions on Software Engineering*, **SE-12**(2).

Bouzegoub M. and Gardarin G. (1986) SECSI: an expert approach for data base design. *Proc. IFIP World Congress*, Dublin.

Bubenko J., Rolland C., Loucopoulos P. and de Antonellis V. (1994) Facilitating 'Fuzzy to formal' requirements modelling, *IEEE International Conference on Requirements Engineering*.

Bubenko J. A. and Wangler B. (1993) Objectives driven capture of business rules and information systems requirements. *IEEE Conference on Systems, Man and Cybernetics*.

Byrd T. A., Cossick K. L. and Zmud R. W. (1992) A synthesis of research on requirements analysis and knowledge acquisition techniques. *IS Quarterly*, March.

Chen P. (1976) The entity–relationship model: toward a unified view of data. *ACM Transactions on Database Systems*, 1(1), 9–36.

Chicofsky E. J. and Cross J. H., II (1990) Reverse engineering and design recovery: a taxonomy. *IEEE Software*, 7(1).

Choobineh M., Manniho J., Nunamaker J. and Konsynsky B. (1988) An expert database system based on analysis of forms. *IEEE Transactions on Software Engineering*, **14**(2).

Coad P. and Yourdon E. (1991) *OOA—Object-oriented Analysis*. Prentice Hall, Englewood Cliffs, NJ.

Crowley D. J. (1982) *Understanding Communication: The Signifying Web*. Gordon & Breach, New York.

Diaper D. (Ed.) (1989a) *Task Analysis for Human Computer Interaction*. Ellis Horwood, Chichester.

Diaper D., (1989b) Task Analysis for Knowledge Descriptions (TAKD): the method and an example. In Diaper D. (Ed.) *Task Analysis for Human Computer Interaction*. Ellis Horwood, Chichester.

Eason K. (1987) *Information Technology and Organisational Change*. Taylor and Francis, London.

Edwards A. (1987) Mining for knowledge. *Accountancy*, April.

Goguen J. (1994) Requirements engineering as the reconciliation of social and technical issues. In Jirotka M. and Goguen J. (Eds) *Requirements: Engineering Social and Technical Issues*. Academic Press, New York.

Goguen J. A. and Linde C. (1993) Techniques for requirements elicitation. *IEEE Symposium on Requirements Engineering*.

Graham I. and Jones P. L. (1988) *Expert Systems: Knowledge Uncertainty and Decision*. St Edmundsbury Press, Bury St Edmunds, UK.

Hall P. A. V. (1991) *Overview of Reverse Engineering and Reuse Research*. Department of Computing, Open University, Milton Keynes, UK.

Hayes-Roth F. D. (1984) The knowledge-based expert system: a tutorial. *IEEE Computer*, **17**(9).

Holbrook H., III (1990) A scenario-based methodology for conducting requirements elicitation. *ACM Software Engineering Notes*, **15**(1).

Hooper J. W. and Hsia P. (1982) Scenario-based prototyping for requirements identification. *ACM SIGSOFT Software Engineering Notes*, **7**(5).

Jones T. C. (1984) Reusability in programming: a survey of the state of the art. *IEEE Transactions on Software Engineering*, **SE-10**(9).

Karakostas V. (1990) Modelling and maintaining software systems at the teleological level. *Journal of Software Maintenance*, **2**.

Karakostas V. (1992) Intelligent search and acquisition of business knowledge from programs. *Journal of Software Maintenance*, **3**.

Karakostas V. and Loucopoulos P. (1989) Constructing and validating conceptual models of office information systems: a knowledge-based approach. *Proc. 3rd Conference Putting into Practice Methods and Tools as Aids to Design Information Systems*, Nantes.

Kersten M. L., Weigand H., Dignum F. and Proom J. (1986) A conceptual modelling expert system. In Spaccapietra S. (Ed.) *Proc. 5th International Conference on the ER Approach*, Dijon.

Loucopoulos P. (1994) Extending database design techniques to incorporate enterprise requirements evolution. In Bubenko J., Caplinskas A., Grundespenkis J., Haav H.-M., and Sølvberg A. (Eds), *Baltic 94*. Vilnius, Lithuania, pp. 8–23.

Loucopoulos P. and Karakostas V. (1989) Modelling and validating office information systems: an object and logic-oriented approach. *Software Engineering Journal*, March.

Macaulay L. (1993) Requirements capture as a cooperative activity, *IEEE International Symposium on Requirements Engineering*. IEEE Computer Society Press, San Diego, CA, pp. 174–181.

Macaulay L. A. (1994) Cooperative Requirements Capture: Control Room 2000. In Jirotka M. and Goguen J. A. (Eds) *Requirements Engineering: Social and Technical Issues* Academic Press, London, pp. 67–86.

Mitroff I. I. (1980) Management myth information systems revisited: a strategic approach to asking nasty questions about system design. In Bjorn-Adnersen N. (Ed.) *The Human Side of Enterprise*. North-Holland, Amsterdam.

Mittermeir R. T., Rousopoulos N., Yeh T. and Ng P. (1990) An integrated approach to requirements analysis. In Ng P. A. and Yeh R. T. (Eds) *Modern Software Engineering: Foundations and Current Perspectives*. Van Nostrand Reinhold, New York.

Mumford E. and Weir M. (1979) *Computer Systems in Work Design – the ETHICS Method. Associated Business Press, London.*

Neighbors J. M. (1984) The DRACO approach to constructing software from reusable components. *IEEE Transactions on Software Engineering*, **SE-10**(5).

Nellborn C., Bubenko J. and Gustafsson M. (1992) Enterprise modelling – the key to capturing requirements for information systems, *SISU, F3 Project Internal Report*.

Prieto-Diaz R. and Arango G. (1991) *Domain Analysis and Software System Modelling*. IEEE Computer Society Press, Los Alamitos, CA.

Reubenstein H. B. and Waters R. C. (1991) The requirements apprentice: automated assistance for requirements acquisition. *IEEE Transactions on Software Engineering*, **17**(3).

Rolland C. and Richard C. (1982) The REMORA methodology for information systems design and management. In Olle T. W. *et al.* (Eds) *IFIP WG8.1 Working Conference on Information Systems Design Methodologies: A Comparative Review*. North Holland, Amsterdam.

Rolland C. and Proix C. (1992) A natural language approach for requirements engineering. In Loucopoulos P. (Ed.) *Proc. 4th International Conference CAISE '92*. Springer-Verlag, Berlin.

Sommerville I., Bentley R., Rodden T. and Sawyer P. (1994) Cooperative systems design, *The Computer Journal*, **37**(5), 357–366.

Sommerville I., Rodden T., Sawyer P., Bentley R. and Twidale M. (1993) Integrating ethography into the requirements engineering process. *Proc. IEEE Symposium on Requirements Engineering*.

Sutcliffe A. G. and Maiden N. A. M. (1992) Supporting component match for software reuse. In Loucopoulos P. (Ed.) *Proc. 4th International Conference CAISE '92*. Springer-Verlag, Berlin.

Telem M. (1988) Information requirements specification I: brainstorming collective decision making approach. *Information Processing and Management*, **24**(5).

Vitalari N. and Dickson G. (1983) Problem solving for effective systems analysis: an experimental exploration. *Communications of the ACM*, **26**(11).

4

MODELLING REQUIREMENTS

4.1 INTRODUCTION

Developing an information system is a design task in which the contents of the final specification cannot be known in advance. In particular, the area of requirements modelling and analysis is characterized by informality and uncertainty. The quality of a requirements specification and ultimately that of the information system depends largely on the ability of a developer to extract and understand knowledge about the modelled domain, the *universe of discourse* (UoD), and the information system itself. Because of the nature of the task, developers are forced to capture large bodies of knowledge about the enterprise that are subsequently abstracted into a 'formal' specification. This specification should represent the central reference point for any development aspect or maintenance procedure of an information system.

The development of a specification involves a mapping of real-world phenomena onto basic concepts of a specification language. Because of the cognitive nature of requirements modelling, the formalisms employed are known as *conceptual models*. A specification developed in terms of a conceptual model represents abstractions, assumptions, and constraints about an application domain.

The aims of this chapter are: (a) to introduce the topic of conceptual modelling as a facilitating mechanism to modelling any aspects of requirements specification; (b) to discuss approaches to modelling phenomena in the context of the intended system, especially objectives that provide the purpose for the system; (c) to discuss approaches to functional requirements modelling; and (d) to discuss approaches to non-functional requirements modelling.

As discussed in Chapter 1 there is a need to take a wider view on requirements specification, going beyond the traditional approach which has concentrated on functional requirements modelling almost to the exclusion of modelling, the context within which the system will function. Section 4.3 is concerned with enterprise modelling, taking the view that requirements need to be articulated in the framework of 'real-world' knowledge which provides the purpose of the intended system as well as the knowledge about the phenomena common to the enterprise and system domains.

A functional requirements specification describes the structure and content of the system supporting the activities of the environment. This is typically a conceptual picture defining structural, static as well as dynamic aspects of the information system and the conditions (rules, constraints, etc.) under which the information system needs to operate. Central to the process of specification is a modelling process that uses as input information elicited from requirements holders, and results in a structured definition of the functions of the intended system or system component. The process itself is neither deterministic nor linear in nature, and the techniques employed are primarily concerned with the way that one progresses from 'fuzzy' expressions to more 'formal' ones that can be analysed and subsequently be used as input to the system design process. As pointed out in Chapter 2, this process involves elicitation, representation, validation, and agreement between the requirements stakeholders. The treatment of functional requirements specification is the subject matter of Section 4.4.

The operation of an information system and its environment is determined not only by its functionality, expressed in a functional specification, but also by other properties, such as development cost, accuracy, performance, robustness, security, etc., often referred to as non-functional requirements. Non-functional requirements can be defined as restrictions or constraints placed on a system service. They differ from functional requirements in that they refer to a characteristic which a system or a sub-system must possess, while functional requirements refer to the way the system behaves or responds. Although the distinction between functional and non-functional requirements can often be blurred, the separation of the two, viewed as separate projections on the total requirements specification, is valuable because of the different influences on the design activity and user acceptability criteria that each class of requirement imposes. Section 4.5 deals with non-functional requirements.

4.2 CONCEPTUAL MODELLING

4.2.1 Overview

The growing demand for information systems of ever-increasing size, scope, and complexity has caused the introduction of various high-level modelling languages, by which functional application requirements and information system components may be modelled at a conceptual level.

The process of conceptual modelling is the activity of formally defining aspects of the physical and social world around us for the purposes of understanding and communication (Mylopoulos, 1992).

The activity of conceptual modelling is a combination of *empirical*, *formal*, and *engineering* problems (Verrijn-Stuart, 1987). Empirical problems are concerned with the fact that in developing a specification one is constantly engaged in observing real-world phenomena. The concepts, processes, rules, etc., that constitute the functioning of a library, for example, is a subject that one may investigate empirically and develop theories about it. In this sense the investigator gains *knowledge* about the library itself. Formal problems are concerned with the abstraction, structure, and representation of this knowledge in a way that makes it possible to reason about this knowledge. Engineering problems arise when one attempts to implement the construction established by the adopted formality principles. Naturally, since an information system is a man-made artefact, many concepts found in such a system are simplifications of concepts found in real systems.

According to ISO (van Griethuysen, 1982), a conceptual specification is defined as follows:

- The description of the possible states of affairs of the Universe of Discourse (UoD) including the classifications, rules, laws, etc., of the UoD.

A conceptual schema can be used as the means of communicating the semantics of an application, through a variety of textual and graphical interfaces, to end users and developers and for reaching a common view and an agreement between these people. A conceptual schema, through the use of a formal notation, captures the semantics of the UoD and therefore has a clear advantage over natural language or other informal ways of describing the UoD. It should be stressed, however, that the formal notation (i.e. the conceptual models) used in developing a conceptual schema is motivated by cognitive considerations, and to this end it has a different orientation to mathematical and other formal notations that one finds in computer science.

In information systems, conceptual modelling has been traditionally associated with the task of database design. In recent years, however, it has been recognized that conceptual modelling can and should be used for specifying the four major domains of information systems, shown in Fig. 4.1, namely the subject world, the usage world, the system world, and the development world (Mylopoulos, 1992; Vassiliou *et al.*, 1990).

The subject world relates to the domain for which the information system is developed—an insurance system, hospital system, etc.,—and conceptual modelling in this context will need to consider the structural and behavioural aspects of the modelled

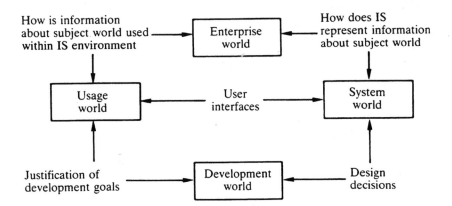

Figure 4.1 The four worlds of information systems.

enterprise. The usage world is concerned with the environment within which the information system will operate—the users of the system, the human–computer interaction, etc. The system world refers to the different details about the information system itself, i.e. specifications of one sort or another, including requirements specification, designs, software code, etc. Finally, the development world is concerned with the process of development itself including aspects such as the methods used, the personnel involved, the languages used, etc.

Conceptual modelling, therefore, can be used for some target UoD for example, for modelling enterprise requirements, functional and non-functional requirements for the system as well as modelling the method by which one might go about carrying out these development activities. The relationship between application dependent and method-dependent conceptual specifications is shown in Fig. 4.2.

Conceptual modelling for the method domain always results in models (actually metamodels) which are application independent and time invariant (assuming that the conceptual model itself is stable). On the other hand, conceptual modelling for the application domain is always dependent on the semantics of the particular application and can be time variant (assuming that changes in the organization will need to be specified in the conceptual schema).

Application domain modelling is concerned with both the modelling of part of the real world for which one is interested in developing a system, and with specifying, at a conceptual level (see the ANSI/SPARC architecture: ANSI/X3/SPARC, 1975) the structure and behaviour of the database. Indeed very often the same conceptual modelling language is used for both activities.

There is an analogous activity of modelling when it comes to specifying the development method itself. A method-dependent specification consists of the *products* (the deliverables at various development phases) as well as the *process* (the development steps) of the method. This description represents a formal way in the use of the method and underpins any computer-assisted tools which may be used in conjunction with the method. Method-dependent modelling is also relevant from a database perspective, often referred to as the

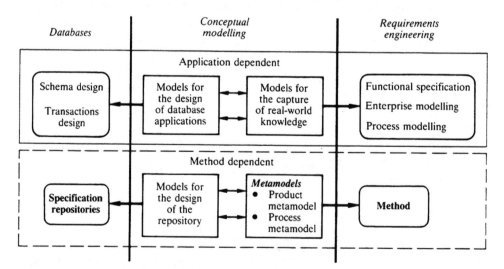

Figure 4.2 Conceptual modelling for applications and methods.

repository, in the context of computer-assisted software engineering (CASE) technology, in that it can be used to determine the structures and behaviour of the database that will store and manipulate a system specification.

The relationship between a conceptual model, the way that the model may be used by a developer to build a specification, and the way that the specification itself may be used to determine the actual operation of an information system gives rise to four levels of abstraction. The highest, most abstract level is that of the *meta-concepts* level, whereby one is using some language for defining a conceptual model. The same language may be used for developing a multitude of different conceptual models. This level of abstraction is of use to developers of conceptual modelling tools, which are found in the more general class of tools known in the field of software engineering as CASE. This is especially so for the class of customizable CASE (these are variously called CASE-shells or meta-CASE). At the next level, the *concepts* level, one is concerned with the syntax and semantics of the conceptual model that may be used for any conceptual modelling activity. For example, in attempting to develop an application specification, a developer (system analyst or designer) will have to use the conceptual model according to the axioms defined at the concepts level. In this sense the next level, the *specification* level, is constrained by the definitions in the concepts level. Similarly the allowable states of the information system (i.e. the next level of detail, the *instance* level) will be constrained by the definitions at the specification level.

Many authors contrast conceptual modelling to other fields such as knowledge representation approaches in the artificial intelligence field and semantic data modelling in the field of databases (Borgida *et al.*, 1985; Hull and King, 1987). Indeed the field of conceptual modelling has benefited from contributions from the following fields:

- Databases (e.g. Mylopoulos *et al.*, 1980; Shipman, 1981)
- Artificial intelligence (e.g. Brachman *et al.*, 1983; Schank, 1975; Sowa, 1984)
- Software engineering (e.g. Dubois *et al.*, 1986a; Hagelstein, 1988; Olle *et al.*, 1983, 1984, 1986)
- Programming languages (e.g. Albano and Orsini, 1985; Buneman and Atkinson, 1986)

There exist, however, a number of differences between these fields. For example, knowledge representation is concerned with different reasoning schemes and in the way that these schemes can be handled computationally, whereas conceptual modelling is more concerned with the semantic richness and simplicity of approaches which assist in the understanding by and communication between humans about a part of the world. Semantic data modelling has similar objectives to conceptual modelling but is motivated primarily by implementation considerations and usually confines itself to the description of objects of the real world that need to be represented in some database.

In conceptual modelling one is interested in separating knowledge concerning general principles in the UoD (referred to as the intension) from actual occurrences of the UoD (referred to as the extension). In attempting to develop a conceptual schema, a developer is concerned with the intension of the UoD. Therefore, a developer analyses some aspects of the world in order to determine relationships between intensions.

The intension of a word is that part of meaning that follows from general principles. An example of an intension is 'employees work in departments'. The extension of a word is the set of all existing things to which the word applies. Extensions are normally large sets which cannot be observed in their entirety. Intension and extension give rise to the syntactical (datalogical) and semantic (infological) aspects of information systems.

Objects are, in general, 'things' in the real world, tangible as well as intangible. Humans communicate about objects in terms of *concepts*. Concepts are *abstract ideas* which are formed from experience or by placing other concepts in a particular context. Each concept in a specification has a particular meaning (*semantics*) and is part of particular structures (*syntax*) whose form depends on the particular conceptual model used by the person modelling the UoD.

4.2.2 Properties of conceptual models

The primary use of a conceptual specification is in understanding a specific application domain (the UoD) and, naturally, this activity involves communication with users of the UoD. Because the communication is to be carried through the specification itself, the concepts must be relevant to the milieu in which the information system is used and not related to its design or implementation. Moreover, the specification should force users to participate actively by stimulating and generating questions as to how reality is abstracted and assumptions are made.

From a database perspective, a conceptual schema can be viewed as a set of rules describing which information may enter and reside in the database. In other words the following should be described: (1) all fact type definitions which refer to the permitted populations of the database; (2) all constraints which refer to the allowable states of the database as well as the permitted transitions on these populations; and (3) all derivation rules which are concerned with the facts that can be derived from the database using these rules.

The characteristics of a conceptual specification can be summarized by the two ISO principles (van Griethuysen, 1982):

Principle 1: the 100 per cent principle All laws and rules governing the UoD must be defined within the conceptual schema. None of these laws or rules must become part of an application program or be distributed among many different application programs. The respective aspects of formulating these rules and of retrieving and manipulating information must be kept strictly separate.

This principle implies that if the rules that govern the behaviour of the information system are distributed among different schemata and different application programs, then the control, verification, and maintenance of these rules becomes an impossible task. This principle gives rise to the requirement for a conceptual modelling language which is capable of permitting the formulation of all rules, although this does not imply that the rules must necessarily be expressed declaratively and that a conceptual schema may very well contain procedures to describe complex rules.

Principle 2: the conceptualization principle The conceptual schema must refer exclusively to rules of the UoD. Rules which govern the implementation of the information system must not be allowed to become part of the conceptual schema.

The motivation behind this principle is the need to simplify the process of conceptual schema design by concentrating only on conceptually relevant details and disregarding everything else. For example, the conceptual schema is not responsible for any aspects of external or internal data representation, physical data organization, or data access strategies.

Based upon these principles, a set of requirements for a conceptual schema has been proposed (Balzer and Goldman, 1979; Borgida *et al.*, 1985; Liskov and Zilles, 1977; Mylopoulos, 1986; Yeh, 1982):

- *Implementation independence* No implementation aspects like data representation, physical data organization, and access, as well as aspects of particular external user representation (such as message formats, data structures, etc.) should be included in a requirements specification.
- *Abstraction* Only general (i.e. not subject to frequent changes), static, and dynamic aspects of an information system and the UoD should be represented in a requirements specification.
- *Formality* Descriptions should be stated in a formalism with unambiguous syntax which can be understood and analysed by a suitable processor. The formalism should come with a rich semantic theory that allows one to relate the descriptions in the formalism to the world being modelled.
- *Constructability* A conceptual schema should be constructed in such a way so as to enable easy communication between analysts and users and should accommodate the handling of large sets of facts. In addition, a specification needs to overcome the problem of complexity in the problem domain, by following appropriate abstraction mechanisms which permit decomposition in a natural manner. This calls for the existence of a systematic approach to formulating the specification.
- *Ease of analysis* A conceptual schema needs to be analysed in order to determine whether it is ambiguous, incomplete, or inconsistent. A specification is ambiguous if more than one interpretation can be attached to a particular part of the specification. Completeness and consistency require the existence of criteria against which the specification can be tested. However, the task of testing for completeness and consistency is extremely hard simply because normally no other specification exists against which the specification can be tested.
- *Traceability* Traceability refers to the ability to cross-reference elements of a specification with corresponding elements in a design specification and ultimately with the implementation of an information system.
- *Executability* The importance of this property is in the validation of the specification. Executability refers to the ability of a specification to be simulated against some facts relevant to the modelled reality. The executability of the descriptions in a schema is subject to the employed formalism.
- *Minimality* Every concept in the model has a distinct meaning and no concept can be expressed in terms of compositions of other concepts.

4.2.3 Abstraction mechanisms

A common feature of almost all contemporary conceptual modelling paradigms is the use of different abstraction mechanisms. Abstraction is the process of emphasizing some particular details of the modelled domain while suppressing other details. Among different abstraction mechanisms those of classification, aggregation, grouping, and generalization are of fundamental use in conceptual modelling. These abstraction forms have their root in knowledge representation schemes within artificial intelligence and in particular in semantic nets (Peckham and Maryansky, 1988).

Classification is an abstraction mechanism which relates types with instances. The inverse of classification, which is used for obtaining entities or facts that conform to the definition of an entity type, is called *instantiation*. Classification results in the 'grouping' of entities which play the same roles (one or more) in the information system. For example, the class PERSON refers to all persons that share the roles of having an age, working for departments, working on projects, etc. The class DEPARTMENT in turn may refer to all the instances of departments that share the roles of having a department name, having a budget, etc. The individuality of the members of a class is established through an identifier role, e.g. persons may be identified in a system by their social security number. A class describes a set of potential entities.

An individual entity may be related to one or more entities of the same or a different class. For example, 'Smith works for Accounts' and 'Smith is managed by Brown' represent two instances of linking the entity 'Smith' to two other entities, where 'Accounts' is an instance of an entity of a different class and 'Brown' is an instance of the same class as 'Smith'. An *association* is therefore an abstraction which describes a group of links between instances of two or more entity classes. An association describes a set of potential links. Associations are inherently bidirectional. For example, an association which describes the employment of persons in departments can be expressed as 'PERSON works_in DEPARTMENT' or equivalently 'DEPARTMENT employs PERSON'.

A special case of association is the abstraction mechanism of *aggregation*. Aggregation is a special form of association in the sense that an aggregate entity is made up of component entities and components are *part_of* the aggregate. Aggregation, therefore, adds special semantics to certain associations; if two entities are considered as independent but are linked in some way, then the relationship is one of association, but if they are related by a part–whole relationship then this is a case of aggregation. For example, the fact that a 'person works_for a company' is regarded as an association since both 'person' and 'company' are independent concepts, whereas 'branch is part_of company' is considered as an aggregation where 'branch' is a component part of 'company'. Aggregation is often referred to as an 'and relationship', e.g. 'vehicle consists of body and chassis and engine'.

Parts may or may not exist in isolation or appear in many different aggregates. Aggregation is *transitive*, that is an aggregate has parts and its part may have other parts, e.g. if A is part_of B and B is part_of C then A is part_of C. Aggregation is also *antisymmetric*, e.g. if A is part_of B then B is not part of A. It is also possible that some of the associations of the assembly propagate to the component parts, e.g. the name of a company is propagated to its branches.

Aggregation can be fixed, variable, or recursive. A *fixed aggregate* has a predefined aggregation structure as well as a predefined number of occurrences of the component parts. For example, the 'vehicle' aggregate defined above has a fixed structure in that its components are those of 'body', 'chassis', and 'engine' and the numbers of these parts are also predefined (one in each case). In the case of a *variable aggregate*, the aggregate structure is predefined but the number of parts may vary. For example, the 'company' aggregate defined above has a predefined aggregate structure, i.e. it has a component part of 'branch' but, the number of branches may be variable. A *recursive aggregate* is the case when the aggregate contains an instance of the same aggregate and therefore the number of potential levels in the aggregation structure may be unlimited.

In order to be able to reason about populations of entities involved in the assembly–parts relationships, each part–whole relationship is treated as separate (this also emphazises that aggregation is a special kind of association). In the 'vehicle' example there are three aggregation relationships defined: between 'body' and 'vehicle', 'chassis' and 'vehicle', and 'engine' and 'vehicle'.

Generalization is used to extract from one or more classes the description of a more general class that captures the commonalities and suppresses some of the detailed differences in their description. Generalization is captured through the special *isa* link in forming directed acyclic graphs between supertype–subtype, where a subtype is contained totally inside its supertype (i.e. the population of a subtype is a subset of the population of its supertype). Common fact types are attached to the supertype and in general a subtype inherits all the facts associated with is supertypes. Generalization is often referred to as an 'or relationship', e.g. an 'employee is a salaried employee or a consultant'.

The usefulness of the above abstraction forms cannot be overstated. They impact in a major way in the manner in which a particular conceptual model can actually be applied in practice, and also provide opportunities for modelling an increased scope of application domains. An example of the use of these abstraction forms in a methodological sense is the use of aggregation and specialization in providing a structure in the modelling process. Used in a complementary fashion, aggregation and generalization allow one to produce two hierarchies which can be thought of as two independent or orthogonal views of the same reality. These abstraction forms can also assist in other important areas such as reusability. Generalization can help to emphasize similarities among objects, abstracting their differences at the generic level and thus defining specific properties at the specialized level; and through aggregation it is possible to define a new object as a composition of existing objects. New kinds of applications such as CAD/CAM and CASE can also benefit enormously from the use of abstraction forms since they permit a developer gradually to make visible the structure of a complex object and the way in which individual components of the object relate to it and to each other.

4.3 MODELLING OF ENTERPRISE REQUIREMENTS

4.3.1 The need for enterprise modelling

The need to take a wider view of requirements specification, beyond and above the modelling of functional requirements, was discussed in Chapter 1. The current thinking in the area of requirements engineering is that requirements need to be articulated in the framework of 'real-world' knowledge which provides the purpose of the intended system as well as the knowledge about the phenomena common to the enterprise and system domains. Elaborating on enterprise aspects delimits the scope of the investigation and also provides a context and justification for the intended system or system component. This is especially useful nowadays as organizations strive to establish 'integration' across organizational boundaries and along a number of different dimensions. A distinguishing feature of enterprise integration is that it seeks *improvement through the co-ordination of interacting organizations, individuals, and systems* (Petrie, 1992).

A specification which incorporates aspects of the enterprise explicitly identifies different stakeholders, their objectives, and the focal point of the requirements for all these stakeholders. For example, in considering an inter-company integration, around the process of 'ticket reservation' one might identify the following stakeholders and their objectives:

Chief executive

- When a flight is full, VIPs are the first to be upgraded and/or given a seat in preference to others.
- Discounted tickets should be offered to politicians since these people make important decisions affecting the airline.
- Information about frequent fliers and executive club members should not be made available to outside contractors.

Chief security officer

- The number of bags in the aircraft's hold should tally against the list of passengers on board.
- Passenger lists should not be made available to the public.
- Passengers should check-in only once.

Catering manager

- The food loaded is dictated by the number of passengers travelling in a particular class, irrespective of the fare they paid.
- A predicted number of passengers on a flight must be available 24 hours prior to departure.
- Passengers requiring special diet must indicate their request 24 hours prior to departure.

Travel agent

- An agent is responsible for holding and cancelling reservations.
- Tickets offered by an agency have different fares to be negotiated with the sales department of the airline.

Airline sales manager

- A ticket may only be issued when a fair is paid.
- For some fares a reservation can be held and not confirmed.
- When a discounted ticket is booked, the normal book-ahead requirements do not apply.
- All tickets must carry appropriate endorsements relating to the terms and conditions of the issue of tickets.

This example shows that even in this very small sample there are many different stakeholders with different concerns, perceptions of problems, and different expectations from the target system. A requirements specification cannot be properly developed without considering all these different viewpoints, and modelling and communicating the understanding gained from the elaboration of these objectives and problems. Objectives or goals rarely occur in isolation. People often find themselves in situations in which they possess several goals simultaneously, either because they have initially more than one or because the execution of a plan for a single goal impinges upon other goals. Thus, in order to develop a requirements specification which meets the objectives of all stakeholders, there is a need to consider the interactions between different goals.

Typically, in any enterprise there will be many, sometimes contradictory, objectives which must be documented, analysed, and reconciled if necessary. The very general and sometimes 'fuzzy' objectives will result, through successive elaboration, in 'hard' functional and non-functional requirements.

An *enterprise* can be viewed as a *social* structure. It includes *organizations* that may be individuals, groups, or even companies. All these participants share *resources* (material and information), and provide *services* that contribute to the overall *objectives* of the enterprise.

An enterprise model is a structured description of important, basic application knowledge and assumptions, about the context within which the planned system will need to operate (Bubenko *et al.*, 1992; Nellborn *et al.*, 1992). An enterprise model typically considers aspects of the following:

- Organizational structures
- Objectives and goals
- Activities, processes, products
- Agents and work roles

There are four major functions, as shown in Fig. 4.3, served by an enterprise model.

The teleological view provides knowledge about the reasons for the required system, i.e. it addresses the 'why' question. The social view considers the roles, responsibilities, obligations, and other interactions between individuals and groups constituting the 'end user' community and customers of the system. The operational view is concerned with the activities, processes, products, etc., of the enterprise, i.e. the current functioning of the

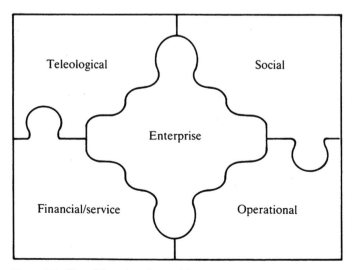

Figure 4.3 Use of the enterprise model.

organization. The financial or service view represents an evaluatory view with respect to the value attached to the current functioning of the enterprise or potential functioning in the future.

Enterprise modelling is about describing, in some formal way, a social system with its agents, work roles, goals, responsibilities, and the like. Early examples of techniques and formalisms for including enterprise models in a requirements specification include MacDonald (1986) and Mercurio *et al.* (1990). More recent approaches tend to expand on the earlier results, recognizing that it is advantageous to examine an enterprise from multiple perspectives (Dobson 1992; Nellborn *et al.*, 1992; Yu, 1993).

The enterprise modelling hypothesis is that it helps in the understanding of the complex interactions among organizations and people. Enterprise modelling enables more peer-to-peer communications, and clearly defines job interactions. Enterprise modelling is also essential to application developers by offering the means of describing business processes, and for defining and structuring the information to support these applications.

The last few years have witnessed major advances in information technology domains such as hardware, software, telecommunication networks, robotics, even smart chips that are used in products to enhance functionality or reliability. The continuing evolution of information technology has now reached a threshold of cost and ease of use that is having widespread organizational impact. Information technology in general, and information systems in particular, exert such a strong influence because they can affect both production and co-ordination. Traditionally information systems dealt with issues relating to cost reduction, productivity increment and quality enhancement of the services offered by the enterprise. These issues bring changes in work roles and skill levels. Work roles may be enriched or extra burdens may be imposed. In recent years information systems have adopted more supervisory and strategic support roles. This brings changes in power structures, while individual privacy or freedom may be curtailed. In such an unstable environment information system developers are challenged to develop systems that can meet the requirements of modern organizations. One of the key elements in their effort is organizational analysis and enterprise modelling. Organizational analysis can help interpret and explain the effects of systems on organizations and can be used to assist developers and organizational participants to make better-informed choices about system alternatives.

The traditional waterfall application development lifecycle is no longer capable of supporting the requirements of information systems that aim to remain effective for more than a limited period (until changes in the enterprise environment declare them out of date).

4.3.2 Approaches to enterprise goal modelling

Enterprise goal modelling has been examined from a number of different perspectives. Prominent among these are efforts in the areas of computer-integrated manufacturing (CIM), enterprise integration (EI), telematics, and of course information/software engineering.

CIM technology links automation systems into a distributed processing system. The need for enterprise modelling in this area is that rather than attempting to deal with the full complexity of a distributed system, one can consider the system from different viewpoints, each representing a different set of abstractions of the original distributed system. The enterprise viewpoint describes the distributed processing system in terms of what is required for the enterprise concerned. The enterprise model describes the overall objectives of the system. It specifies the activities that take place within the organization using the system and the interactions between the organization, the system, and the environment in which they are placed. It concentrates on aspects relevant to distributed information systems. The enterprise units that support and participate in the information systems under consideration are explicitly identified and described.

In EI one is interested in the co-ordination of different individuals, or groups that share a common goal. This integration can happen at intra-company, inter-company, or even at virtual-company level. For example, the manufacture of cars and aeroplanes requires the co-ordination of not only thousands of people within the manufacturing organization, but also a large number of subcontractors and suppliers. In this domain, enterprise modelling is considered as a corporate activity that produces models of the information resources, information flows, and business operations that occur in the enterprise (Goranson, 1992; Petrie, 1992; Scheer and Hars, 1992). The resultant models describe the business environment in such a way so as to provide a common language to describe the heterogeneous enterprise components and their functions, to predict the effects of change, and to support strategic decision making.

Telematics is the combined technology of computing and communications. It is the key to the creation, management, transmission, storage, and eventually use of information in any form—voice, data, textual, or graphical. One of the components of telematics is electronic data interchange (EDI). EDI is paperless, or electronic trading. Although the emphasis of EDI is largely on inter-company electronic trading, it does not preclude the possibility of intra-company trading. One of the problems with the standardization of electronic documents is the lack of specification of the business function of the document. Work currently under way in the standards area focuses as much on the business procedures as on the documents.

In the area of information systems engineering an early example can be found in MacDonald (1986). Typically, one considers the development of an information system in terms of four levels: planning, analysis, design, and construction. The first two levels emphasize strategic planning, modelling of the enterprise, and business area analysis. During strategic planning, several business areas are identified, which are subsequently treated individually in the business area analysis phase. Entity types and their relationships, business functions, and interactions between data and functions are represented using entity models, function hierarchy diagrams, and process diagrams. More recently, repository technology has also advocated the use of enterprise modelling (Hazzah, 1991; Mercurio et al., 1990) in that an enterprise sub-model supports a high-level definition of business processes and data, and represents the definitions of the kinds of information necessary to describe a business and its business operations. This sub-model is a large data model with more than 100 entity types, over 600 relationship types, and hundreds of attribute types. It is a data model for defining allowable data in the repository. This enterprise sub-model is divided into 18 component models each focusing on a topic of enterprise system modelling. Together they form a unified model for defining the enterprise.

From a requirements engineering point of view, many of the techniques advocated in the areas outlined above have been used in one form or another. Again there are different proponents of techniques for use in requirements depending on one's viewpoint.

By focusing on social aspects, one can reason about organizational goals, policies, and structures, and the work roles of intended end users in a way that will facilitate the identification and expression of organizational requirements for systems. In Dobson *et al.* (1994) the organization is described as a set of work roles based on the premise that any system contains within it two kinds of resource: technical and social—and these are so interrelated that any attempt to optimize only one of these sets of resources may well adversely affect the other. The concept of agency is introduced to differentiate between social and technical objects. A machine may perform the same tasks as a person, but the person will take responsibility for those tasks. These responsibilities are structural or social in nature, arising from responsibilities that relate to the other agent.

Other authors prefer to take a multiple view to the task of enterprise modelling (Bubenko *et al.*, 1994; Nellborn and Holm, 1994; Yu, 1993; Yu and Mylopoulos, 1994). These approaches tend to consider enterprise modelling as a facilitating task to gradually arriving at better functional and non-functional requirements specifications and tracing these to enterprise requirements. Concepts such as objective and goal dependencies provide teleological links between high-level strategic requirements and operational requirements and provide opportunities for analysing the correspondence between high-level expectations and actual processes (Anton *et al.*, 1994). Objectives and goals modelling leads to the incorporation of requirements components which should support them. They justify and explain the presence of requirements components which may not otherwise be obvious to the requirements engineering participants.

The need for goals analysis when developing an information system is broadly accepted (Mittermeir *et al.*, 1990; Mylopoulos *et al.* 1992; Dardenne *et al.*, 1993; Yu and Mylopoulos, 1994). Information systems developers need to understand not only what they are developing, but also the purpose of the intended system. Goals express intention and capture the reason of the system to be built. Goals analysis can assist the process of eliciting information systems requirements, since it helps analysts clearly to define the purpose that the new system should serve in the organization. However, the process of eliciting goals is far from straightforward since the process is likely to involve multiple participants who will hold multiple perspectives on a single domain. The *private goals* of members of an organization (its owners, employees, etc.) must all be considered and harmonized. Maintaining consistency in multi-perspective software development may not always be possible. At times, this may not even be desirable, since it can unnecessarily constrain the development process and lead to loss of important information. Instead of eradicating inconsistencies, one can consider inconsistency handling explicitly, where rules that specify how to act in the presence of consistency are explicitly specified (Nuseibeh *et al.*, 1994).

In the *teleological* approach information systems functions can be derived progressively from organizational objectives through a process that is called goals *operationalization*. Operationalization is the process of refining goals so that the resulting sub-goals have an operational definition (Anton *et al.*, 1994). In this sense, a required system is considered as the realization of a set of enterprise goals. The derived interrelated goal network will inevitably give rise to a variety of implementation alternatives. These alternatives should be evaluated in some way to determine the degree to which a set of goals is supported by a particular operationalization. An example of this approach for an industrial project is reported in Potts (1994).

A key activity in enterprise goal modelling is the conceptualization and abstraction mechanisms used for reasoning about goals. The results from this activity provide the basis for further exploration of the operationalization process in terms of 'scenarios' for alternative implementations.

According to their degree of specificity, enterprise goals can be organized into goal hierarchies. Vague objectives need to be refined into concrete, formal goals. The refinement of enterprise objectives into less abstract goals is necessary because only simple primitive goals can be operationalized. One disadvantage of goal decomposition is that the distinction between primitive goals and the means to achieve them is not always clear.

Goals can also be grouped in different categories, depending on their context, owner, priority and so on. Several goal classifications have been proposed (Mittermeir *et al.*, 1990; Mylopoulos *et al.*, 1992; Dardenne, *et al.*, 1993; Yu and Mylopoulos, 1994). According to diRoccaferrera (1973), each objective forming the multiple goals set can be considered to belong to one of the following three general categories: enterprise objectives (reflecting general policy, strategy, and tactics), problem-solving objectives, and innovative objectives. A pragmatic classification of goals (Anton *et al.*, 1994) differentiates between *prescriptive* and *descriptive* goals. A prescriptive goal is offered by the stakeholder to account for organizational structures and processes that should be observed. A descriptive goal, in contrast, emerges from analysis of actual processes. Another distinction is that between *objective* goals and *adverbial* goals. The former refer to the object of the business, while the latter refers to the manner of achieving an objective goal. Adverbial goals often serve as the rationale for the non-functional requirements.

Another approach to goal analysis problem is that of *goal reduction*. The idea is borrowed from the problem-reduction method used in problem solving (Nilsson, 1971). As for the problems, for the goals to be reached, they have to be ranked in order of importance and priority. As there are corresponding and related solutions to problems, so there are connected objectives. The theme to this approach is to reason backward from the objective to be met, establishing goals and sub-goals until, finally the original objective is reduced to a set of trivial primitive goals. For any given objective more than one alternative set of sub-goals can be produced. Some of the sub-goals may not be satisfiable (unrealistic, too expensive, etc.), thus requiring the testing of several alternatives in order to reach a set of sub-goals that are all satisfiable.

In summary, enterprise goal modelling is important for several reasons. It leads to the incorporation of requirements components which should support the goals; it justifies and explains the presence of requirements components; it may be used to assign responsibilities of agents in the system and commitments of requirements stakeholders with respect to the intended system; it can provide basic information for detecting and resolving conflicts that arise from multiple viewpoints among human agents (Dardenne *et al.*, 1993). Teleology embodies a specification of possible behaviours, not the description of a single behaviour. In other words, there may exist several alternative behaviours that satisfy a given teleology. Teleological knowledge allows the description of the system both from the representation and reasoning perspectives. Analysing goals helps stakeholders raise 'what if' questions about specific cases or situations, and answer questions that have already been raised (scenario analysis).

Once the goals graph has been constructed, it can be traversed either forward to lead from the objectives to the systems goals that motivate systems requirements, or backwards from the systems goals to the organizational objectives that justify them. In that sense, the goals graph assists *requirements traceability*. Requirements traceability refers to the ability to describe and follow the life of a requirement, in both forwards and backwards direction

(Gotel and Finkelstein, 1993; Morris *et al.*, 1994). In particular, goals modelling endeavours the *pre-requirements traceability*, which is concerned with those aspects of a requirement's life prior to its inclusion in the requirements specification.

4.3.3 An example

The example used in this section is about an air traffic control environment. It is not possible to cover the entire enterprise situation. However, the chosen part is sufficient for demonstrating the concepts, especially those of objectives modelling. The example is also used to show the relationships between enterprise, functional, and non-functional requirements and the tracing possible among the different modelling orientations. To this end the example is carried forward in Sections 4.4 (dealing with functional requirements) and 4.5 (dealing with non-functional requirements).

A view of the major concepts of the part of the environment under consideration is shown in Fig. 4.4. Figure 4.4 shows that the subject matter under investigation involves air traffic controllers who interface with a console which is part of the control unit of the air traffic control (ATC) system. The control unit also involves a sequencer (SQC) and a radar data processor (RDP). This model provides a view of the different concepts that one

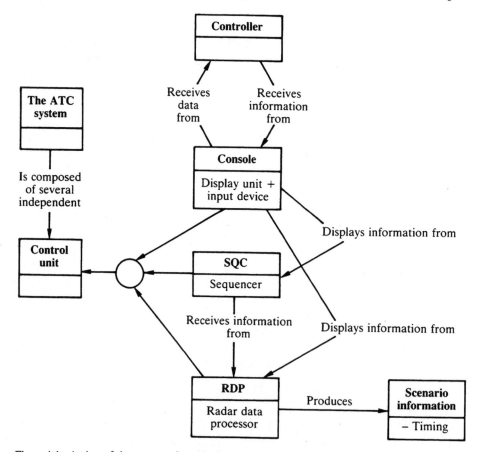

Figure 4.4 A view of the concepts found in the air traffic control environment.

reasons about in the portion of the enterprise about which is attempting to develop a requirements specification.

Although this view is useful in delimiting the problem space, it leaves a number of unanswered questions. For example, there is still no explicit view about the reasons behind the requirements for the system, or an explanation of the role of the different actors found in the enterprise or even the activities that take place and which make use of the concepts detailed in Fig. 4.4.

This additional information about the enterprise requires a set of different viewpoints on the enterprise. An objectives model is shown in Fig. 4.5, which provides a view on the goals established by requirements holders within an enterprise context.

The main objective is shown as the 'need to guarantee a high degree of safety'. In order for this to be met there is a need to meet another goal, 'decrease risk of human error' which can be achieved by providing automated control facilities in terms of 'better visualization of air traffic scenarios'.

It is this enterprise requirement which is directly related to defining specific functional and non-functional requirements for a number of system components, one of which will be considered for the purpose of this example, namely the *display system*. This enterprise requirement can also act as the 'link' between the system itself and the role of the system in the wider context of the enterprise and in particular its participation in meeting the overall objective of 'providing a high degree of safety'.

The model shown in Fig. 4.6 provides a different viewpoint. It gives an insight into the activities that take place in the enterprise and the information sets that are required by each activity. For example, the model shows that the 'planning sequence' activity requires some information (which would normally be constructed in terms of a more detailed view of the concepts defined in the model of Fig. 4.4) and this process generates some other type of information used by another process and so on.

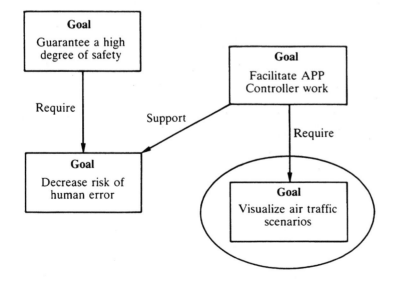

Figure 4.5   An objectives view of the air traffic control environment.

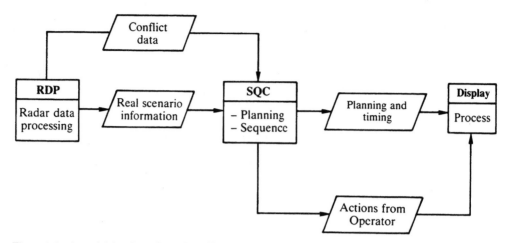

Figure 4.6 An activities view of the air traffic control environment.

4.4 MODELLING OF FUNCTIONAL REQUIREMENTS

4.4.1 Overview of functional requirements models

A large variety of different conceptual models have been proposed for the purpose of describing application domains. These approaches can be classified according to different viewpoints as *structural* or *behavioural*. The structural viewpoint emphazises the modelling of *information structures* (semantic data modelling) found in the application together with rules (constraints and derivations) which determine the allowable states of these structures. The behavioural viewpoint is concerned with the specification of *activities* operating on the information structures and a part that specifies *events* that trigger these activities.

The relationship between the three fundamental conceptual cornerstones of data, activities, and events is shown graphically in Fig. 4.7.

Since the early 1970s a number of different approaches to conceptual modelling have been proposed. The field of information systems development in general and functional requirements modelling specifically is dominated by the so-called 'structured development methods'. Examples of these methods include the following:

- SADT (Ross and Schoman, 1977)
- SASD (DeMarco, 1978; Yourdon, 1989; Yourdon and Constantine, 1979)
- Information Engineering (MacDonald, 1986, 1988)
- JSD (Jackson, 1983)

the list is almost inexhaustible.

More recently developments in the area of object-orientation are beginning to impact on the following areas:

- Programming domain (Rentsch, 1982)
- Database domain (Beeri, 1989; Dittrich, 1986)

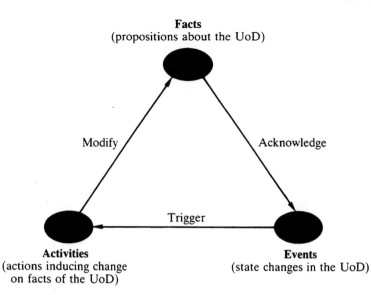

Facts
(propositions about the UoD)

Modify

Acknowledge

Trigger

Activities
(actions inducing change
on facts of the UoD)

Events
(state changes in the UoD)

Figure 4.7 Relationship between data, activities, and events.

- System specification approaches (Bailin, 1989; Booch, 1991; Henderson-Sellers and Edwards, 1990; Hoza *et al.*, 1989; Kappel and Schrefl, 1990; Rumbaugh *et al.*, 1991; Shlaer and Mellor, 1988; Troyer, 1991).

At the functional requirements specification level, the majority of these methods employ conceptual models of a graphical nature.

4.4.2 Structural viewpoint modelling

A large variety of different conceptual models have been proposed for the purpose of modelling information structures. (The term 'semantic data models' is commonly used to refer to those conceptual models whose orientation is towards the description of structural components of the application domain and information system.) An overview of language features is given in Hull (1987) and Peckham and Maryansky (1988).

The main motivation for the emergence of semantic data modelling was data independence and abstraction. In this sense conceptual models represent a major improvement in capturing additional semantics of the modelled application rather than through data structures.

Data independence implies that the conceptual schema should be free from the physical structure of the database. This makes possible a change at the data physical level without involving any modification of the conceptual schema. Furthermore, the conceptual model is closer to human perception of the UoD.

The major advantage of abstraction is in the provision of techniques for organizing knowledge about the UoD and reasoning about it. For example, by using generalization one can emphasize similarities among objects, abstracting their differences at the generic level and leaving specific properties for the specialized level. Another example, using aggregation, is in the ability to define a new object as a composition of existing objects.

Two basic approaches dominate semantic data modelling: the entity–relationship–attribute and object–role approaches. The entity–relationship–attribute formalism owes its heritage to the work of Bachman (1969) and has led to the development of a large number of conceptual models, most notably the entity–relationship model (Chen, 1976) and the infological model (Langefors, 1973). The object–role formalism avoids the distinction between attributes and relationships and its origin can be traced to Abrial (1974) and Smith and Smith (1977). This approach has given rise to models such as NIAM (Nijssen and Halpin, 1989), Predicator (van Bommel *et al.*, 1991), and PSM (ter Hofstede *et al.*, 1993).

Typically, modelling of structural aspects of the UoD is concerned with defining relationships between tangible or abstract objects (at the intensional level) of the UoD, together with the rules that determine the allowable states of the target information system during its lifetime.

For example, Fig. 4.8 shows a number of entity classes (shown as rectangles) related in some ways according to the modelled UoD, i.e. employees are allocated a tax reference code, invoices are authorized by managers, managers are allocated company cars, etc. The involvement of instances of each entity class in a relationship is shown through cardinality constraints. Specialization is shown by distinguishing employees as managers, staffers, and freelancers, indicating also that the population of the subtypes are mutually exclusive and collectively exhaustive. Aggregation is also used by modelling the concept of car as being composed of the concepts of engine capacity and doors.

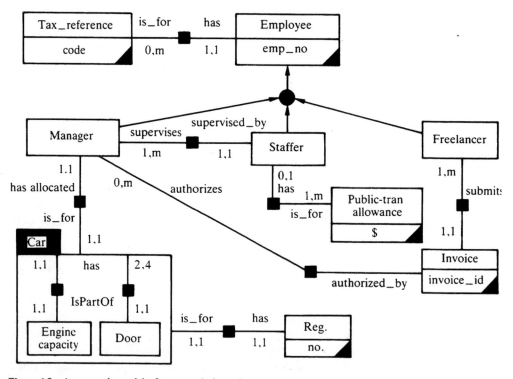

Figure 4.8 An example model of structural viewpoint.

A number of constraints can be shown in models using this diagrammatic convention. For example, it is stated that one invoice corresponds to one and only one freelancer. The specialization is also constrained to indicate that it is total (i.e. employees are made up of managers, staffers, and freelancers, and no more) and non-overlapping (i.e. an employee cannot be at the same time more than one of a manager, staffer, or freelancer).

A number of conventions have been put forward to represent constraints, from graphical notations to textual ones (Loucopoulos, 1989; Nijssen and Halpin, 1989; Tanaka *et al.*, 1991; Theodoulidis *et al.*, 1991).

4.4.3 Behavioural viewpoint modelling

The purpose of behavioural modelling is to provide a conceptual formalism for expressing how and when changes occur to objects. Behavioural modelling is orthogonal to structural modelling. An information system can be viewed as an artefact with certain functionality, defined by a set of actions, and with certain behaviour, which is observed in terms of the triggering of these actions by some events. Events may be generated either by the environment or by the various parts of the information system. For example, in a stock control system, a happening in the real world, such as the arrival of new stock for a product, affects the system by triggering the actions that perform the updating of the stock quantity of the received product. Obviously, the system responds only to certain happenings of the real world. Furthermore, the execution of some actions in one part of a system could affect another part of it and trigger some other actions at that part. For example, referring again to the stock control system, the result of satisfying a customer order may result in the stock quantity of a product to fall below the reorder level, which will affect the actions in the part of the system that takes care of the reordering of low stock products.

In modelling behavioural aspects of the UoD one is interested in specifying the interaction of the application with its environment, the input and output of each process, the sequencing of the processes, and the conditions under which a process may be invoked. Typical modelling concepts that deal with these issues are *processes*, *external agents*, *events*, *conditions*, and *views on the object model*.

A *process*, at an appropriate level of abstraction, is performing some identifiable task in the information system. It is an orderly or established series of steps or operations towards a desired result or product, and can denote anything from a vague activity taking place in an organization to a simple hardware process in a computer. *External agents* are physical entities external to the information system under consideration, that interact with it by sending or receiving information. An external agent may be a person, an organization, or another system outside the scope of the application domain under consideration, interacting with the target system. *Events* determine when a process should be considered for firing. *Conditions* determine when a process should be fired. They are checked when the triggering conditions have been established, i.e. an event condition is evaluated to true, in order to determine whether the execution of the process may start. A condition is always an expression referring to the object model. Finally, an *object view* is a selected part of the object model, which corresponds to either the input or output flows of the process.

Behavioural modelling has been dominated by 'data flowing' models, which are concerned with the specification of activities in an application area. An activity is informally defined as a set of partially ordered sub-activities which themselves can be further decomposed. There are many variations of representation but basically they all conform to the same underlying semantics as advocated in Ross and Schoman (1977). Taxonomic abstraction is achieved via composition and decomposition of processes. The structural emphasis of the data flow formalism is on *procedural* decomposition and therefore it encourages top-down development.

In general, behavioural modelling can be considered as either *operational* or *declarative*. Operational modelling involves the specification of the system's behaviour in terms of processes which are explicitly invoked by events, whereas declarative modelling specifies a set of rules which are invoked through object accesses.

The operational approach has been strongly influenced by database notions such as that of 'transaction'. Examples of the operational approach include the following:

- REMORA (Rolland and Richard, 1982)
- TAXIS (Mylopoulos *et al.*, 1980)
- OBCM (Wand and Weber, 1989).

In the operational approach, changes in the information system correspond to changes in the real world. These changes are defined in terms of events and operations. An occurrence of a real-world external event triggers the execution of a set of transactions and produces a state transition. The logic and control aspects of an application are both mixed. An operational specification has the following general form:

When ⟨event occurrence identified⟩
if all ⟨conditions⟩ met
then ⟨transaction execution⟩ on ⟨objects⟩

Events express when a state change on entities in the environment must happen; operations define how the entities are modified. Conditions must be defined in a way which guarantees that the transition is permitted. The transaction (set of operations) must produce a new valid state.

In practice, the operational approach is dominated by the so-called 'data flow' approaches. Complexity of systems is handled by using functional decomposition. For example, Fig. 4.9 shows a process being decomposed into two further processes together with the flow of data between these lower-level processes.

A number of extensions on the basic data flow model have been proposed in order to increase its expressiveness, in particular by adding control concepts such as triggering ports (Krogstie *et al.*, 1991).

Because of the difficulty inherent in the early phases of functional requirements modelling it is not always possible to identify the parts of a process. To decrease the level of shallow knowledge of top-level processes, some approaches advocate the use of causal networks (Hayes, 1985). Causal networks are aimed at describing the behaviour of a process instead of the flow of information and material.

In contrast to the operational approach, the declarative approach is concerned with expressing a system's behaviour in terms of its logical components, thus avoiding saying anything about control aspects. To this end, a declarative specification consists of a specification of facts, a set of constraints which determine the validity of facts, and a set of

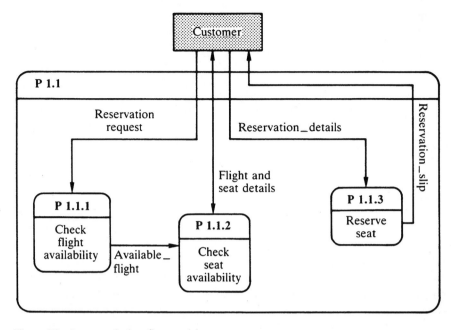

Figure 4.9   An example data flow model.

derivation rules which express the conditions which should have been true for a fact to hold at any time. Examples of declarative approaches include the following:

- CIAM (Gustafsson *et al.*, 1982)
- ERAE (Dubois *et al.*, 1989; Fiadeiro *et al.*, 1992)

The declarative approach using the CIAM conceptual model is demonstrated in Fig. 4.10. For each entity type, a set of stored or derived attributes are defined and in addition, some of the stored attributes are designated as the entity identifier. Each attribute function of an entity type may have a time argument, e.g. price(D). If the function is assumed to be derivable, then a derivation rule must be defined. For example, the price of a product is defined as the price stated in the last *price change* event referring to the particular product instance.

A number of declarative models use a combination of graphical and textual notation. For example, the ERAE model consists of two parts, the *declaration* part where concepts are identified and classified similarly to structural modelling, and the *statement* part where the concepts defined in the declaration part are further constrained using a typed first-order language with equality.

4.4.4 Trends in functional requirements modelling

Integrating structural and behavioural models In recent years the modelling dichotomy (structural vs. behavioural) has been seriously questioned. It is evident that any conceptual modelling activity concerned with representing functional requirements needs to involve both viewpoints. Also, new application requirements have highlighted the importance of

```
entity      PRODUCT
  attribute functions
    pno : PNO;
    pname : PNAME;
    price(D) : MONEY;
      derivation rule: ∀x ∀t ∀d (PRODUCT (x,t) ∧ D(d) ∧ day(t)=d
          ∧ ∃y (PRICE-CHANGE(y) ∧ product(y)=x ∧ day(y) ≤ d
          ∧ ∃z (PRICE-CHANGE(z) ∧ product(y)=product(z) ∧ day(z) ≥ day(y)))
        → price(x,d) = price(y));
    qty(t): NONNEGATIVE-INTEGER:
      derivation rule: .........
  identifier: pno;
end;
```

Figure 4.10 The specification of **product** in CIAM.

modelling complex objects as well as dealing with structural and behavioural components of an information system in a uniform modelling way.

These requirements have given rise to the object-oriented paradigm in specifying functional requirements. The trend of object-oriented programming languages and object-oriented database management systems (DBMS) is beginning to influence work in the conceptual modelling area. The arguments put forward by the object-oriented paradigm in the database area are also applicable to conceptual modelling. For example, the modelling of complex objects arises from the need to deal with applications which require the management of objects of arbitrary complexity. In applications such as CAD/CAM or CASE, one needs to be able to deal with objects that consist of a number of components and to reason about them while being able to deal with their components.

Traditional semantic data models fail to deal with this requirement; the structural constraints, for example, of the relational model (Codd, 1970, 1979) force a developer to decompose the representation of a complex object into a set of relations. Extensions to the relational model include new types of attributes (Haskin and Lorie, 1982) and the relaxation of the first normal form constraint (Abiteboul et al., 1989). In both cases modelling of complex objects is carried out from an implementation rather than a conceptual modelling perspective.

In conceptual modelling many authors have advocated the use of the object-oriented paradigm in order, primarily, to deal uniformly with structural and behavioural aspects of information systems (Booch, 1991; Fiadeiro et al., 1990, 1992; Sernadas and Ehrick, 1990; Wieringa, 1991). In object-oriented approaches, object descriptions are the units of design that encapsulate all structural and behavioural aspects local to that object.

The concept of 'object' is considered as a knowledge unit which describes an object in terms of three perspectives:

- The structural perspective is centred on objects, their properties, and structural relationships among objects.
- The behaviour perspective (or dynamic perspective) is specified by the object lifecycle and includes the definition of events which may occur in the object lifecycle.
- The process perspective focuses on the dynamic and temporal relationships between objects, dealing with triggering of operations when some event occurs and with synchronization rules between events.

Within the object-oriented framework the above three perspectives are treated in a variety of ways (Wirfs-Brock and Johnson, 1990). These can be classified as the functional approach, the data approach, and the object-centred approach.

The *functional approach* advocates the use of functions and data flows as an initial step, the results of which are subsequently transferred to an object view at the design stage. Naturally, this approach owes much to the operational view of behavioural modelling approaches. More specifically, from a methodological perspective this represents an evolutionary approach to object-orientation from the well-known 'structured analysis and design' methods. The relationship between structured techniques and object-oriented approach implies that there is a need for transformations from one approach to the other (Alabiso, 1988). Another approach is to combine the functional and object-oriented approaches at the requirements specification stage (Bailin, 1989; Ward, 1989).

The *data approach* is strongly influenced by classical conceptual data models (Hoza *et al.*, 1989; Rumbaugh *et al.*, 1991; Shlaer and Mellor, 1988). The definition of objects is based on well-known techniques of semantic data modelling such as the E–R model. This approach emphasizes the structural view of objects but augments this view by incorporating dynamic and functional properties.

The *object-centred approach* makes use of object-oriented concepts from the outset of the modelling process. The resulting conceptual schema is defined as a collection of objects that can interact with each other. The use of the same concepts for both requirements analysis and system design is seen by many as one of the strengths of an object-oriented approach.

Dealing with temporal aspects Time is an important aspect of real-world phenomena which is intimately tied to the description of dynamic aspects of the world. The need for modelling time explicitly arises from the need of many applications to retain historical information. The lack of temporal support raises serious problems in many cases. Without temporal support, many applications have been forced to manage temporal information in an *ad hoc* manner. Clearly many applications, from traditional employee record-keeping, inventory control, and accounts payable and receivable, to more sophisticated computer-aided design, decision support, and expert system applications, could all benefit from models and DBMSs with built-in features for modelling and organizing information across time and for accessing that information in time-dependent ways.

The traditional approach to dealing with temporal issues is to treat dates as ordinary entities or attributes in semantic data modelling. Thus, there was no need to provide built-in mechanisms in information systems to record and process time-varying information. When the application programmer is faced with the need to record and use time-varying information, then the appropriate constructs for time representation and manipulation need to be defined. This extends to the area of requirements specification. Without any general concepts supported by a conceptual model, the task of modelling time becomes application dependent, thus requiring a special treatment for every application with temporal requirements.

Over the years researchers in disciplines as varied as database systems, artificial intelligence, logic, natural language processing, and distributed processing have studied the role that time plays in information processing. Rather than abating, the interest in this subject has been increasing steadily. For instance, researchers in artificial intelligence have pointed out that any realistic model of the real world should not only include snapshot descriptions, but also their evolution over time (Allen, 1983, 1984, 1987; Allen and Hayes, 1985; Dean, 1987). Additionally, the modelling of planning problems dictated that a model should provide the ability to reason about disjunctive and incomplete temporal knowledge (Dean, 1984; Dean and McDermott, 1987). Many different algorithms have been proposed for reasoning with temporal information, but none of them has been widely acceptable in practice due to efficiency problems.

Conceptual modelling has generally addressed the problem of time modelling with two main objectives:

- To define time models
- To use temporal languages in the modelling of the behaviour of systems

Various classifications of time modelling consider the task from the following viewpoints:

- Modelling of state transitions and events
- Modelling of temporal rules
- Modelling of temporal data

Based on these characteristics, conceptual modelling approaches can be distinguished as static, dynamic, temporal, and full-time perspective approaches.

Static approaches Static approaches cater only for the description of a snapshot of the application domain, and therefore none of the features that were identified above are explicitly modelled. Some variants of this class include the modelling of processes which can be interpreted as computer instructions.

This class includes approaches where only one particular state of reality is considered at a time. The application domain is considered as a snapshot of interrelated classes of entities and a set of processes that operate on the model. These approaches are simple and straightforward, offering a low development cost. The use of processes for the description of the dynamic aspects of the application domain has, however, a number of drawbacks. These descriptions are imperative rather than declarative, thus reducing the design space of the later development stages. Additionally, the semantics of the real-world behaviour are presented in sequences of instructions creating descriptions that are difficult to understand and maintain. Examples of this class are all the second- and third-generation languages that were developed during the mid-1970s.

Dynamic approaches This class of conceptual modelling formalisms offers more suitable means for describing the dynamic aspects of an application domain. These are described using state transitions which are modelled explicitly. The behaviour of the application domain is described by a pair consisting of a precondition and a postcondition. The establishment of the latter is independent of the conceptual model description.

This class allows the designer to use whatever platforms and mechanisms he/she wants in order to implement the specification opting for a higher system performance. Since any implementation details are suppressed, the resulting description is easier to understand and maintain. An example of this class is ACM/PCM (Brodie and Silva, 1982).

Temporal approaches These approaches allow for the specification of time-dependent constraints such as 'salaries must never decrease'. This class also considers the sequence of states, and makes use of the notion of event. Rather than a property which can take on different values over time, an event is an object that prevails for only one time unit. Events are central to the description of the application domain since one is not only interested in modelling an enterprise but also its environment and the interaction between the two. This interaction is easily interpreted through events that have preconditions, triggering conditions and resulting actions.

This category of formalisms offers the capability also to define constraints between states, between events and states, and between events. These approaches mainly provide support for the last two of the three features that are identified as the basis for this classification. Examples of such approaches are Infolog (Sernadas, 1980), SDM (McLeod and Hammer, 1981), and LBM (Lundberg, 1982).

Full-time perspective approaches This category of approaches fully realizes the importance of time in conceptual modelling and provides—at different levels—support for the modelling of many aspects of the interaction between time and information, including the modelling of historical or temporal data. Examples of such approaches are the ERAE model (Dubois *et al.*, 1986b; Elmasri *et al.*, 1993) and the TEER model (Elmasri *et al.*, 1993).

One of the major issues involved in designing a conceptual model for information systems that has a built-in notion of time is *'what is the nature of time and its interaction with information?'*.

The nature of time There are three core issues reflecting the nature of time which need examination:

Time elements An essential issue when considering a model or system for handling the temporal dimension of data is the nature of the time dimension itself. Basically, this issue comes down to whether time should be modelled as *discrete elements* (such as integers) or as *dense elements* (such as rationals or reals). While there are proposals for both types of time, it appears that the use of discrete time points is more widespread. A related issue concerns whether data values are associated with *points* in time or with *intervals*. Clearly this issue disappears when using discrete time, since the two representation schemes are equivalent.

Absolute and relative time Most approaches to date have focused on modelling and managing *absolute time* in some form, i.e. exact time points or intervals are associated with each data value. In artificial intelligence, however, a great deal of attention has been placed on *relative time*, e.g. dealing with phrases such as 'last week', and 'a year ago', which appear in natural language understanding and story understanding systems. Clearly, the issue of relative time modelling impinges on the modelling of information systems and has to be considered alongside absolute time modelling.

Linear and non-linear time An issue of importance with respect to the nature of time in a scheduling context, such as might take place in an office automation or job scheduling environment, is that of *periodic time*. Any system that supports time should be able to model requirements which refer to the periodicity of the familiar time units of weeks, months, etc., and also to user-defined periods such as work-weeks, weekends, payroll periods, etc. Non-linear time also appears when there is a need to make assertions in alternative futures. This is useful in forecasting models and requires the use of *branching time*.

Recent approaches to conceptual modelling dealing with time have focused mainly on increasing the capabilities of conceptual modelling languages—mostly along the structural dimension—by incorporating a temporal modelling dimension. The ERAE data model (Dubois *et al.*, 1986b, 1989) is an attempt to extend the semantics of the entity-relationship model with a distinguished type 'event' in its basic set of constructs. The TEMPORA model (Loucopoulos *et al.*, 1991; McBrien *et al.*, 1992; Theodoulidis *et al.*, 1990) includes time as a primitive notion and provides facilities for the modelling of time along the structural, processing, and event dimensions through the use of three interrelated models. A temporal extension of the extended entity relationship model that incorporates the idea of lifespan for entities and relationships has been proposed by Elmasri and Wuu (Elmasri *et al.*, 1990; Elmasri and Wuu, 1990).

Extending traditional conceptual models with concepts that enable one to model temporal aspects of requirements is an area that is receiving increased attention, as evidenced by published bibliographies in this area (McKenzie and Snodgrass, 1986; Soo, 1991; Theodoulidis and Loucopoulos, 1991).

Interaction of time with information In the first approaches to modelling time it was considered that its interaction with traditionally non-time-varying information was straightforward and the incorporation of time in the models was enough to solve all problems in the area. Extensive research in the area has shown, however, that there are a variety of different ways that time interacts with information, not all of which are yet well understood. Various aspects of these interactions are presented in the following paragraphs.

Attribute types and properties Three relationships have been identified between time and the values or attributes or properties. Some properties can be constant, such as NAME. Usually in the context of extensions to the relational model, key attributes are assumed to belong to this category. Other attributes are time varying, such as STATUS. Finally, a third category of properties is that of attributes which take their values from the domain of times, such as BIRTH-DATE.

Object identification across time An important issue is the ability to recognize uniquely and unambiguously any individual object that is modelled. In database technology this is achieved through the use of key attributes. This becomes more important and complicated in the context of temporal models, since one must know whether or not an object that is currently being examined is the same one as another that is already known through some existing facts in the model. This requires that the identifier attributes be time invariant. In some cases this has led to artificial identifiers provided by the users or the systems. These identifiers have no connection with the reality being modelled but their introduction and use is based on design considerations.

An additional complication is caused by the fact that a temporal model keeps a more or less permanent record of objects that are or even were of interest to the enterprise. For example employees in a company may be hired, fired, and subsequently rehired. The temporal model must be able to capture and represent these 'births' and 'reincarnations' of objects in order to be able to keep track of the objects that are actively of interest.

Object and/or property timestamping A controversy exists relating to the level at which the temporal dimension should be incorporated. This has its roots in the relational extensions where one of the main issues was the introduction of tuple or attribute timestamping or both. This continued in the third generation of temporal models where some researchers choose to attach timestamps to the object and relationship level, while others timestamp the objects' properties.

Continuous and discrete changes Some information changes at a precise point in time, e.g. the STATUS of a supplier might change from 10 to 20 at the beginning of a precise day. Other changes, however, take place continuously, i.e. in chemical reactions, and are only occasionally monitored. Both cases are different, although probably both of them are usually represented as discrete changes. It has been suggested, however, that even though the representation is the same, one needs to keep track of the each different type of change (Clifford and Rao, 1987).

Valid, transaction, and user-defined time A major aspect of the relationship between time and information is that there exist multiple such relationships. There are three orthogonal kinds of time that a data model may support: valid time, transaction time, and user-defined time (Snodgrass and Ahn, 1985, 1986). Valid time concerns modelling a time-varying reality; it is the time that something happened in the real world. The valid time, for example, of an event is the clock time at which the event occurred in the real world, independent of the recording of that event in some database. Other terms with similar meaning found in the literature include intrinsic time (Bubenko, 1977a), effective time (Ben-Zvi, 1982), and logical time (Dadam *et al.*, 1984; Lum *et al.*, 1984). Transaction time, on the other hand, concerns the storage of information in the database. The transaction time for an event identifies the transaction that stored the information about the event in the database. Other terms with similar meaning that have been used are extrinsic time (Bubenko, 1977b), registration time (Ben-Zvi, 1982), and physical time (Dadam *et al.*, 1984; Lum *et al.*, 1984). User-defined time is an uninterpreted domain for which the data model supports the operations of input, output, and perhaps comparison. As its name implies, the semantics of user-defined time is provided by the user or application program. The relational model already supports user-defined time because it is simply another domain, such as integer or character string (Overmyer and Stonebraker, 1982).

Events Although the notion of event was not considered in the initial approaches to dealing with temporal modelling, events are the main reason that one is interested in time. Without events there would be no changes to model over time, and the snapshot models would have been adequate for modelling reality. In contrast to time-varying properties, events happen at real time. Events are considered as constituting evolution rules which describe the dynamics of an information system and in particular the dynamics of the integrity constraints expressed by ⟨event–action⟩ sequences. A lot of different definitions for events can be found in the literature (i.e. Bubenko, 1977a; Rolland and Richard, 1982) where the event has been defined as: decision / change in the world / observation or decision / action or activity / begin, end, or change of an atomic state / happening / change of conditions / value change of conditions / instantaneous message / creation, change, extinction, of entities.

Generally, however, events represent a change of interest in the environment or the information system and are, therefore, usually classified as internal or external events. Events have triggering conditions (WHEN something happens), preconditions (IF a condition is true), and postconditions (what is the next state of the model) or actions (what process takes place if both triggering condition and precondition hold). Usually events are considered as instantaneous in the literature, though some approaches deal with duration events as well (McLeod and Hammer, 1981).

Evolving schemas Although it is clear that in the area of conceptual modelling both the data and the metadata are of interest, and that both may evolve over time, this issue has received little attention in its own right. While schema evolution has been investigated, the issue of temporal management of evolving schemas has been addressed by very few researchers (Clifford and Croker, 1987; Shiftan, 1986). Schema evolution is associated solely with transaction time since it is concerned with how the reality is modelled by the schema.

Dealing with business rules The approach of specifying business rules during functional requirements modelling is based on the need for formalizing, documenting, encoding, and maintaining 'business' knowledge externally to application programs. The major efforts in addressing *business policy* modelling involve the use of a rule-based paradigm which provides a 'natural' mapping from enterprise to information systems concepts, and which can also be used to carry out formal analysis of requirements (Bubenko and Wangler, 1993; Loucopoulos *et al.*, 1991; Petrounias and Loucopoulos, 1994; Tanaka *et al.*, 1991; Tsalgatidou and Loucopoulos, 1991). The view put forward is that a major aspect of information systems development is about formalizing and documenting knowledge about the application domain, and this knowledge should be represented explicitly (Bubenko and Wangler, 1992).

Typically the role of a specification language that models the UoD in terms of rules is twofold. Firstly, it is concerned with constraints placed upon information structures and with the derivation of new information based on existing information. Secondly, it is concerned with the eligibility for the execution of different activities and constraints placed on their order of execution.

It is possible, therefore, to place a rule, at the conceptual level, in one of the following categories:

- *Constraint rules* which are concerned with the integrity of the information structure components.
- *Derivation rules* which are expressions that define the derived components of an information structure in terms of concepts that are already present in the information base of the modelled system. Derivation rules are introduced as a means of capturing

structural domain knowledge that need not be stored and that its value can be derived dynamically using existing or other derived information.

- *Event–action rules* which are concerned with the invocation of activities. In particular, action rules express the conditions under which the activities must be taken, i.e. a set of triggering conditions and/or a set of preconditions that must be satisfied prior to their execution.

Constraints can be further specialized into static constraints and transition constraints. *Static constraints* apply to every state of the database and are time independent. They represent conditions which must hold at every state of the database. *Transition constraints* define valid state transitions in the database, thus specifying restrictions on the behaviour of the system.

An example of a static constraint rule specifying that 'employees with a company car are not allowed public transport reimbursement' is shown in Fig. 4.11.

The objective of transition constraint rules is to provide the means for describing business rules that refer to the past or the future. For example, consider a rule stating that a company decides (now) that it will never allow a reduction of its number of employees. Such a rule enforces the number of employees in past state (from now) to be less or equal to the number of employees in any future state of the company (and eventually the information system). Such types of constraints do not refer to the current state of the information; they rather reflect a part of business policy across time and they represent the connections between states of the evolution of the intended system, as they develop across time.

Two examples shown in Fig. 4.12 demonstrate the above concepts.

The purpose of derivation rules is to specify a way in which one can obtain information when needed, instead of having it explicitly stored. For example, consider the schema of Fig. 4.13 expressed in an E–R type notation. According to this schema, the derived fact type of profit could be defined in terms of a derivation rule as follows:

A sales item (SI) has profit (P) if (SI) has a wholesale price (WP) and (SI) has a retail price (RP) and $P = RP - WP$

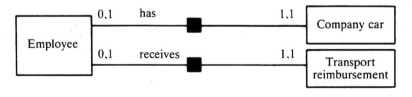

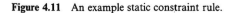

employee that has a **company car**

is disjoint from

employee that receives **monthly public transport reimbursement**

Figure 4.11 An example static constraint rule.

> **always_in_the_future always_in_the_past** Salary is_of EMPLOYEE >
> 10,000
>
> This rule specifies that in every state of the business world the salary of an employee for every previous state was greater than £10 000.

> **always_in_the_future number_of** EMPLOYEE works_for DEPARTMENT > 10
> **after end_of_next_month** (3)
>
> This rule states that, after the end of the next month and always thereafter, the number of employees that work for a department must be greater than 10.

Figure 4.12 Example transition rules.

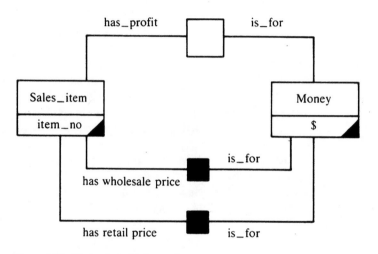

Figure 4.13 Derivation of information.

Event–action rules express the control of an activity and thus are represented as WHEN...IF...THEN rules. The WHEN part of an event–action rule contains the triggering expression and the IF part the preconditions for the invocation of a process. The following example shows an event–action rule:

When Cancellation_request
If (Reservation [reserves Ticket [has Ticket_basis (T)]] and
T in {'F', 'C', 'CP', 'Y'}) or
Reservation [reserves Ticket [has Ticket_basis (T)]] and
T = 'YAP') and
(Reservation [refers_to Flight [has Departure_date (D)]] and D
starts_after Today – 7 * days)
Then Remove_Reservation.

4.4.5 An example

Section 4.3.3 introduced the example of the air traffic control system. A 'concepts' model, an 'objectives' model, and an 'activities' model were defined in order to describe some important views of the enterprise. With respect to functional requirements the following observations can be made. First, the goal 'visualize air traffic scenarios', shown in Fig. 4.5, will motivate an information system goal which in turn will drive the process of deriving functional requirements. Second, for each functional requirement a description of the system function in terms of at least its input, output processing, and data will need to be defined.

The relationship between enterprise goal, information system goal, and system functional requirements is shown in Fig. 4.14. Note that the example is limited to only the 'display scenarios' requirement.

The model shown in Fig. 4.14 relates the IS-goal 'the system should display scenarios' with a set of functions, shown in the diagram by the boxes labelled 'IS-FR' that need to be incorporated by the intended system in order for the system to meet this goal. This model shows no details about the data required by the system or the details of the functions themselves in terms of input, output, and processing. These two aspects are modelled separately, examples of which are shown in Figs 4.15 and 4.16 respectively.

Figure 4.15 shows the main entity types and their relationships for this application. This entity–relationship model shows that the displayed information is made up of different types of entities such as alerts (which themselves can be software failure, hardware failure, or other radar alerts), maps and airways, radar signals, tables, and tracks (note that there are different types of radar signals, tables, and tracks).

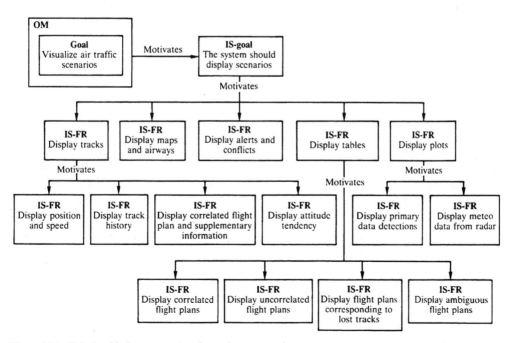

Figure 4.14 Relationship between enterprise and system goals.

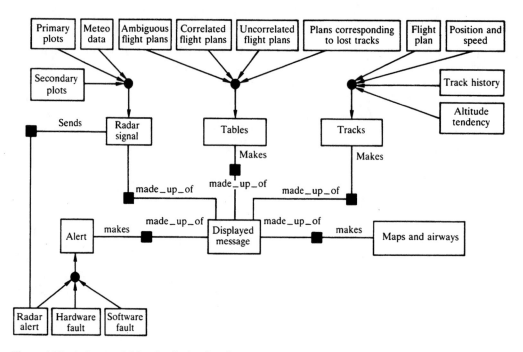

Figure 4.15 A data model for the display function.

Details of the function that deals with displaying the various required data are given in Fig. 4.16.

4.5 MODELLING OF NON-FUNCTIONAL REQUIREMENTS

4.5.1 Definition of non-functional requirements

Non-functional requirements play a crucial role in the design and development of an information system. Errors, omissions, or failure to take properly into account non-functional requirements are generally considered to be among the most expensive and difficult to correct once the system has been completed. Failure to meet, or satisfy, non-functional requirements has resulted in cancelled projects, unprofitable products, unhappy users, chaotically structured systems, and budget and schedule overruns as continuous changes need to be made.

Non-functional requirements can be defined as restrictions or constraints placed on a system service (Sommerville, 1992). Non-functional requirements have also been termed 'quality requirements' (Boehm, 1976; Deutsch and Willis, 1988) or non-behavioural requirements in contrast to behavioural, i.e. functional requirements (Davis, 1993).

According to IEEE-Std.'830' (1984), non-functional requirements are considered in terms of performance, external interfaces, design constraints, and quality attributes. Performance requirements are concerned with the static and dynamic requirements placed on the system and its interaction with its users. External interface requirements address issues such as user interface, hardware and software interface, and communication

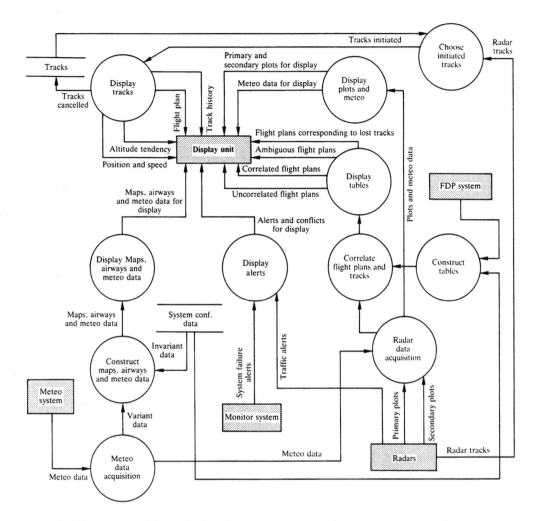

Figure 4.16 Description of the display function.

interface. Design requirements refer to the various constraints that may be imposed on the design of the system through various external or internal standards. Finally, quality attributes refer to those requirements that are concerned with the characteristics of the system such as security, maintainability, availability, etc. Similar definitions are also given in NCC (1987).

Undeniably, non-functional requirements have a great influence on the quality of the system to be developed. However, there are cases where the relative importance of a specific non-functional requirement, or rather its value, is determined by the nature of the system itself. This is apparent in the case of embedded systems, i.e. systems integrated in larger systems, such as industrial process-control systems, air traffic control systems, patient-monitoring systems, etc. (Zave, 1982). The nature of the larger systems impose certain non-functional requirements on the embedded components. For example, it is normally required that these systems exhibit a very fast response time (i.e. performance requirements), and have very high fail-safe mechanisms (i.e. reliability requirements). This influence of the nature of the system to the relevance of a non-functional requirement is extended also to other types of non-functional requirement apart from safety and performance. For instance, if the system is to be long lived, then portability and modifiability are usually critical considerations (Davis, 1993).

A report published by the Rome Air Development Centre (Bowen, 1985) separates non-functional requirements into two classes: (i) consumer oriented, i.e. non-functional requirements considered from a user's perspective, called *quality factors*, e.g. efficiency, interoperability, and correctness; and (ii) technically oriented non-functional requirements called *quality criteria*, e.g. anomaly management and completeness.

In general, user needs from a software system can be classified as shown in Fig. 4.17 (Deutsch and Willis, 1988).

Operational needs deal with the use of the system to perform a task for which it was intended. Maintenance needs are primarily concerned with modifications to the system either to correct errors or to add new functionalities.

Several classifications of non-functional requirements have been proposed in recent years. An early classification of non-functional requirements was proposed in Boehm (1976) which referred to qualities that a software must exhibit. However, several more general classifications of non-functional requirements, covering all aspects of an information system, have been proposed in recent years.

Roman's (1985) classification identifies six general classes of non-functional requirements: interface constraints, performance constraints, operating constraints, lifecycle constraints, economic constraints, and political constraints. This classification covers non-functional requirements related to all aspects of a system development. Desired goals of the system are expressed as non-functional requirements—accessibility for maintenance, maintainability, etc. The STARTS classification (NCC, 1987) distinguishes four principal classes of non-functional requirements: performance and reliability requirements, interface requirements, design constraints, and other non-functional requirements. According to the classification proposed by Yeh and Ng (1990), three classes of non-functional requirements are identified: target system constraints, system development, evolution

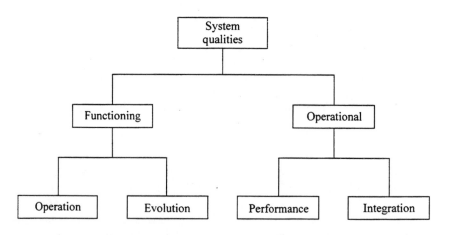

Figure 4.17 Classification of system qualities.

and maintenance constraints, and system development economic constraints. This classification is made from a management point of view and more emphasis is placed on the management issues concerning the development of the system rather than the system itself.

Although the non-functional requirements hierarchies proposed in these classifications have many common components, they differ according to their authors' viewpoints so that a classification may emphasize some aspects at the expense of some others. A general classification which seems to capture most of the elements of other classifications is that of Sommerville (1992). According to this classification (see Fig. 4.18), three general classes of non-functional requirements are distinguished, namely product, process, and external requirements.

Product requirements These are requirements which specify the desired characteristics that a system or a subsystem must possess. Some, such as performance and capacity, can be

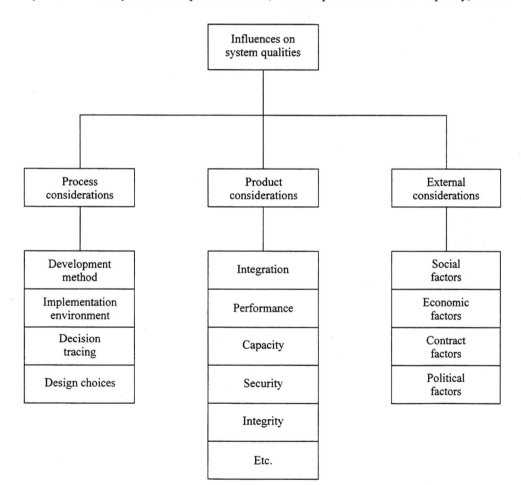

Figure 4.18 Process, product and external considerations.

formulated precisely, and thus easily quantified, while others, such as usability, are more difficult to quantify and consequently are often stated informally. The following statement 'The type of recording media (i.e. high density tapes) should guarantee one week of continuous data recording without manual operation (i.e. tape cartridge replacement)' is an example of a product requirement referring to the capacity of a subsystem, the data recording system, of the ATC system.

Process requirements These are constraints placed upon the development process of the system. These include requirements for a particular development method, implementation tool, or standards to be followed. Thus, the statement 'The system must achieve compliance with all relevant ISO-9000 standards' is an example of a process requirement referring to a particular standard to be followed. Since there is an increasing emphasis on process modelling and development standards, it is highly probable that there will be an increasing demand to meet such requirements.

External requirements These are constraints placed on both product and process and they arise from within or without the enterprise. These include constraints derived from enterprise policies, legislative requirements, etc. The statement 'radiation emitted by the display must meet European Union regulations' is an example of an external constraint, and specifically a legal constraint.

The difficulty of dealing with non-functional requirements is exemplified in Charette (1986):

- There are no rules and guidelines for determining when a non-functional requirement is optimally met. Every 'solution' might provoke a proposal for a more refined solution; the end might never be apparent.
- Non-functional requirements have only good and bad solutions, not right and wrong ones.
- Non-functional requirement problems may not be definitively tested.
- Problems related to non-functional requirements may be symptoms of higher-level problems. For example, if the schedule or the budget are unreasonable or the technology is unavailable, the non-functional requirement might not be met in any way, shape, or form.

4.5.2 Approaches to modelling non-functional requirements

Although the importance of non-functional requirements in the development of information systems is recognized, the field of information systems specification methods is almost entirely dominated by approaches that concentrate much more on functional requirements modelling and rather tangentially on non-functional requirements. These shortcomings are primarily due to the informal representation of non-functional requirements. Even with the growing interest in developing higher-level models and design paradigms, current technology is not yet fully developed for adequately representing non-functional requirements, reasoning about them, and using them to generate designs (Chung, 1991).

Unlike functional requirements, non-functional requirements are treated rather informally and there are few methods that provide any guidelines for capturing and representing or showing the influence that these requirements can have on the design process. Formality and detail is increased as one turns towards those approaches that concentrate on specific aspects of non-functional requirements particularly those of performance (Borderwisch *et al.*, 1993; Nixon, 1993; Puigjaner *et al.*, 1993) and security (Chung, 1993; Cole, 1990; Thuraisingham, 1990). There are, of course, a number of standards that provide a number of useful definitions (Dorfman and Thayer, 1990), but little exists in the form of methodological frameworks.

In expressing non-functional requirements, it is important to relate general objectives, or 'soft' goals into statements that can refer to measurable properties of the system. A statement of the type 'the display must accommodate all necessary data for the scenario', related to the ATC system, is an example referring to the system's capacity and usability. The problem with such a statement is that it is expressed in such a way so as to make testing for usability a difficult undertaking since it contains no tangible information about the properties which would be critical for achieving usability. This is true of most other non-functional requirements (most of the 'ilities' such as portability, evolvability, flexibility, reliability, etc.). The concept of ease of use is indeed subjective and the above statement expresses a high-level requirement that needs further analysis in order to derive a measurable constraint.

The only way to overcome this problem is to state non-functional requirements in such a way that satisfies two attributes that all non-functional requirements must possess (Deutsch and Willis, 1988; Sommerville, 1992), namely:

- They must be objective
- They must be testable

A non-functional requirement is objective if it does not express a wish, a goal, or a personal opinion, and is testable if there is some process by which the requirement is tested. Thus, a better expression for the NFR of the ATC system would be 'the display must be able to handle 100 tracks, 200 vectors and 500 table symbols.

Examples of properties for the ATC system are shown in Fig. 4.19.

One of the causes of the complexity of non-functional requirements is that they participate in many different types of relationship with other requirements, non-functional as well as functional. As an example consider the non-functional requirement of cost effectiveness. Three major components could be involved with cost requirements:

- Operation cost—e.g. training cost, salaries, etc. It can be further refined according to either job positions or job categories.
- Equipment cost—the cost of physical resources.
- System cost—the running cost for the information system, including the cost for hardware and software components.

These three components are interdependent, i.e. a decision taken for one may affect negatively the other(s). Trying, for example, to minimize the equipment cost could increase operation cost, or trying to increase the system cost may decrease the operation cost. However, cost must be also considered in the time interval. Trying, for example, to minimize short-term cost may increase long-term cost. A cost requirement may be also affected by accuracy requirements, i.e. accuracy acts negatively on cost in the sense that in order to achieve higher accuracy, a higher cost may be incurred, but on the other hand, higher accuracy means reduced long-term cost.

As shown in Fig. 4.20, the process of specifying non-functional requirements is essentially a process which involves knowledge acquired in the form of verbatims from requirements holders, and knowledge about the context within which the target system will

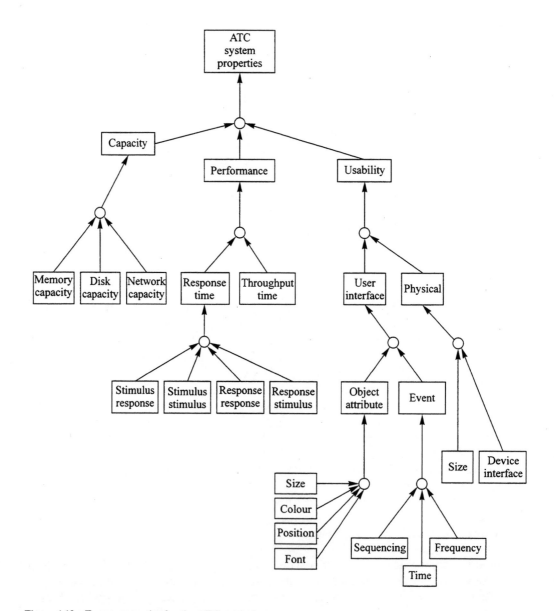

Figure 4.19 Target properties for the ATC example.

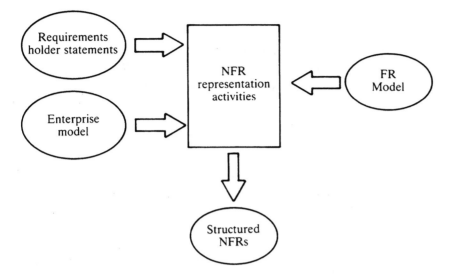

Figure 4.20 Capturing non-functional requirements.

operate, i.e. the enterprise specification, and knowledge about the functionality of the target system, i.e. the functional requirements specification.

When people express a requirement, be it functional or non-functional, they are hypothesizing, or imagining, a system that is not yet in existence. In the case of a functional requirement the issue of concern is the behaviour of the system, whereas for non-functional requirements one is concerned with the characteristics of the system or the process to be followed in developing and maintaining the system or some component of it. Therefore, even more so than in the case of functional requirements, correct identification of non-functional requirements (in the sense of objectivity and measurement) needs to make reference to a system architecture and to the relationship between components of this architecture and their functionality.

An important consideration, particularly applicable to complex situations, is the interrelationships between different non-functional requirements. It is not inconceivable that there may be contradictory non-functional requirements or dependencies between them such that the satisfying of one depends on the satisfying of another. It is important that these conflicting or synergistic relationships between requirements are identified and clearly documented so that appropriate design decisions can be made.

4.5.3 An example

To demonstrate the modelling of non-functional requirements, consider again the air traffic control system.

A number of viewpoints are shown in this section. First, a relationship between enterprise goals and non-functional requirements is shown in Fig. 4.21. This view is analogous to that shown in Fig. 4.14, between enterprise goals and functional requirements goals.

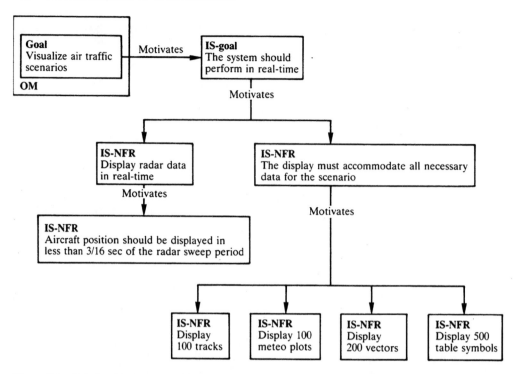

Figure 4.21 Relationship between enterprise and system goals.

The system requirement is that it should perform in real time. This leads to a number of non-functional requirements that are primarily concerned with performance and capacity. For example, the non-functional requirement 'radar data should be displayed in real time' motivates the more detailed non-functional requirement 'aircraft position should be displayed in less than 3/16 sec of the radar sweep period'. Further analysis of non-functional requirements results in successively more specific statements represented as the leaves of the tree diagram shown in Fig. 4.21.

The view shown in Fig. 4.21 has therefore two objectives: to relate non-functional requirements to the objectives of the enterprise, and to examine successively these requirements until a measurable statement has been defined. Again, as in the case of functional requirements, it is possible to trace non-functional requirements back to originally stated, vague expressions in the enterprise domain.

All the non-functional requirements stated in Fig. 4.21 refer to one of the components of the target system, the display unit. It would be useful therefore to gain an understanding of the architecture of at least part of the system to which the display unit belongs. Such a view is shown in Fig. 4.22.

By expressing non-functional requirements at the architectural level one gets a clear view of the interdependencies and conflicts between these requirements at the system component level. For example, the requirement that the display unit 'should display tracks up to a maximum number of 100' has design implications not only for the display unit (in terms of layout, size of screen, etc.) but also on the memory capacity of the RDPC in its ability to hold enough information about a maximum of 100 tracks.

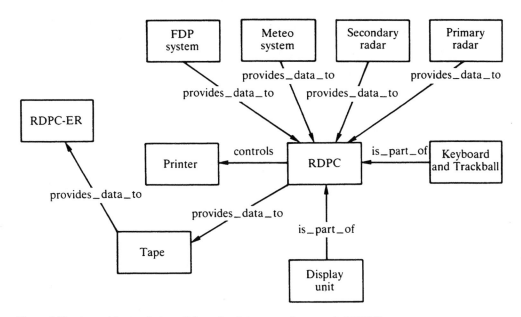

Figure 4.22 An architectural view of the radar data processing console (RDPC).

Since the functionality of the display unit is defined in the functional specification and since there is an obvious impact of non-functional requirements on both the system component and its functionality, another important consideration is the view that articulates architectural requirements, as shown in Fig. 4.23.

Figure 4.23 shows the influence of non-functional requirements on the system component under consideration, the display unit, on the component's two main functions, i.e. 'display position and speed' and 'display tracks', as well as the data required by these functions, i.e. 'tracks' and 'aircraft position and speed'.

4.5.4 Influence of non-functional requirements on the design process

The formal treatment of non-functional requirements is characterized by two approaches (Mylopoulos *et al.*, 1992): product-oriented and process-oriented approaches.

- *Product-oriented approach* This approach deals with non-functional requirements from the evaluation point of view, i.e. evaluation of the final product. This approach attempts to elaborate formal definitions of non-functional requirements so that a system can be evaluated with respect to the degree to which it meets its requirements. Evaluation occurs at the end of the development process.
- *Process-oriented approach* This approach attempts to develop techniques for justifying decisions during the development process. Instead of evaluating the final product, this approach tries to rationalize the development process in terms of non-functional requirements. Design decisions may affect positively or negatively particular non-functional requirements. These dependencies can serve as a basis for arguing that a system meets a certain non-functional requirement or explaining why it does not.

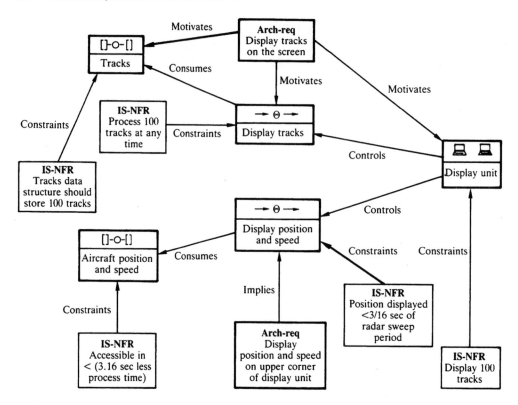

Figure 4.23 Relating non-functional requirements to system components, functions, and data.

Perspective	Purpose
Product • What qualities should the system exhibit?	*System testing* • Explicit statement about system characteristics
Process • How does a designer specify an IS that meets the quality characteristics defined in the NFRs? • Does the system satisfy the stated NFRs?	*Process guidance* • Identify critical FR components whose 'executable' equivalent must have some specified properties • Guide the designer to choose from a set of possible alternative solutions • Define relevant measurement procedures and data for testing

Figure 4.24 Use of product- and process-oriented approaches.

These approaches lead to two complementary views of non-functional requirements with respect to their influence on the design process. These views are summarised in Fig. 4.24.

The product view concentrates on the qualities that the system should have. Its purpose is to use explicit constraints expressed on system components and to test these components against these constraints.

The process view is concerned with the way that a designer may use non-functional requirements to make design choices out of a number of potential options as well as devising testing criteria for evaluating these designs against the stated requirements.

Each non-functional requirement can be attached to a single evaluation component, the characteristics of which are determined by the nature of the requirement in question, i.e. by reasoning about a particular constraint it should be possible to construct an evaluation component that is capable of determining whether a system component meets that constraint. This requires that for each type of constraint there is a corresponding test procedure, and that for each group of non-functional requirements constraining a particular system component, a corresponding test is attached to the evaluation component responsible for the evaluation of that system component.

In attempting to define a system that meets a set of constraints, a designer can regard these constraints as representing design goals that must be satisfied. Therefore, the satisfiability of a functional requirement can be broken down into a decision tree of subordinate requirements. There may be, however, several alternatives of doing this, thus leading to AND/OR decision trees of non-functional requirements. Each hierarchy that is created in this way is confined to a single type of non-functional requirements and successive levels in the hierarchy direct the designer to lower levels of detail corresponding to the functional specification. A small example is represented in Fig. 4.25 which shows that the non-functional requirement of performance for a system component 'track warning' is a design goal that can be met by satisfying the two performance goals corresponding to 'data to be displayed' and 'interface of display window'.

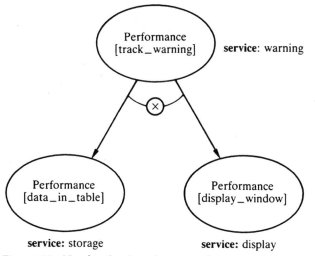

Figure 4.25   Non-functional requirement goals.

Table 4.1 Conflicting non-functional requirements

Security vs. flexibility	Security vs. performance	Usability vs. performance
Since flexibility requires very general structures, security might be harder to ensure in such cases	The additional design and processing required to control the access of the system usually lengthens run-time	The additional design and processing required to ease an operator's task usually lengthens run-time

All requirements, either functional or non-functional, act as constraints on the design process. Thus, a non-functional requirement does not only constrain a service of the system to be developed but also constrains the design process itself. In fact, if one considers design as a search problem in a multidimensional solution space, then non-functional requirements can be viewed as constraints of the searching space within which the designer seeks a functionally correct solution (Borderwisch *et al.*, 1993).

However, this process is further complicated by the fact that very often non-functional requirements conflict with each other. To illustrate the point, three examples in Table 4.1 show the potential conflicts between the non-functional requirements of security, flexibility, usability, and performance.

The complication in the design process, derived from conflicting non-functional requirements, arises from the fact that the result of a decision taken in order to satisfy a particular non-functional requirement is in conflict with another requirement and in this case there is the risk of failure to meet that particular requirement with consequences that may be difficult to predict.

One possible way to overcome this problem is to relate each non-functional requirement to a conceptually higher-level goal, usually found in the enterprise. Since these goals have different priorities and criticalities, then the goal with the highest priority must be satisfied. Consequently, the relative non-functional requirement will have to be satisfied to a higher degree compared to the others. The following example concerning an air traffic control system shows the above 'principle'. One of the main goals of an airport authority is to ensure the safety of the aeroplanes and passengers. This goal is of the highest priority and thus the system controlling the air traffic must display to the controller, all the data relative to flight plans, tracks, etc., as quickly as possible. The desired degree of response time (performance of the system) must therefore be satisfied over all other requirements. The resolution of the conflict through the use of knowledge about the context within which the system is required is another example of the importance of taking a broad view of requirements.

Of course, non-functional requirements are not only potentially conflicting but also potentially synergistic, i.e. the achievement of one or more non-functional requirements influences positively the achievement of other requirements. For example, to increase flexibility may result in an increase of interoperability or, for a software component, increasing reusability may result in increased portability.

4.6 SUMMARY

The process of specifying requirements can be viewed as a sequence of model-building activities. These models can fall into three general categories: enterprise models, functional requirements models, and non-functional requirements models.

The quality of each set of models depends largely on the ability of a developer to extract and understand knowledge about the UoD which needs to be acquired from a diverse user population. This sensitive activity needs to be supported by appropriate conceptual modelling formalisms. The purpose of these formalisms is to specify unambiguously the UoD in such a way so as to enable developers to ascertain the validity of their understanding of the UoD.

This chapter has introduced the context within which these different models are used, together with the major orientations currently in practice.

REFERENCES

Abiteboul S., Fischer P. C. and Schek H.-J. (Eds) (1989) *Nested Relations and Complex Objects in Databases. Lecture Notes in Computer Science.* Springer-Verlag, Berlin, Vol. 361.

Abrial J. R. (1974) Data semantics database management. In Klimbie and Koffman (Eds) *Data Base Management.* North Holland, Amsterdam.

Alabiso B. (1988) Transformation of data flow analysis models to object-oriented design. *OOPSLA '88*, San Diego, CA.

Albano A. and Orsini R. (1985) A software engineering approach for database design: the GALILEO project. In *Computer-aided Database Design.* North Holland, Amsterdam.

Allen J. (1987) *Natural Language Understanding.* Benjamin Cummings, Menlo, CA.

Allen J. F. (1983) Maintaining knowledge about temporal intervals. *Communications of the ACM*, **26**(11), 832–843.

Allen J. F. (1984) Towards a general theory of action and time. *Artificial Intelligence*, **23**, 123–154.

Allen J. F. and Hayes P. J. (1985) A common-sense theory of time. *International Joint Conference on Artificial Intelligence.* Los Angeles, CA.

ANSI/X3/SPARC (1975) Study group on data base management systems: interim report 75-02-08. *ACM SIGMOD Bulletin*, **7**(2).

Anton A. I., McCracken W. M. and Potts C. (1994) Goal decomposition and scenario analysis in business process reengineering. In Wijers G., Brinkkemper S. and Wasserman T. (Eds) *Sixth International Conference on Advanced Information Systems Engineering (CAiSE '94).* Springer-Verlag, Utrecht, pp. 94–104.

Bachman C. W. (1969) Data structure diagrams. *Data Bases*, **1**(2), 4–10.

Bailin S. C. (1989) An object-oriented requirements specification method. *Communications of the ACM*, **32**(5).

Balzer R. M. and Goldman N. (1979) Principles of good software specification and their implications for specification languages. *IEEE Conference on Specifications of Reliable Software.* IEEE Computer Society Press, Washington, DC. pp. 58–67.

Beeri C. (1989) Formal models for object oriented databases. In Kim W. (Ed.) *First International Conference on Deductive and Object Oriented Databases.* North Holland, Kyoto, pp. 405–430.

Ben-Zvi J. (1982) The time relational model. Ph.D. dissertation, University of California, Los Angeles.

Boehm B. (1976) Software engineering. *IEEE Transactions on Computers*, **25**(12), 1226–1241.

Booch G. (1991) *Object-oriented design.* Benjamin-Cummings, Menlo, CA.

Borderwisch R., Foeckeler W., Schwarmer B. and Stewing F.-J. (1993) Non-functional aspects: system performance evaluation. In Thomé B. (Ed.), *Systems Engineering: Principles and Practice of Computer-based Systems Engineering.* Wiley, Chichester, pp. 223–271.

Borgida A., Greenspan S. and Mylopoulos J. (1985) Knowledge representation as the basis for requirements specification. *IEEE Computer*, **18**(4) 82–91.

Bowen T. P. (1985) Specification of software quality attributes. RADC-TR-85-37. Rome Air Defense Centre, Griffiths Air Force Base, NY, February.

Brachman R. J., Fikes R. E. and Levesque H. J. (1983) Krypton: a functional approach to knowledge representation. *IEEE Computer*, **16**(10) 67–73.

Brodie M. L. and Silva E. (1982) Active and passive component modelling (ACM/PCM). In Olle T. W., Sol H. G. and Verrijin-Stuart A. A. (Eds) *Information System Design Methodologies: A Comparative Review*. North Holland, Amsterdam.

Bubenko J. A. J. (1977a) The temporal dimension in information modeling. In *Architecture and Models in Database Management Systems*. North Holland, Amsterdam, pp. 93–118.

Bubenko J. (1977b) Validity and verification aspects of information modeling. *Third International Conference on Very Large Data Bases*, Tokyo.

Bubenko J. A. and Wangler B. (1992) Research directions in conceptual specification development. In Loucopoulos P. and Zicari R. (Eds) *Conceptual Modelling, Databases and CASE: An Integrated View of Information Systems Development*. Wiley, New York, pp. 389–412.

Bubenko J. A. and Wangler B. (1993) Objectives driven capture of business rules and information systems requirements. *IEEE Conference on Systems, Man and Cybernetics*.

Bubenko J., Dahl R., Gustafsson M., Nellborn C. and Song W. (1992) Computer support for enterprise modelling and requirements acquisition. SISU, Kista, Stockholm, Sweden, F3 Project Internal Report.

Bubenko J., Rolland C., Loucopoulos P. and de Antonellis V. (1994) Facilitating 'fuzzy to formal' requirements modelling. *IEEE International Conference on Requirements Engineering*.

Buneman P. and Atkinson M. (1986) Inheritance and persistence in database programming languages. *Proc. ACM SIGMOD International Conference on Using of Data*. ACM, Washington, DC, pp. 4–15.

Charette R. N. (1986) *Software Engineering Environments: Concepts and Technology*. McGraw-Hill, New York.

Chen P. P. (1976) The entity–relationship model—toward a unified view of data. *ACM Transactions on Database Systems*, 1(1), 9–36.

Chung L. (1991) Representation and utilization of non-functional requirements for information system design. In Andersen R., Bubenko J. A., Jr and Solvberg A. (Eds) *Third International Conference on Advanced Information Systems Engineering (CAiSE '91)*. Springer Verlag, Berlin, pp. 5–30.

Chung L. (1993) Dealing with security requirements during the development of information systems. In Rolland C., Bodat F. and Cauvet C. (Eds) *Fifth International Conference on Advanced Information Systems Engineering (CAiSE '93)*. Springer-Verlag, Paris, pp. 234–251.

Clifford J. and Croker A. (1987) The historical relational data model (HRDM) and algebra based on lifespans. *IEEE Data Engineering Conference*.

Clifford J. and Rao A. (1987) A simple general structure for temporal domains. *Conference on Temporal Aspects of Information Systems*. France, pp. 23–30.

Codd E. F. (1970) A relational model of data for large shared data banks. *Communications of the ACM*, 13(6), 377–387.

Codd E. F. (1979) Extending the database relational model to capture more meaning. *ACM Transactions on Database Systems*, 4(4), 397–434.

Cole R. (1990) A model for security in distributed systems. *Computers & Security*, no. 9, 319–330.

Dadam P., Lum V. and Werner H. D. (1984) Integration of time versions into a relational database system. In Dayal U., Schlageter G. and Seng L. H. (Eds) *VLDB*. Singapore, pp. 509–522.

Dardenne A., van Lamsweerde A. and Fickas S. (1993) Goal-directed requirements acquisition. *Science of Computer Programming*, 20, 3–50.

Davis A. M. (1993) *Software Requirements: Objects, Functions and States*. Prentice Hall, Englewood Cliffs, NJ.

Dean T. (1984) Planning and temporal reasoning under uncertainty. *IEEE Workshop on Principles of Knowledge Based Systems*, Denver, CO.

Dean T. (1987) Large-scale temporal databases for planning in complex domains. *Tenth International Joint Conference on Artificial Intelligence*, Milan.

Dean T. and McDermott D. V. (1987) Temporal database management. *Artificial Intelligence*, no. 32.

DeMarco T. (1978) *Structured Analysis and System Specification*. Yourdon, New York.

Deutsch M. S. and Willis R. R. (1988) *Software Quality Engineering: A Total Technical and Management Approach*. Prentice Hall, Englewood Cliffs, NJ.

diRoccaferrera G. M. F. (1973) Behavioral aspects of decision making under multiple goals. In Cochrane J. L. and Zeleny M. (Eds) *Multiple Criteria Decision Making*, pp. 635–656.

Dittrich K. R. (1986) Object-oriented database systems: the notion and the issues. *International Workshop on Object-oriented DB*. Pacific Grove, CA.

Dobson J. (1992) A methodology for managing organisational requirements. University of Newcastle upon Tyne, UK.

Dobson J. S., Blyth A. J. C., Chudge J. and Strens R. (1994) The ORDIT approach to organisational requirements. In Jirotka M. and Goguen J. A. (Eds) *Requirements Engineering: Social and Technical Issues*. Academic Press, London, pp. 87–106.

Dorfman M. and Thayer R. H. (Eds) (1990) *Standards, Guidelines, and Examples on System and Software Requirements Engineering*. IEEE Computer Society Press, Los Alamitos, CA.

Dubois E., Hagelstein J., Lahou E., Ponsaert F. and Rifaut A. (1986a) A knowledge representation language for requirements engineering. *Proceedings of the IEEE*, 74(10), 1431–1444.

Dubois E., Hagelstein J., Lahou E., Rifault A. and Williams F. (1986b) A data model for requirements engineering. *Second International Conference on Data Engineering*, Los Angeles, pp. 646–653.

Dubois E., Hagelstein J. and Rifaut A. (1989) Formal requirements engineering with ERAE. *Phillips Research Laboratory*. Brussels, Belgium **43**(3/4), 393–414.

Elmasri R., El-Assal I. and Kouramajian V. (1990) Semantics of temporal data in an extended ER model. *Ninth International Conference on Entity–Relationship Approach*. Lausanne, pp. 249–264.

Elmasri R. and Wuu G. (1990) A temporal model and query language for ER databases. *IEEE Data Engineering Conference*.

Elmasri R., Wuu G. T. J. and Kouramajian V. (1993) A temporal model and query language for EER databases. In Tansel Clifford A., Gadia J., Jajodia S., Segev S., Snodgrass R. (Eds) *Temporal Databases: Theory, Design and Implementation*. Benjamin Cummings, Menlo, CA.

Fiadeiro J., Sernadas C., Maibaum T. and Saake G. (1990) Proof-theoretic semantics of object-oriented specification constructs. In Meeersman K. (Ed.) *Object Oriented Databases: Analysis, Design and Construction*. North Holland, Amsterdam.

Fiadeiro J., Sernadas C., Maibaum T. and Sernadas A. (1992) Describing and structuring objects for conceptual schema development. In Loucopoulos P. and Zicari R. (Eds) *Conceptual Modelling, Databases and CASE: An Integrated View of Information Systems Development*. Wiley, New York, pp. 117–138.

Goranson H. T. (1992) Dimensions of enterprise integration. In Petrie C. J. (Ed.) *Proc. 1st International Conference on Enterprise Integration Modeling*. MIT Press, Cambridge, MA, pp. 101–113.

Gotel, O. C. Z. and Finkelstein, A. C. W. (1993) An analysis of the requirements traceability. Technical Report TR-93-41. Department of Computing, Imperial College, 1993.

Gustafsson M. R., Karlsson T. and Bubenko J. A., Jr (1982) A declarative approach to conceptual information modeling. In Olle, T. W., Sol H. G. and Verrijn-Stewart A. A. (Eds) *Information Systems Design Methodologies: A Comparative Review*. North Holland, Noordwijkerhout, The Netherlands, pp. 93–142.

Hagelstein J. (1988) Declarative approach to information systems requirements. *Journal of Knowledge-based systems*, **1**(4), 211–220.

Haskin R. L. and Lorie R. A. (1982) On extending the functions of a relational database system. *ACM SIGMOD Conference*. Orlando, FL.

Hayes P. J. (1985) The second naive physics manifesto. In Hobbs J. R. and Moore R. C. (Eds) *Formal Theories of the Commonsense World*. Ablex, Norwood, NJ, pp. 1–36.

Hazzah A. (1991) DRC and DRM: the repository meets the database. *Database Programming & Design*, August, 29–39.

Henderson-Sellers B. and Edwards J. M. (1990) The object-oriented systems life cycle. *Communications of the ACM*, **33**(9), 142–159.

Hoza B. J., Smith M. K. and Tockey S. R. (1989) An introduction to object-oriented analysis. *Fifth Structured Techniques Association Conference*. Chicago.

Hull R. (1987) A survey of theoretical research on typed complex database objects. In Paredaens J. (Ed.) *Databases*. Academic Press, London.

Hull R. and King R. (1987) Semantic database modeling: survey, applications and research issues. *ACM Computing Surveys*, **19**(3), 201–260.

IEEE-Std.'830' (1984) *IEEE Guide to Software Requirements Specifications*. Institute of Electrical and Electronics Engineers, New York.

Jackson M. A. (1983) *System Development*. Prentice Hall, London.

Kappel G. and Schrefl M. (1990) Using an object-oriented diagram technique for the design of information systems. In Sol H. G. and van Hee K. M. (Eds) *IWC on Dynamic Modelling of Information Systems*. Delft University of Technology, Noordwijkerhout, The Netherlands, pp. 97–130.

Krogstie J., McBrien P., Owens R. and Seltveit A. H. (1991) Information systems development using a combination of process and rule based approaches. In Andersen R., Bubenko J. A. Jr and Solvberg A. (Eds) *Third International Conference on Advanced Information Systems Engineering (CAiSE' 91)*. Springer-Verlag, Trondheim, pp. 319–335.

Langefors B. (1973) *Theoretical Analysis of Information Systems*. Student Literature, Lund.

Liskov B. and Zilles S. (1977) An introduction to formal specifications of data abstractions. In Yeh R. T. (Ed.) *Current Trends in Programming Methodology—Vol. 1: Software Specification and Design*. Prentice Hall, Englewood Cliffs, NJ, pp. 1–32.

Loucopoulos P. (1989) The RUBRIC project—integrating E–R, object and rule-based paradigms. *European Conference on Object Oriented Programming (ECOOP)*, Workshop Session on Design Paradigms, Nottingham.

Loucopoulos P., Wangler B., McBrien P., Schumacker F., Theodoulidis B. and Kopanas V. (1991) Integrating database technology, rule based systems and temporal reasoning for effective information systems: the TEMPORA paradigm. *Information Systems*, **1**(1).

Lum V., Dadam P., Erbe R., Guenauer J. and Pistor P. (1984) Designing DBMS support for the temporal dimension. In Yormark B. (Ed.) *ACM SIGMOD International Conference on Management of Data*. ACM Press, Boston, MA, pp. 115–130.

Lundberg B. (1982) An axiomatisation of events. *BIT*, no. 3.

MacDonald I. G. (1986) Information engineering. In Olle T. W., Sol H. G. and Verrijn-Stuart A. A. (Eds) *Information System Design Methodologies: Improving the Practice*. Elsevier/North Holland, Amsterdam.

MacDonald I. G. (1988) Automating the information engineering methodology with the information engineering facility. In Bhabuta L. (Ed.) *Computerized Assistance During the Information Systems Life Cycle*. Elsevier/North Holland, Amsterdam.

McBrien P., Seltveit A.-H. and Wangler B. (1992) An entity–relationship model extended to describe historical information. In Majumdar A. K. and Prakash N. (Eds) *International Conference on Information Systems and Management of Data—CISMOD '92*. Indian National Scientific Documentation Centre, Bangalore, pp. 244–260.

McKenzie E. and Snodgrass R. (1986) Bibliography: temporal databases. *ACM SIGMOD Record*, **15**(4), 40–52.

McLeod D. and Hammer M. (1981) Database description with SDM: a semantic database model. *ACM Transactions on Database Systems*, **6**(3).

Mercurio V., Meyers B. F., Nisbet A. M. and Radin G. (1990) AD/cycle strategy and architecture. *IBM Systems Journal*, **29**(2).

Mittermeir R. T., Rousopoulos N., Yeh R. T. and Ng P. A. (1990) An integrated approach to requirements analysis. In Ng P. and Yeh R. T. (Eds) *Modern Software Engineering: Foundations and Current Perspectives*. Van Nostrand Reinhold, New York, pp. 450–461.

Morris P., Coombes A. and McDermid J. (1994) Requirements and traceability, 1st *International Workshop on Requirements Engineering: Foundation of Software Quality REFSQ '94*. Utrecht, The Netherlands, 1994.

Mylopoulos J. (1986) The role of knowledge representation in the development of specifications. In Kugler H.-J. (Ed.) *Information Processing 86*. Elsevier, Amsterdam.

Mylopoulos J. (1992) Conceptual modelling and telos. In Loucopoulos P. and Zicari R. (Eds) *Conceptual Modelling, Databases and CASE: An Integrated View of Information Systems Development*. Wiley, New York, pp. 49–68.

Mylopoulos J., Bernstein P. A. and Wong H. K. T. (1980) A language facility for designing database intensive applications. *ACM Transactions on Database Systems*, **15**(2).

Mylopoulos J., Chung L. and Nixon B. (1992) Representing and using nonfunctional requirements: a process-oriented approach. *IEEE Transactions on Software Engineering*, **SE-18**(6), 483–497.

NCC (1987) *The STARTS Guide: A Guide to Methods and Software Tools for the Construction of Large Real-time Systems*. National Computing Centre, Manchester.

Nellborn C., Bubenko J. and Gustafsson M. (1992) Enterprise modelling—the key to capturing requirements for information systems. SISU, F3 Project Internal Report.

Nellborn C. and Holm P. (1994) Capturing information systems requirements through enterprise and speech act modelling. In Wijers G., Brinkkemper S. and Wasserman T. (Eds) *Sixth International Conference on Advanced Information Systems Engineering (CAiSE '94)*. Springer-Verlag, Utrecht, pp. 172–185.

Nijssen G. and Halpin T. (1989) *Conceptual Schema and Relational Databases—A Fact-oriented Approach*. Prentice Hall, Englewood Cliffs, NJ.

Nilsson N. J. (1971) *Problem-solving Methods in Artificial Intelligence*. McGraw-Hill, 1971.

Nixon B. A. (1993) *Dealing with Performance Requirements During the Development of Information Systems*. IEEE Computer Society Press, San Diego, CA. pp. 42–49.

Nuseibeh B., Krammer J. and Filkenstein A. (1994) A framework for expressing the relationships between multiple views in requirements specification. *IEEE Transactions on Software Engineering*.

Olle T. W., Sol H. G. and Tully C. J. (Eds) (1983) *Information Systems Design Methodologies: A Feature Analysis*. North Holland, Amsterdam.

Olle T. W., Sol H. G. and Verrijn-Stuart A. A. (Eds) (1984) *Information Systems Design Methodologies: A Comparative Review*. North Holland, Amsterdam.

Olle T. W., Sol H. G. and Verrijn-Stuart A. A. (Eds) (1986) *Information Systems Design Methodologies: Improving the Practice*. Elsevier/North Holland, Amsterdam.

Overmyer R. and Stonebraker M. (1982) Implementation of a time expert in a database system. *ACM SIGMOD Record*, **12**(3), 51–59.

Peckham J. and Maryansky F. (1988) Semantic data models. *ACM Computing Surveys*, **20**(3).

Petrie C. J. (Ed.) (1992) *Proc. 1st Conference on Enterprise Integration Modeling*, Scientific and Engineering Computation Series. MIT Press, Cambridge, MA.

Petrounias I. and Loucopoulos P. (1994) A rule based approach for the design and implementation of information systems. In Jarke M. (Ed.) *EDBT '94*. Springer-Verlag, Cambridge.

Potts C. (1994), Requirements completeness, enterprise goals and scenarios. Internal Report, College of Computing, Georgia Institute of Technology, August 1994.

Puigjaner R., Benzekri A. and Ayache S. (1993) Estimation process of performance constraints during the design of real-time and embedded systems. In Rolland C., Bodart F. and Cauvet C. (Eds) *Fifth International Conference on Advanced Information Systems Engineering (CAiSE' 93)*. Springer-Verlag, Paris, pp. 629–648.

Rentsch T. (1982) Object oriented programming. *SIGPLAN Notes*, September, 51–57.

Rolland C. and Richard C. (1982) The REMORA methodology for information systems development and management. In Olle T. W., Sol H. G. and Verrijn-Stuart A. A. (Eds) *Conference on Comparative Review of Information System Design Methodologies*. North Holland, Amsterdam.

Roman G.-C. (1985) A taxonomy of current issues in requirements engineering. *IEEE Computer*, **18**, 14–23.

Ross D. T. and Schoman K. E. (1977) Structured analysis for requirement definition. *IEEE Transactions on Software Engineering*, **SE-3**(1), 1–65.

Rumbaugh J., Blaha M., Premerlani W., Eddy F. and Lorensen W. (1991) *Object-oriented Modelling and Design*. Prentice Hall, Englewood Cliffs, NJ.

Schank R. C. (1975) *Conceptual Information Processing*. North Holland, Amsterdam.

Scheer A.-W. and Hars A. (1992) Extending data modelling to cover the whole enterprise. *Communications of the ACM*, **35**(9), 166–175.

Sernadas A. (1980) Temporal aspects of logical procedure definition. *Information Systems*, **5**(3), 167–187.

Sernadas A. and Ehrick H.-D. (1990) What is an object after all?. In Meersman K. (Ed.) *Object Oriented Databases: Analysis, Design and Construction*. North Holland, Amsterdam.

Shiftan J. (1986) An assessment of the temporal differentiation of attributes in the implementation of a temporally oriented DBMS. Ph.D. dissertation. Information Systems Area, Graduate School of Business Administration, New York University.

Shipman D. (1981) The functional data model and the data language DAPLEX. *ACM Transactions on Database Systems*, **6**(1).

Shlaer S. and Mellor S. J. (1988) *An Object Oriented Systems Analysis: Modelling the World in Data*. Yourdon Press, Prentice Hall, Engelwood Cliffs, NJ.

Smith J. M. and Smith D. C. P. (1977) Database abstractions: aggregation and generalization. *ACM Transactions on Database Systems*, **2**(2), 105–133.

Snodgrass R. and Ahn I. (1985) A taxonomy of time in databases. In Navathe S. (Ed.) *ACM SIGMOD International Conference on Management of Data*. ACM Press, Austin, TX, pp. 236–246.

Snodgrass R. and Ahn I. (1986) Temporal databases. *IEEE Computer*, **19**(9), 35–42.

Sommerville I. (1992) *Software Engineering*. Addison-Wesley, Reading, MA.

Soo M. D. (1991) Bibliography on temporal databases. *ACM SIGMOD Record*, **20**(1), 14–23.

Sowa J. F. (1984) *Conceptual Structures—Information Processing in Mind and Machine*. Addison-Wesley, Reading, MA.

Tanaka A. K., Navathe S. B., Chakravarthy S. and Karlapalem K. (1991) ER-R: an enhanced ER model with situation action rules to capture application semantics. *Tenth International Conference on Entity Relationship Approach*, San Mateo, CA.

ter Hofstede A. H. M., Proper H. A. and van der Weide T. P. (1993) Formal definition of a conceptual language for the description and manipulation of information models. *Information Systems*, **18**(7), 489–523.

Theodoulidis C. and Loucopoulos P. (1991) The time dimension in conceptual modelling. *Information Systems*, **16**(3).

Theodoulidis C., Loucopoulos P. and Wangler B. (1991) The entity relationship time model and the conceptual rule language. *Tenth International Conference on Entity Relationship Approach*, San Mateo, CA.

Theodoulidis C., Wangler B. and Loucopoulos P. (1990) Requirements specification in TEMPORA. In Steinholtz B., Solvberg A. and Bergman L. (Eds) *Second International Conference on Advanced Information Systems Engineering (CAiSE '90)*. Springer-Verlag, Stockholm, pp. 264–282.

Thuraisingham M. B. (1990) Towards the design of a secure data/knowledge base management system. *Data & Knowledge Engineering*, no. 5, 59–72.

Troyer O. D. (1991) The OO-binary relationship model: a truly object oriented conceptual model. In Andersen R., Bubenko J. A., Jr and Solvberg A. (Eds) *Second International Conference on Advanced Information Systems Engineering (CAiSE '91)*. Lecture Notes in Computer Science. Springer-Verlag, Trondheim.

Tsalgatidou A. and Loucopoulos P. (1991) Rule-based behaviour modelling: specification and validation of information systems dynamics. *IST (Information and Software Technology)* **33**(6), 425–432.

van Bommel P., ter Hofstede A. H. M. and van der Weide T. P. (1991) Semantics and verification of object-role models. *Information Systems*, **16**(5), 471–495.

van Griethuysen J. J. (1982) ISO—concepts and terminology for the conceptual schema and the information base. N695, ISO/TC9/SC5/WG3.

Vassiliou Y., Marakakis M., Katalagarianos P., Chung L., Mertikas M. and Mylopoulos J. (1990) IRIS—a mapping assistant for generating designs from requirements. In Seinholtz B., Sølvberg A. and Bergman L. (Eds) *Lecture Notes in Computer Science: Advanced Information Systems Engineering*. Springer-Verlag, Stockholm, pp. 307–338.

Verrijn-Stuart A. A. (1987) Themes and trends in information systems. *Computer Journal*, **30**, 97–109.

Wand Y. and Weber R. (1989) An ontological evaluation of systems analysis and design techniques. In Falkenberg E. D. and Lindgreen P. (Eds) *Information Systems Concepts: An In Depth Analysis*. Elsevier/ North Holland, Amsterdam.

Ward P. (1989) How to integrate object orientation with structured analysis and design. *IEEE Computer*, March.

Wieringa R. (1991) Steps towards a method for the formal modelling of dynamic objects. *DKE*, **6**, 509–540.

Wirfs-Brock R. J. and Johnson R. E. (1990) Surveying research in object-oriented design. *Communications of the ACM*, **33**(9), 105–124.

Yeh R. T. (1982) Requirements analysis—a management perspective. *COMPSAC '82*, pp. 410–416.

Yeh R. T. and Ng P. A. (1990) Software requirements—a management perspective. In Thayer R. H. and Dorfman M. (Eds) *System and Software Requirements Engineering*. IEEE Computer Society Press, Los Alamitos, CA, pp. 450–461.

Yourdon E. (1989) *Modern Structured Analysis*. Prentice Hall, Englewood Cliffs, NJ.

Yourdon E. and Constantine L. L. (1979) *Structured Design*. Prentice Hall, Englewood Cliffs, NJ.

Yu E. and Mylopoulos J. (1994) Understanding 'why' in software process modeling, analysis and design. *Sixteenth International Conference on Software Engineering*, Sorrento.

Yu E. S. K. (1993) Modelling organizations for information systems requirements engineering. *IEEE International Symposium on Requirements Engineering*. IEEE Computer Society Press, San Diego, CA, pp. 34–41.

Zave P. (1982) An operational approach to requirements specification for embedded systems. *IEEE Transactions on Software Engineering*, **8**(3), 250–269.

5

VALIDATING REQUIREMENTS

5.1 INTRODUCTION

Chapter 4 discussed a number of modelling formalisms which can be used to create a functional requirements model. The use of a single formalism or a combination of them, e.g. entities/relationships, rules, state transition diagrams, results in a model of what the analyst perceives to be the user requirements for a software system. With careful checking, possibly with some help from an automated CASE tool (such as those discussed in Chapter 6), the analyst can become fairly convinced that the requirements model is a *correct* one, i.e. the model does not contain illogical or self-contradicting definitions.

There is a problem with the above approach, however. *A correct requirements model is not necessarily the right requirements model.* What has been thought to be the user's problem can sometimes be something totally irrelevant, i.e. a situation can occur where time and effort is spent analysing the wrong problem. Such a situation is illustrated in Fig. 5.1.

Chapter 3 identified the main causes for such misconceptions to be the following:

- Difficulty in eliciting the requirements from a user. (In expert system terminology this is called the *knowledge acquisition bottleneck.*)
- Difficulty in establishing a common framework of understanding between the analyst and the user, i.e. *making them speak the same language.*

Obviously, wasting precious time and resources in solving the wrong problems is something ill-afforded. It is therefore important to make sure at a fairly early stage that the analysed problem is indeed the user's problem and that the resulting requirements

Figure 5.1 Solving the wrong problem.

model will be a faithful representation of the user's demand for a computer solution to his/her problem.

- Requirements validation is the process of certifying the requirements model for correctness against the user's intention.

As such, requirements validation helps *to do* the right thing, in contrast with the careful following of a modelling approach which helps *in doing* the thing right.

Section 5.2 provides more arguments in favour of an early validation of requirements which will avoid correcting expensive mistakes later on in the software life cycle. Section 5.3 gives guidelines on issues that should be considered when validating the requirements model. Section 5.5 introduces techniques for requirements validation, namely prototyping, simulation/animation, the use of natural language in validation, and finally expert system approaches.

Prototyping provides the users with a mock-up version of the software system as a means of acquiring their correct requirements.

Simulation and animation are techniques for 'bringing life' into the requirements model, taking it through different states and generally testing it under different scenarios in order to see how well it copes in real-life situations.

Natural language paraphrasing is a technique for translating the requirements model into the user's own language (i.e. natural language) in the hope that this will make it easier for the user to judge the validity of the requirements.

Expert system approaches to validation introduce the concept of an *assistant*, i.e. a system containing knowledge about the problem domain which it uses in order to bring to the attention of the human analyst contradictions, omissions, unresolved issues, etc., about the requirements model.

5.2 THE NEED FOR REQUIREMENTS VALIDATION

This section stresses the importance of an early validation of the requirements model. In addition, validation is distinguished from the more usually practised *verification*. It must be emphasized that in contrast to verification, validation cannot be performed by the analyst and software tools alone; the user's active participation is always necessary.

The *IEEE Glossary* (IEEE, 1983) defines validation as the process of evaluating software at the end of the software development process to ensure compliance with software requirements. The same glossary defines verification as 'The process of determining whether or not the products of a given phase of the software development cycle fulfil the requirements established during the previous phase.'

Some attention must be paid to the above definition. First, validation is defined as taking place only after the software has been developed. Second, verification is always carried out with respect to some requirements. The questions raised as a result of these definitions are as follows:

- Is it sufficient to validate software only after it has been developed?
- Against what can requirements be verified, i.e. what are the 'requirements for the requirements model'?

Statistics have proved the answer to the first question to be 'no'. A price has to be paid if software validation is left until late. The longer software validation is postponed, the more expensive (in terms of testing, debugging, and redevelopment) it becomes to correct mistakes. In a survey carried out by Boehm in the 1970s (Boehm, 1980) it was revealed that up to 50 per cent of the bugs in software systems were results of errors in the requirements. Moreover, the cost of fixing a bug which was a result of an error in requirements definition was up to five times the cost of errors in designing or coding. Such findings are justifiable, considering that most software systems are developed today using a 'waterfall' lifecycle approach (see Chapter 2), and the reasons are as follows. Suppose that an error occurs during the requirements specification phase. This will result in some part of the requirements model being erroneous and the rest being correct. As the development of software progresses, a portion of the design will be based in part on the erroneous requirements and in part on the correct requirements. Such a design will not be partially wrong; it will be completely wrong. Similarly, code which will be derived partially in erroneous and partially in correct design will be wrong. This 'snowball' effect can have catastrophic consequences. A single error in the requirements specification may cause the need to redesign, recode, and retest a large part of the software system. Therefore:

- Validating at the requirements specification phase can help to avoid fixing expensive bugs after the software has been developed.

In a similar manner, the answer to the second question asked at the beginning of this discussion ('is there some other model against which the requirements model can be verified?') is, again, 'no'. There is no such a thing as the requirements' requirements. While code can be verified against the design and design itself can be proved correct with respect to the requirements, there is no way we can formally verify the latter. If such a thing as a 'requirements' requirements' model existed it would have been inside the users' heads. In reality, however, users do not know what they want, neither (sometimes) what is best for them, nor (unless they are computer experts themselves!) what is feasible. This leads to another conclusion:

- It cannot be proved formally that a requirements model is correct.

What can, however, be achieved instead is a well-justified *belief* that the solution specified in the requirements model is the right one for the user. This can only be achieved by the set of techniques known as requirements validation which can be now defined as follows:

- The processes which establish and justify our (and the user's) belief that the requirements model specify a software solution which is right for the user's needs.

5.3 GUIDELINES ON WHAT TO VALIDATE IN A REQUIREMENTS MODEL

Requirements validation should be thought as more of a 'debugging' activity rather than a 'proving correct' one. The aim of requirements validation is not to prove the requirements correct, but instead to identify and correct all the errors (inconsistencies, omissions, incorrect information) now rather than later on when the software will be designed and coded. In Chapter 3 validation was defined to be a process which proceeds in parallel with other processes of requirements engineering, i.e. elicitation and specification. Indeed, validation is an 'ever present' activity which takes place every time a piece of requirement is acquired, analysed, or integrated with the rest of the requirements model. Validation of requirements is also mainly an *unstructured* process. This means that it is not possible to apply an algorithmic procedure which will obtain a validated requirements model. However, there is a set of tasks that are performed during validation which apply equally well to all methodologies and formalisms used to construct the requirements model. The purpose of these tasks is to identify the existence of a number of desirable properties in the requirements model, namely:

- Internal consistency
- Non-ambiguity
- External consistency
- Minimality
- Completeness
- Redundancy

The above properties of requirements models are discussed below.

5.3.1 Internal consistency

A requirements model is *internally consistent* if no contradicting conclusions can be derived from it. Consider as an example a requirements model for a payroll application. If some requirement in the model states that 'employees who earn less than £10 000 should not be taxed' and at the same time a different requirement states that 'for all employees tax should be deducted from their salaries' then the model is inconsistent. It must be noticed here that it is not necessary for both contradicting requirements to be explicit in the model; one (or both of them) may be implied from other requirements. This of course makes the validation task difficult since it is not always possible to check all the implications of the requirements model.

Faced with the problems of checking consistency, some researchers have suggested that a requirements model should be specified using *mathematical logic* (Dubois and Hagelstein, 1987). In logic we can view requirements as *logic sentences* which can be either *true* or *false*. Complex requirements statements can be constructed from more simple ones using logic connectors such as *and, or, not,* and *implies.* An example of a complex requirement formed from two simple ones is as follows:

'a book is available for borrowing'
'a book is out of the library'
'a book is available for borrowing' *or* 'a book is out of the library'

Being able to manipulate the requirements in a logical way when possible has a number of advantages. A *theorem prover* is a program which can infer new logic sentences by combining existing ones, using rules of *inference*. A theorem prover applied to a logic requirements model can help the analyst discover certain types of contradictions.

5.3.2 Non-ambiguity

Non-ambiguity is another important characteristic for which a requirements model should be checked. Non-ambiguity means that a requirement cannot be interpreted in more than one way. Unfortunately, ambiguities can be easily introduced in a requirements model, especially when natural language is used. The following example will show the potential disastrous effect that ambiguous requirements can have. Imagine a model of requirements for a software-controlled furnace. One particular requirement states

When the furnace temperature reaches 200°C or the environment temperature falls below 5°C and the water valve is turned on, then the oil valve must be turned on.

The above requirements statement is ambiguous because it can be interpreted in two different ways:

When the furnace temperature reaches 200°C and the water valve is turned on, the oil valve should be turned on. When the environment temperature falls below 5°C and the water valve is turned on the oil valve should be turned on.
or

When the furnace temperature reaches 200°C the oil valve must be turned on. When the environment temperature falls below 5°C and the water valve is turned on, the oil valve must be turned on.

While there seems to be little difference between the two interpretations, in fact the second one is wrong and if implemented in a software system could have devastating consequences. According to the second interpretation, the oil should start flowing in the furnace when its temperature reaches 200°C. This, however, ignores the requirement that the furnace's temperature must be controlled by a cooling mechanism. According to the second interpretation, this cooling system would never come into operation, allowing a possible overheating and explosion of the furnace.

The above is only one possible example of the risks brought by ambiguous requirements. One of the most important jobs of the analyst is therefore to eliminate ambiguities from the requirements model by using common sense, rules of logic, and by clarifying ambiguous specifications in conjunction with the users.

5.3.3 External consistency

External consistency is the agreement between what is stated in the requirements model and what is true in the problem domain. In a study by the Naval Research Laboratory, documented in Basili and Weiss (1981) it was revealed that 77 per cent of all the requirement errors for the A-7E aircraft's flight program were non-clerical. Forty nine per cent of these errors were incorrect facts. Every effort must be therefore put on ensuring that what is said in the requirements model is in accordance with the problem domain. Most of the facts appearing in the requirements model will come from interviewing the user's or studying the literature about the problem domain, etc. (see Chapter 3). If the facts about the domain are volatile (i.e. change frequently—something that usually happens when, for example, the software is going to be embedded in a new piece of hardware, yet to be developed), then every attempt should be made to keep the facts in the requirements model up to date.

5.3.4 Minimality

Minimality is an important feature which should be present in our requirements document. The opposite of minimality is called *over-specification*, which is simply the tendency to include more in the requirements model than is necessary. Usually, over-specification is an attempt to prescribe a design solution at the same time as we specify the requirement. This is, however, wrong because it constrains the possible solutions which the designers can choose from. An example of overspecifying the problem of a heating control system is as follows:

When the furnace temperature exceeds 200°C the master controller module should send a request of the type to the valve controller. The valve controller should use a first-in, first-out queue to store the requests it receives from the master controller.

The above statement belongs more to a design rather than to a requirements document as it introduces concepts (modules, queues, etc.) and solutions which are not essential to specify the heating control problem. In general, anything that should limit the designer's choices, unnecessarily, should not be included in the requirements module.

5.3.5 Completeness

A requirements model is complete when it does not omit essential information about the problem domain which could result into a system not meeting the user's needs. Completeness is a difficult thing to check in a requirements model, since there is no formal procedure to do so. A requirements model contains goals to be achieved in a problem domain, as well as rules, facts, and constraints that apply to the domain and to the software system that will be operating in the domain. Failure to capture any of these ingredients of a requirements model will have an impact on the correctness of the model.

- The omission of an objective, for example, will result in a model that will not represent all the user's needs.
- Failure to capture a rule or fact of the modelled domain will prohibit the software system from being a correct model of that domain.
- The absence of a constraint from the requirements model can lead to incorrect behaviour of the software system.

Some types of completeness checking can be performed fairly easily, and even be automated using a tool (see Chapter 6). These are usually checks for definition of all the names that appear in the requirements model. If, for example, process *xyz* is mentioned in the requirements model, then the tool should be able to check whether the process is described somewhere in the model or not.

The most difficult kinds of completeness checking, i.e. checking for missing goals, facts, or constraints, can be assisted in a number of ways, such as the following:

- By looking at systems with similar requirements to the one being analysed, we can identify 'forgotten' requirements (goals).
- By assuming a hierarchical organization of the requirements, we can identify requirements which do not have any corresponding 'higher-level' ones. If the justification for including some particular requirement is missing, then this missing justification could be some other, forgotten, requirement.

A good, general way to check for completeness in the requirements model is to use *prototyping* (described in Section 5.5.1). By prototyping the requirements model, obvious omissions (as well, of course, as inconsistencies, ambiguities, etc., can be found by the analyst and the participating users).

5.3.6 Redundancy

A requirement is redundant if it can also be obtained from some other part of the requirements model, or if it is simply some property or behaviour not wanted in the software system. Multiple definitions of requirements are not desirable features of a requirements model, since ideally a requirement should be identifiable in one and only one place in the requirements model. Care, however, is required when a requirement is *implied*

from other stated requirements. If a requirement is implied (in a logical sense) from other requirements and, at the same time, is stated explicitly, then one of the following conditions apply:

- The explicit statement of the requirement can be removed, as long as there is no fear that the implied requirement will be ignored.
- The explicit requirement can remain in the document together with a reference to the requirements by which it is implied. If any of those requirements is subsequently removed, the analyst should re-examine the status of the implied requirement.

Deciding on whether a requirement is redundant or not is an activity which requires an understanding of the users' expectations from the system (sometimes called a 'wish list'), the feasibility of the proposed requirements and also assigning priorities to requirements. A way to do so is to assign to each requirement a value from a range, starting from 'absolutely essential' through 'a nice thing to have in your system' down to 'redundant'.

5.4 RESOURCES NEEDED FOR REQUIREMENTS VALIDATION

It is fair to describe validation as the *quality assurance* process which can be applied to the requirements model. Quality is a sought-after property of every computer artefact—design, code, documentation, etc. The need for quality raises two issues of practical importance, i.e. the time and resources spent on requirements validation and the quality criteria which can be applied to a requirements model.

In an ideal world, the validation process should take as long as is necessary. The requirements model should be checked thoroughly by the analyst (in conjunction with the users and software tools when necessary) for all the points we mentioned before (omissions, inconsistencies, violation of constraints, etc.). The model's behaviour should be exhibited using techniques such as prototyping, animation, etc., and the model should be modified until it corresponds to the users' expectations. Additions, deletions, or modifications of requirements should be checked for their impact on the rest of the requirements model.

In the real world, however, the situation is different. Software projects have to meet budgets and deadlines. Requirements validation takes up only a small percentage of the overall project lifecycle and it cannot possibly last forever. Moreover there is usually a tendency among the developers to get requirements specification over with in order to move to more 'challenging' issues such as design. Finally, the users do not always have all the time and willingness in the world to collaborate with the analysts in endless requirements validation (inspections, walkthroughs) sessions.

The analyst is thus coming under time and resource constraints to perform a daunting and critical job such as requirements validation. As assistants to the validation task, the analyst can employ a number of tools and practices:

- Logical organization of the requirements model, which shows the interdependencies among the requirements.
- Automated tools, which help avoiding clerical errors and speed up some aspects of validation.

- Communication with the user at any opportunity using techniques such as simulation and prototyping.
- Bringing in experience of analysis of similar systems; reuse of previous requirements models.

Naturally, the duration and effort spent on requirements validation will vary with the modelled application. Also tools and techniques for validation may appear to be more suitable for some kinds of applications than for others. Nevertheless some sort of formal validation procedure is beneficial for all types of applications, since 'getting the requirements right' is the single most important step towards a successful software project.

5.5 TECHNIQUES FOR VALIDATING REQUIREMENTS

5.5.1 Prototyping

Prototyping (Chapter 2) is the term used to describe the process of constructing and evaluating working models of a system, in order to learn about certain aspects of the required system and/or its potential solution. Prototyping is a common technique in engineering disciplines, where a scaled-down model of the artefact (aeroplane, car, etc.) under production is first created and used for experimentation in order to arrive at a production model.

In software engineering, prototyping (also called *rapid prototyping*) has been advocated as the paradigm of producing software as quickly and cheaply as possible at some stage of the development. The actual uses of prototype vary, depending on the phase of the lifecycle in which it is used, as well as on the particular lifecycle model followed. The software prototype can be throw-away (used only for understanding and assessing solutions, performances, risks, etc.) or it can be transformed into the final production system (Balzer *et al.*, 1983). In order for a model (of any artefact, including software) to be characterized as a prototype, the following must be attainable:

- It must be possible to obtain information about the behaviour and performance of the production system from the prototype. To provide such information, prototypes should be capable of being fully instrumented; the result of such instrumentation is that the execution of a prototype results in the generation of data from which needed information can be inferred.
- Prototyping should be a *quick* process. In a well-supported environment, producing a working prototype should take significantly less time and effort than it would take to produce a full-scale artefact.

Use of prototyping in requirements validation In Chapter 2 the process of requirements engineering was said to have a lifecycle, consisting of three major phases: *elicitation, specification*, and *validation*. Prototyping can assist in all three phases of requirements engineering. It has already been discussed (Chapter 3) how prototyping techniques can help in acquiring (eliciting) and formalizing the requirements. This section is more concerned with the application of prototyping to validation, i.e. to the process of certifying the requirements model for correctness against the user's intention.

Since, by necessity, validation is a process in which users are very heavily involved, the prototype model must provide the user with meaningful information. There are two kinds of such information, namely *behavioural* and *structural*. A behavioural prototype models what the prototyped software system is supposed to do. In this respect, a behavioural prototype is a black-box model of the software system which exhibits responses to stimuli. It can be said that a behavioural prototype models the *functional requirements* (see Chapter 4) of the software. In contrast, a structural prototype models how the system being prototyped will accomplish its black-box behaviour. A structural prototype is thus a 'glass-box' model which exhibits aspects of the internal structure and organization of the system being prototyped, and in this respect it can be said that a structural prototype models the *non-functional requirements* (see Chapter 4) of the software.

Techniques for prototyping A requirements model can be created using a variety of different languages and formalisms as discussed in Chapter 4. However, in order to be used for prototyping, the modelling formalism (language) must exhibit a number of properties as follows:

- It must allow the inference of information 'hidden' in the requirements model.
- It must have the notion of 'state' as well as 'state transition'.

The first property (inferencing) essentially means that not only must someone be able to look at what is stated in the requirements model, but they must also be able to examine the implications of such statements. One way to make this possible is to use some *logic* language together with an inference mechanism to create the prototype. A very suitable language for this purpose is *PROLOG* and an extensive literature on prototyping using PROLOG now exists (Budde, 1984). The major advantage of PROLOG is that (by virtue of being a programming language) it allows the execution of the requirements specification. As a very high level language (VHLL) PROLOG permits incompleteness in the specifications and does not force the use of strong typing or procedural control structures. In addition, it is possible to transform the initial requirements prototype into an efficient production system, without having to leave PROLOG. Among the disadvantages of the PROLOG (or more generally, logic programming) approach to prototyping are the following:

- There is no graphical notation associated with it.
- Users do not always find logic specifications easy to understand.

The first problem can be overcome by using some graphical formalism (e.g. an entity–relationship model) as the front-end and having PROLOG translating E–R definitions to equivalent PROLOG structures in the background.

The second problem can be overcome by paraphrasing PROLOG definitions using some sort of 'IF–THEN–ELSE' rules and pseudo-English.

The following example (taken from a library specification problem) illustrates the use of PROLOG in prototyping requirements specifications. Part of the natural language requirements model for the library case is as follows:

In a university library there are two kinds of users, namely staff and students. Staff can perform two kinds of activities, namely check-out a book for a student who wants to borrow it and check-in a book returned by a student. Once a book is checked out it is not available for borrowing until it is checked-in again. A student cannot have more than ten books borrowed at any time.

The above requirements specification translated to PROLOG looks as follows:

user(X) :- staff(X) *or* student(X).

check_out(Book, Borrower) :- student(Borrower) *and not* checked_out(Book) *and not* borrowing_limit_exceeded(Borrower) *and* assert(checked_out(Book)) *and* update_borrowing_record(Borrower, borrowed).

check_in(Book, Borrower) :- student(Borrower) *and* book(Book) *and* retract(checked_out(Book)) *and* update_borrowing_record(Borrower, returned)

update_borrowing_record(Borrower, borrowed) :- borrowing_record(Borrower, Number_of_Books) *and* New_Number_of_Books is Number_of_Books + 1 *and* retract(borrowing_record(Borrower, Number_of_Books) *and* assert(borrowing_record(Borrower, New_Number_of_Books)).

update_borrowing_record(Borrower, borrowed) :- borrowing_record(Borrower, Number_of_Books) *and* New_Number_of_Books is Number_of_Books + 1 *and* retract(borrowing_record(Borrower, Number_of_Books) (*and* assert(borrowing_record(Borrower, New_Number_of_Books)).

borrowing_limit_exceeded(Borrower):- borrowing_record(Borrower, Number_of_Books) *and* Number_of_Books = 10.

This PROLOG requirements specification follows closely the English specification, making at the same time some additional statements which are usually taken for granted in the natural language specification (such as, for example, that if a person wants to check-out something, then that person must be a student and the thing to check-out must be a book).

Despite looking like a conventional program, the above PROLOG specification conforms to the quality criteria set for a requirements specification; it describes the problem domain, rather than the solution domain. As it is, the above specification says nothing about design decisions, e.g. decisions about the choice of data structures to hold the borrowing record of students. However, by virtue of its executability, the above specification provides the second necessary ingredient for prototyping, namely *states* and *state transition*.

In order to create a state in the above PROLOG specification, a number of *facts* must be defined. Facts are supposed to represent a (hypothetical) state in the real library, as follows:

student(student1).
student(student2).
book(book1).
book(book2).

{stating that the individual students 'student1', 'student2', as well as the individual books 'book1', 'book2' exist in the library}
checked_out(book2). {stating that book 'book2' has been checked out}
borrowing_record(student1, 0).
borrowing_record(student2, 1). {stating the borrowing records of students}

The above library state can be transformed to another state by invoking one of the rules describing the activities of checking-in and checking-out in the library. If for example, rule 'check_in' is invoked as follows:

check_in(student2, book2).

The new state of the library will be as follows.

student(student1).
student(student2).

book(book1).
book(book2).

borrowing_record(student1, 0).
borrowing_record(student2, 0).

In this new state, 'book2' is no longer borrowed and the 'student2' borrowing record has been amended to show that the student has currently borrowed no books. In a similar way, by invoking other rules the present state can be transformed to a number of other allowable states.

The value of this approach lies in the fact that users are asked to validate something which is closer to their real experience than a static requirements document. Users are more capable of detecting anomalies (in terms of inconsistencies, omissions, etc.) when they have hands-on experience with a dynamic executable requirements model. As an example, consider the above library state in which 'student1' is trying to check-in 'book1' (i.e. a book which is not borrowed!). If the execution of such request (i.e. check_in(student1, book1)) is refused by PROLOG, then this is obviously positive evidence for the quality of the specification, since a correct specification should not allow the creation of meaningless library states. On the other hand, the execution of the above request by PROLOG would mean that there are problems with the specification, since obviously the latter does not model the reality in a realistic manner. A possible remedy to this problem would be to redefine the rule describing the activity of 'checking-in'. A precondition could be added to the rule stating that in order for a book to be checked-in, it must be currently in a 'checked-out' state, as follows:

Check_in(Book, Borrower) :- student(Borrower) *and* book(Book)
and checked_out(Book) /*the precondition*/
and retract(checked_out(Book)) and update_borrowing_record(Borrower, returned).

It is up to the analyst to devise a number of suitable test cases which can lead to the identification of flaws in the requirements model.

Apart from running test cases, another prototyping technique known as *static validation* can be used with PROLOG requirements specifications. With static validation, the specification is analysed in order to check a number of possible flaws such as missing definitions. In the above case study, for example, it could be discovered that the 'check-in' activity can never take place because there is no corresponding rule for the 'check-out' activity defined. Static validation can save the user from going through too many test cases, but like dynamic validation is not a sufficient technique on its own. Here it must be noted that static analysis is also supported by many CASE tools for a variety of specification formalisms (data flows, entity–relationship models, etc.). Such tools will be also discussed in Chapter 6.

In summary, prototyping is a technique whose importance in requirements validation cannot be easily dismissed. However, whether prototyping is achievable at all depends on the modelling formalism and supporting environment used.

5.5.2 Animation

Animation is a technique which can be effectively brought into use for the validation of real-time systems. Real-time systems have a common set of notions such as *processes, process synchronization, messages,* and *timers.* An important concern in validating real-time systems is that the requirements for concurrent and time-constrained activities are correctly captured. With the advent of new technology such as personal high-speed workstations with high-resolution display devices, the graphical representation of concepts such as processes and the dynamic display of their behaviour has become possible.

Animation is a multiple graphical view of a process in action. In an animation environment, the analyst is given the ability to depict graphically all the major objects of the requirements model (processes, timers) and interact with them (using a mouse or pointing device) in terms of messages. For example, the user can change the state of a process from active to suspended and see the effects of that on the rest of the system. The objects usually have some way of graphically showing the state they are in (e.g. by using colour) and in addition numerical information is available on the screen. By animating the processes, the analyst can identify problems of performance and also detect situations such as deadlocks, starvation, etc.

In the context of information systems development, a prototype specifications animation approach described in Lalioti and Loucopoulos (1994) aims to provide a visual environment for validating and symbolically executing conceptual specifications (in terms of entity, process, and rule models) of an information system. The term *conceptual prototype* is used by this approach to emphasize the difference between executing the specifications and creating a prototype of the information system. In conceptual prototyping there is no need to make any design decisions prematurely. By animating the conceptual prototype, all the actors in the requirements engineering process can understand and inspect the behaviour of the system under development as early as possible in the process.

Visualization has been applied successfully in programming environments in order to provide an indication of the behaviour of the program. In the context of conceptual specifications, visualization involves the animation of the behaviour of a system and a visual interface reflecting the results of events upon the graphical—and where appropriate the textual—components of the specification.

The advantage of visualization over prototyping is that design decisions will not have to be made prematurely during requirements engineering when things are still vague. A requirements specification is likely to change many times before proceeding to design, and visualization should help in deriving a succession of specifications.

Experiences from the use of visual environments in programming tasks has encouraged researchers in requirements engineering to make use of similar techniques, normally referred to as animation techniques, in assisting the activity of validating conceptual specifications (Kramer and Ng, 1988; Tsalgatidou, 1988) .

Animation of a specification is the process of providing an indication of the *dynamic* behaviour of the system by walking through a specification fragment in order to follow some scenario. Animation can be used to determine causal relationships embedded in the specification or simply as a means of browsing through the specification to ensure adequacy and accuracy by reflection of the specified behaviour back to the user.

5.5.3 Natural language paraphrasing

The technique of natural language paraphrasing has being devised in order to tackle the problem caused by two conflicting concerns in requirements engineering, namely the concern of the analyst to develop a formal requirements model, and the users' need to communicate their requirements in their own terminology. Paraphrasing is a technique which compromises the two concerns by providing a 'user-friendly' version of a formal requirements model. Since paraphrasing sometimes summarizes parts of the requirements model, it can come to the aid of not only the user but the analyst as well, who can see the specification from a new perspective.

As with prototyping, paraphrasing does not need to be applied to the whole requirements model, as it can instead focus on those parts of the model which need clarification and reconsideration by the user. Naturally, paraphrasing should be an automated activity so that it does not occupy more valuable time than necessary. Such an automatic paraphrasing tool has been developed by a research project (Myers and Johnson, 1988) to target specifications of the language GIST. A typical GIST specification together with its English paraphrase produced by the tool is shown in Fig. 5.2.

5.5.4 Expert system approaches

This category of approaches includes a number of automated (CASE) prototype tools which assist the validation of requirements. What justifies the characterization of such tools as 'expert systems' is the knowledge of some aspect of the requirements engineering process that they embody. This can be either *method knowledge*, i.e. knowledge of how to apply a method for requirements engineering (e.g. structured analysis—see Yourdon, 1989), or *domain knowledge*, i.e. knowledge about the domain which the software system is supposed to model (see Chapter 3). Expert approaches are still at the prototype stage but they are certainly expected to have an impact on the functionality of the next generation of commercial CASE tools.

In general, there are three modes at which an expert system tool can act in the requirements validation process:

- The *expert*. At this mode the tool is expected to carry the validation process on its own.

GIST specification

```
type driver
   subtype of person
type car
   subtype of mobile object
WITH {relation running()
   invariant in-motion()=>
   self: physical-object-location is a location
PROCEDURE start[']
DEFINITION
   atomic {
   insert in-motion().
   update self: physical-object-location to a location
   }.
```

English paraphrase

All cars are mobile objects. All drivers
are people.
Each car can be in the state of running.

Start is a procedure of car.
Start a car simultaneously
(atomically) does the following. It asserts
that the car is in-motion. It updates the
physical-object-location of the car
to any location.

Figure 5.2 An English paraphrase of the car specification.

- The *assistant*. At this mode the tool is asked to assist the analyst validate some aspect of the requirements, i.e. by checking for some specific kind of inconsistency in the model.
- The *apprentice*. At this mode the tool is asked to perform the low-level clerical activities of validation, i.e. keeping track of all the names used in the requirements model, checking for multiple definitions, and so on.

The current generation CASE tools function at the level of the apprentice. However, the next generation of CASE tools is expected to show performance at the level of the *assistant* (see also Chapter 6). Below is a scenario showing a typical interaction between a human analyst and a requirements validation assistant tool.

The following is the scenario for the analysis of the library system introduced in Section 5.5.1. In the session the human analyst text is in normal font, the tool's output is in bold and the comments are in italic.

The analyst has created a first-cut mode of the problem using the entity–relationship analysis method and is asking the Assistant tool to perform certain types of validation:

<ANALYST>: Validate model LIBRARY
<ASSISTANT>: **Select one of the following types of validation:**
Syntactic validation
Consistency with domain knowledge
<ANALYST>: Syntactic validation
<ASSISTANT>: **I notice that the cardinality of relationship BORROWS**
from STUDENT to BOOK has not been defined. You can
do one of the following:
Define the cardinality of the relationship
Consult KB 'libraries' for typical cardinality of relationship
BORROWS

At this stage the analyst has the option to supply the missing cardinality or be advised by the library domain knowledge-base on what the cardinality should be like.

< ANALYST > :	Consult KB 'libraries'
< ASSISTANT > :	**The typical cardinality of relationship BORROWS is 0 TO MANY. Action?**
< ANALYST > :	. . .

Some of the typical prototype tools belonging to the category of expert assistants are ASPIS (Pietri *et al.*, 1987) the Requirements Apprentice (Reubenstein and Waters, 1991), KATE (Fickas, 1987), and the Analyst Assist (Loucopoulos and Champion, 1988). All these systems help not only in validating the requirements but also in tasks such as requirements acquisition and formal specification (see also Chapter 6).

5.6 SUMMARY

This chapter tackled the important issue of validating the requirements model. Important ideas discussed in this chapter include the following:

- Validation is a process whose importance cannot be easily dismissed. Errors that pass through the requirements engineering phase to design and coding can have catastrophic consequences on the software system.
- Validation of requirements can only be performed against the user's intention; thus the user's participation in the validation process is paramount.
- Requirements can never be proved correct in a formal manner. They can, however, be checked for qualities such as consistency, minimality, non-redundancy, etc.
- Validation is a time-consuming process that can be greatly assisted by automated tools.
- One of the biggest problems in requirements validation is getting the user to understand the formal models created by the analyst. A number of techniques to overcome this problem are prototyping, simulation/animation, and paraphrasing.
- All the above techniques presuppose the use of suitable modelling languages and environments in which the requirements can come closer to the user's experience through execution, animation, and simulation and thus be more easily validated.
- Expert tools are expected to play a significant part in the near future in validating requirements by drawing upon method and domain knowledge.

REFERENCES

Balzer R., Cheatham T. E. and Green C. (1983) Software technology in the 1990's: using a new paradigm. *IEEE Computer*, November.

Basili V. and Weiss D. (1981) Evaluation of a software requirements document by analysis of change data. In *Fifth IEEE International Conference on Software Engineering*. IEEE Computer Society Press, Washington, DC.

Boehm B. W. (1980) *Software Engineering Economics*. Prentice Hall, Englewood Cliffs, NJ.

Budde R. (Ed.) (1984). *Approaches to Prototyping*. Springer-Verlag, Berlin.

Dubois E. and Hagelstein J. (1987) Reasoning on formal requirements: a lift control system. *Proc. 4th International Workshop on Software Specification and Design.* IEEE, New York.

Fickas S. (1987) Automating the analysis process: an example. In *Proc. 4th International Workshop on Software Specification and Design,* Monterey, CA. IEEE.

IEEE (1983) *Glossary of Software Engineering Terminology,* IEEE Std. 729. IEEE, New York.

Kramer J. and Ng K. (1988) Animation of requirements specification. *SPE (Software Practice and Experience),* **18**(8), 749–774.

Lalioti V. and Loucopoulos P. (1994) Visualisation of conceptual specifications. *Information Systems,* **19**(3), 291–309.

Loucopoulos P. and Champion R. (1988) A knowledge-based approach to requirements engineering using method and domain knowledge. *Journal of Knowledge-based Systems,* June.

Myers J. J. and Johnson W. L. (1988) Toward specification explanation: issues and lessons. *Proc. 3rd Annual Rome Air Development Center Knowledge-Based Software Assistant Conference,* Ithaca, NY.

Pietri F., Puncello P. P., Torrigiani P., Casale G., Innocenti M. D., Ferrari G., Pacini G. and Turini F. (1987) ASPIS: a knowledge-based environment for software development. In *ESPRIT '87: Achievements and Impact.* North Holland, Amsterdam.

Reubenstein H. B. and Waters R. C. (1991) The requirements apprentice: automated assistance for requirements acquisition. *IEEE Transactions on Software Engineering,* **17**(3).

Tsalgatidou A. (1988) Dynamics of information systems modelling and verification. Ph.D. thesis, UMIST, Manchester.

Yourdon E. (1989) *Modern Structured Analysis.* Prentice Hall, Englewood Cliffs, NJ.

CASE TECHNOLOGY

6.1 INTRODUCTION

The overall aim of CASE technology is to improve the productivity and quality of the resulting systems by assisting the developer throughout the different stages of the development process—from the acquisition of the functional and non-functional system requirements to the design and implementation of the system considering all the relevant technical and operational features.

CASE provides the software tools that support methodologies used in modelling all levels of an organization. In this sense it is more appropriate to consider CASE in a wider context than just software production, as has normally been the case. Therefore, CASE may be described as software tools for enterprise support consisting of enterprise strategic planning, information systems strategic planning, project planning, systems development, documentation, and maintenance.

This chapter is organized as follows. Section 6.2 presents the possible advantages of the CASE technology and the need for CASE as part of system development and especially requirements engineering. Section 6.3 provides a classification of CASE technology. Distinctions are made between stand-alone CASE tools and integrated environments. Section 6.4 presents a generic architecture for CASE. Despite the plethora of CASE tools and supported methodologies in use today, the typical CASE architecture is built around the concept of a repository used for storing the various types of models which are created during software development, which are accessed by a number of assorted tools such as editors, diagrammers, etc. The same section therefore specifies the requirements for repository functionality as part of CASE for requirements engineering. Issues to consider when selecting and integrating CASE tools for requirements are discussed in Section 6.5. Finally, Section 6.6 is concerned with the properties and future of research-oriented CASE tools for requirements engineering. Many such tools are based on the principle that utilization of the problem domain and the methodical knowledge stored in the tool can automate (at least to an extent) many of the human labour-intensive tasks of requirements engineering.

In summary, this chapter presents an overview of the role of CASE technology within requirements engineering, keeping the discussion as much as possible free from references to specific tools and technologies. CASE is an indispensable feature of any modern software development approach and will be even more so in the future as its potential applicability within the requirements engineering process increases.

6.2 THE NEED FOR COMPUTER-AIDED SOFTWARE DEVELOPMENT

Requirements engineering is one of the software development phases for which CASE is particularly suitable. This fact was realized in the early days of CASE and it was soon put into practice in the form of research prototypes first and commercial tools soon after. There are, of course, good reasons why CASE is particularly applicable to requirements engineering. Requirements engineering produces vast amounts of information (in both textual and graphical forms). Obviously this information must be managed, captured, stored, retrieved, disseminated, and changed. However, the manual capture, storage, manipulation, etc., of requirements increases the risk of errors creeping into the process and into the final outcome. Such errors can manifest themselves in various forms, i.e. as outdated, inconsistent, or incomplete or erroneous requirements models.

Another serious practical problem with requirements engineering concerns the difficulty of enforcing certain software standards. As it happens, users and software engineers have their individual ways of communication in textual or pictorial form. This, however, can cause serious communications problems in the context of software development. User reports written in a variety of formats and styles can be a nightmare for those responsible for their editing and translation into technical descriptions.

CASE tackles the problems related to software requirements in the following ways:

- By providing automated management of all the requirements-related information.
- By enforcing standards. CASE tools provide standard formats for inputting, retrieving, or changing information. Such standards can be, for example, document formats for textual requirements, diagrammatic notations, etc. The use of a uniform set of standards across the software development team ensures that problems such as inconsistency and misinterpretation are eliminated or greatly reduced.

CASE also affects the speed with which a requirements model is produced and updated. This is important, as requirements engineering has to deal with two contradicting demands, namely to involve the user as little as possible in the process (since users are probably too busy doing other things to participate in software development), and at the same time obtain all the information required from the user, including feedback on the specified requirements. In resolving this conflict, CASE is invaluable since it offers easy communication with the user through graphical models and prototyping. CASE allows the quick construction of graphical models which are easily understood by the user, and can be quickly and easily modified. Prototyping is also valuable in putting the user through life-like interactions with the software system in order to understand the user's true requirements (see also Chapter 5).

Most of the arguments in favour of using CASE in requirements engineering apply equally to the use of systematic methods for requirements engineering. As a matter of fact, CASE started as nothing more than an attempt to automate paper-and-pen software methods, which in turn provided the much-needed standardization of documents and models, procedures for requirements change, etc., to software development. It is a truism, therefore, that CASE and software methodologies have been dependent on each other for their success. Methods require automation in order to be practical; CASE, on the other hand, is of little help unless used in a systematic way within the development process, i.e. within a *method*. In a 'chicken and egg' fashion, therefore, structured methodologies and CASE are responsible for each other's rapid growth in popularity in the 1980's and 1990's.

However, as the state of the art moves beyond the structured approaches and into object-oriented and knowledge-based paradigms, the importance of CASE as the enabling technology for requirements engineering is moving into new areas. Sections 6.4 and 6.6 discuss the new role of CASE as a component of a requirements engineering approach, in both commercial and research-oriented settings.

6.3 CLASSIFICATION OF CASE TECHNOLOGY

Several classifications of CASE exist in the literature. One of the first and most important classified CASE as *language-centred*, built around a programming language; *structure-centred*, based on the idea of environment generation; *toolkit environments*, primarily consisting of tools that supported the programming phase of the development; and *method-based*, centred around a specific methodology for developing software systems.

Another classification (Fuggetta, 1993) is based on a framework consisting of three parts: *tools* that support only specific tasks in systems development, *workbenches* that support one or more activities, and *environments* that support a large part of the software process. According to this classification, tools can be further classified into editing, programming, verification and validation, configuration management, metrics and measurement, and project management tools. Workbenches are classified depending on the activities that they support as business planning and modelling, user interface development, programming, verification and validation, maintenance and reverse engineering, configuration management, and project management workbenches. Finally, environments are classified as either toolkits which are integrated collections of products, language-centred, integrated, fourth-generation environments, or process-centred environments.

6.3.1 UpperCASE and lowerCASE

The most popular classification of CASE technology and tools is based on the distinction made between the early and late stages of systems development. Many of the current CASE tools deal with the management of the system specification only by supporting strategy, planning, and the construction of the conceptual level of the enterprise model. These tools are often termed *upperCASE tools* because they assist the designer only at the early stages of system development and ignore the actual implementation of the system. The emphasis in upperCASE is to describe the mission, objectives, strategies, operational plans, resources, component parts, etc., of the enterprise and provide automated support for defining the logical level of the business, its information needs and designing information systems to meet these needs.

UpperCASE tools support traditional diagrammatic languages like entity relationship diagrams, data flow diagrams, structure charts, etc., providing mainly drawing, storage as well as documentation facilities. They support a limited degree of verification, validation, and integration of the system specifications due to the inherent lack of formal foundations for the requirements modelling formalisms.

Other CASE tools deal with the application development itself with regard to the efficient generation of code. These are termed *lowerCASE tools* because they assist the developer at the stage of system generation and ignore the early stages of system requirements specification. The starting point of the system development with lowerCASE tools is the conceptual model of the information system. The conceptual modelling formalism is usually based on formal foundations in order to allow for automatic mapping to executable specifications and efficient validation and verification of the system specification itself.

LowerCASE tools employ mapping algorithms to automatically transform formal specifications into an executable form. This includes, among others, transformation of specifications to relational database schemas, normalization of database relations and SQL code generation. The majority of these tools facilitate rapid prototyping of specifications in terms of the functionality of the system. They do not support the development process itself, but rather they offer a powerful tool for making system design more effective and efficient.

The state-of-the-art products of the CASE market nowadays claim to provide support for both the early stages as well as the implementation stages of information systems development. Clearly, from a users' perspective, this move towards *integrated CASE (ICASE)* is far more important (Gibson *et al.*, 1989). In this architecture, the repository plays a more active role in that all tools can interface and exchange data with it. A repository holds data fields and definitions and ensures that data integrity is maintained throughout the development lifecycle. As a consequence, ICASE allow tools to work together relatively seamlessly and alleviates much of the stop–start nature of non-ICASE environments.

All the CASE environments mentioned above are often rigid and do not support the users' native methodology or different methodologies. To avoid this, more flexible and customizable tools, called *CASE shells*, are emerging. These allow customization of the CASE shell to a given methodology. Users are able to describe their methodology, either through a set of meta-modelling editors or through a set of formal languages, and tailor it to their specific requirements in order to create dedicated CASE tools. Many of the products and research prototypes of CASE shells move towards the support of different methodologies during the development of a single information system.

6.3.2 Integrated software development environments

Central to the issue of CASE integration is the concept of an integrated software development environment (*ISDE*). ISDE, as the term implies, provides support for the coordination of all the different activities that take place during a software project. There are different types of support that an ISDE can provide. Typical examples of ISDE support include the following:

- Automated coordination of development activities. For example, mechanisms may be provided which trigger the design activity at the end of the specification activity.
- Mechanisms for inter-activity communication. This means that data produced, for example, by a specification tool can be filtered and subsequently transmitted to the design tool, to the project planning tool, etc.

A major approach towards ISDEs is the European (Portable Common Tool Environment (*PCTE*) (Boudier *et al.*, 1988). The PCTE approach is similar to the idea of a modern operating system such as Unix which offers a set of standard facilities such as text formatters, filters, process communications, etc., which can provide the building blocks for creating sophisticated applications. Analogously, PCTE provides common building blocks to the developers of CASE tools which will run under PCTE. In turn, this can facilitate compatibility between the tools since they all use common facilities for storing and communicating their data.

6.4 A GENERIC CASE ARCHITECTURE

6.4.1 Overview

Central to any CASE architecture is the concept of the *data dictionary* or *repository* (Bruce *et al.*, 1989; Burkhard, 1989; Martin, 1989b). The role of the repository is to store all the logical and physical objects whose task is to provide control and integration in the development and maintenance of information systems. Essentially, the repository is the single point of definition in the software lifecycle. In this role, the repository holds the meta-data (data about data) which not only defines what and where the data is, but how it relates to other data and how the logical manipulation of data is mapped across physical structures like databases, file systems, and, ultimately, physical objects such as networks and CPUs (McClure, 1988; Martin, 1989a). In terms of the development lifecycle, this means that any program or flowchart which is used in the building of an application and any tools which are employed in its construction must receive and enter data to and from the repository.

The repository provides true integration of specifications from the different tools because it permits the sharing of specifications rather than converting and passing them between tools. CASE tools connect directly with the repository for specification storage and retrieval. The repository uses these specifications to drive an application generator and to generate operating systems commands, database calls, communication commands, and user documentation.

A generic architecture for CASE tools is shown in Fig. 6.1. According to the architecture of Fig. 6.1, a CASE tool consists of the following major components:

The repository This is usually a database or file system in which all the information about the current status of the development process is held. Depending on the particular phase of software development (i.e. analysis, design, testing, etc.) different types of data are

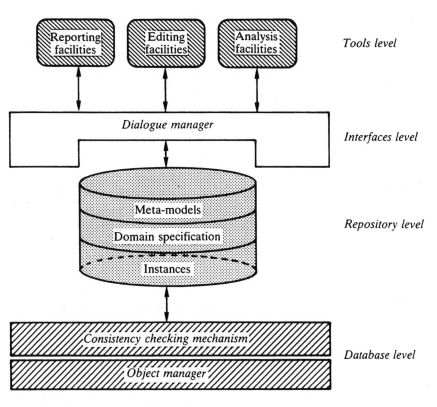

Figure 6.1 Architecture of a CASE tool.

recorded (diagrams, text, test data, etc.) in a CASE repository. Note that a repository is frequently shared among different CASE tools. When all the tools are used within the same development phase (e.g. analysis) the repository must be capable of maintaining data about the individual projects that go on concurrently as well as about their intercommunication requirements. A repository that holds data from different development phases (analysis, design, etc.) must make them accessible from all tools which require them (i.e. analysis data must be accessible by the design tools, design data by the program generation tool, etc.).

The assistant modules These can be considered as tools in their own right, responsible for performing some task within the particular development phase either in an entirely automatic fashion, or by assisting the user of the tool. In the requirements phase, assistant tools can, for example, automatically produce drawings (graphical models) from textual descriptions, check for consistency and completeness of the requirements models, and propagate the changes in some of the models to the rest of the models (e.g. redrawing the corresponding graphical models when the user changes some textual descriptions). In the following sections we will distinguish between assistant modules, which are responsible for the most mundane/clerical tasks (such as screen drawing), and the ones which are capable of completely or in part undertaking intelligent tasks such as model validation, consistency maintenance, etc.

The human–computer interface (HCI) component This component is responsible for handling the tool's communication with the user. The HCIs for CASE tools follow the general trends in user interface technology. There has been therefore a continuous evolution in the HCI technology employed by CASE tools from the early teletype style of interaction to the latest types of interaction using graphical user interfaces (GUIs) in multitasking environments.

The communications component The communications component is responsible for exchanging data with other CASE tools. This usually implies that the communications component receives data about the software project which was created in a previous development phase and transmits data for use by tools in subsequent development phases. Effective communication between CASE tools is a problem still to be solved in a satisfactory manner for a variety of reasons. The lack of widely acceptable standards between the CASE tool developers has resulted in a plethora of proprietary and often mutually incompatible formats used by the tools for the internal storage of development information.

6.4.2 Architecture and functionality of a repository for requirements engineering

The task of a repository is to help manage requirements engineering data by offering a variety of services that promote data sharing, data integrity, and convenient access. The repository can perform the following tasks:

- Help users logically associate the various products of the process (documentation, formal specifications, etc.).
- Keep track of users' annotations which contain explanations and assumptions.
- Manage different versions of requirements, and the associated documentation.
- Control different views of the system under development.
- Help the managerial side of a team development (e.g. estimate required development effort).
- Maintain historical data about the decisions taken through the process of eliciting, specifying requirements.

A CASE environment places specific demands on the repository technology used, especially in the case of large-scale team projects. It must support simultaneous access by team members, editing, and authorship in a computer network. Different versions of requirements must coexist, where team members work independently and then merge their specifications back into the main project. Analysts must be allowed to build specific configurations and version trees, and subsequently merge versions together. In summary, a CASE repository supporting requirements engineering must exhibit functionality in terms of the following:

Complex information modelling A repository for requirements engineering must be able to store large variable-length objects, such as documents and graphical specification models.

Integrity constraints and triggers Due to the size and complexity of the requirements models, the maintenance of data consistency should be performed by enforcing constraints as the data evolves over time.

Transaction management Advanced transaction management features for collaborative requirements engineering must be provided. The classical notion of serializability of a transaction is no longer adequate, as it significantly reduces concurrency and is largely unsuitable for requirements engineering environments at large.

Specification updates The process of requirements engineering is incremental by nature. It is therefore compulsory to provide the means for changing and updating freely the structure of a preliminary requirements model as modelled by the schema of the repository.

Data sharing One of the key issues in collaborative requirements engineering is the sharing of data between various analysts. As in client–server architectures, requirements data may be partitioned based on various criteria. However, data must be accessible by all.

Distribution and co-operative work Effective communication protocols between analysts are essential, since they are often unaware of each other's developments. This sometimes results in lack of co-ordination, reduced parallelism, a considerable waste of time and resources, and faulty specifications due to misinterpretations of data. Mechanisms to support the distribution of tools such as distribution of the repository itself or at least distributed access to a repository residing on a database server are needed. In the same spirit, tools for handling and controlling the distribution must also be provided.

Concurrency The repository should offer the same services as current database systems with respect to the handling of multiple users.

Recovery In case of hardware or software failures, the system should recover, i.e. bring itself back to some coherent state of the data.

6.4.3 Features of CASE technology

This section discusses the properties of contemporary CASE tools used in the requirements engineering phase. The common characteristic of all such tools is that they are built in order to automate aspects of software methodologies. Most of these methodologies existed before the introduction of CASE, albeit in a manual form. The origin of such methodologies is the paradigm of structured development which was initially applied to programming and subsequently to the design and analysis phases (Jackson, 1983; Yourdon, 1989). Structured methodologies are based on the principle of 'divide and conquer', i.e. on the stepwise decomposition of data and functional elements of a system to their parts. This approach ensures the efficient dealing of tasks of arbitrary size since the original task is progressively decomposed into smaller and easier to deal with sub-tasks. One serious drawback of the structured methodologies (especially when practised without tool support) is that they are usually cumbersome to apply, mainly because of the large amounts of information (documents, drawing, etc.) they generate. The most important task of a CASE tool which supports a structured methodology, therefore, is to provide automated functions for the storage and manipulation of the information generated during software development.

The major application of CASE tools developed in the 1970s and early 1980s, therefore, was to assist in the collection and manipulation of the voluminous information generated by structured methodologies. The progress in the ability of CASE tools to store and manipulate project information closely followed the progress in areas such as hardware (processor and graphics technologies), databases, and computer communications.

Early CASE tools for requirements engineering support were handling requirements specifications, either as free text (in which case they were little more than word processors) or in a stylized form which allowed for some limited automatic processing of the requirements. Such automatic processing of requirements specifications usually included checking for *inconsistencies* (e.g. terms with multiple definitions) and *incompleteness* (i.e. terms which are used but not defined).

Advances in hardware technology such as high-resolution graphics screens made possible the development of tools capable of manipulating graphical requirements models. The ability to manipulate graphical definitions has given an important boost to the acceptability of CASE technology since the structured methodologies which the early CASE tools support rely heavily on the use of graphical requirements models. Even in today's CASE the ability to draw and manipulate graphical specifications models on the screen remains the most heavily used and essential feature.

Technological progress, together with a more mature understanding of the requirements engineering (and more generally of the software development) process, guided the incorporation of additional functionality into CASE technology. Today's requirements engineering tools utilize the latest advances in processing, graphical user interfaces, database, and communications facilities in order to provide effective support for the most fundamental activities of requirements engineering. While proprietary tools differ on a number of issues such as the methodology they support, whether they are stand-alone or parts of an integrated environment, etc., they nevertheless share a number of features such as the following:

Facilities for prototyping The importance of prototyping in activities such as requirements acquisition and validation is now generally accepted. The increased use of prototyping as an important technique within requirements engineering persuaded CASE developers to incorporating facilities for prototyping in their tools. Basic prototyping facilities usually encountered in CASE tools include report generation and screen painting. More advanced prototyping facilities include animation and symbolic execution of the requirements models. Also limited code generation (which allows for a crude program to be quickly generated from the specifications) is a facility offered by the more sophisticated tools.

Facilities for data management While the early CASE tools used simple file structures for storing the requirements models, contemporary ones utilize database technology in order to offer facilities such as concurrent access to the data by many developers, version control, etc.

Inter-tool communications facilities As the relationship between requirements engineering and other development phases becomes better understood, so does the ability of the requirements CASE tool to communicate with other CASE tools responsible for tasks such as project planning, configuration control, design, etc.

Graphical user interface This allows the representation of requirements models using the graphical notations used by the methodology which the tool supports. Usually the tool proves the facility for dynamic redrawing of the model on the screen, each time the user changes some part of it. This facility significantly reduces the time it would take manually to redraw the model from scratch.

Data administration Managing the data generated during requirements engineering entails tasks such as keeping lists of the various types of data, enforcing standards (e.g. that the names of the various concepts follow certain naming conventions), and checking for inconsistencies and omissions (e.g. duplicate names).

Utilities for requirements animation and prototyping Such utilities may include screen painters, program generators, etc., which support the requirements validation process (Chapter 5).

Data communication facilities This includes facilities for importing and exporting data to and from other tools. A requirements engineering tool usually exports data to design tools and to project planning tools which use such data to produce information about the current progress with the project and to plan ahead.

6.5 SELECTING, INTEGRATING, AND USING CASE TOOLS FOR REQUIREMENTS ENGINEERING

6.5.1 Desired features of requirements engineering CASE

Modern CASE technology integrates the different categories of CASE that were mentioned before into the concept of an *integrated software development environment* (ISDE). Very often, therefore, the prospective buyer/user of CASE has these days to choose between different ISDE options rather than the stand-alone CASE which is gradually becoming a rarity. Assuming that the dilemma of choosing between the ISDE and the stand-alone option is circumvented, a number of technical and organizational issues that must be considered in the CASE selection process arise:

Support for specific formalisms and methodologies The vast majority of commercial CASE support only one or two of the mainstream software methodologies—Structure Analysis (Yourdon, 1989), Jackson System Development (Jackson, 1983), Structured Systems Analysis and Design Method (SSADM) (NCC, 1990), Information Engineering (Macdonald, 1986), etc. Usually, there is little flexibility for customization of the models used by the tool to suit the individual user's need. One exception, to this is the class of generic or Meta-CASE (Alderson, 1993) tools which allow the customization of existing models or even the creation of entirely new ones to support methods developed in-house.

Support for specific types of applications Although most CASE tools can be used with varying degrees of success for any type of application (e.g. data intensive, real time, process control, expert system), some formalisms and methods better accommodate the needs of specific application types. It is essential therefore that, for example, CASE used for real-time applications should provide support for formalisms such as StateCharts, Petri Nets, etc., while data-intensive CASE should be able to handle the entity-relationship model or some of its variants.

Repository capabilities The majority of modern CASE tools provide repository facilities similar to those discussed in Section 6.4. It is important, however, that a checklist is drawn up by the prospective user which includes the following capabilities: full integration of data in the repository, database facilities, project management information, shareability of data among developers, automatic report generation and support for *ad hoc* querying, import/export capabilities to other repositories, automatic analysis and control of changes in the data.

In the majority of real-life software projects, even the most sophisticated CASE or ISDE tool on its own will fail to meet completely the demands of the requirements phase. One possible way to overcome this is by acquiring and using a set of different CASE with complimentary abilities, e.g. a diagramming tool combined with a prototyping tool and an executable formal specification language. An obvious problem in this approach is cost, since three times as many tools (compared with the one-tool option) will have to be purchased. Even if cost is not an obstacle, communication between the tools is also a potential source of difficulty. In many cases, special software (called *bridges*) will have to be written to allow the transfer of data between tools. Hopefully, this situation will gradually become a rarity as we move towards standard environments and repositories for CASE.

6.5.2 Integrating CASE tools

Integration and communication can be aimed at three levels. The first level is that of *tool integration*. An example approach for tool integration is presented in Fig. 6.2. The tools themselves are responsible for data structuring and control activities; in this way co-operation between tools is achieved through passing of streams of bytes. The advantage of this approach is that tools can be developed almost independently, and generic file transfer utilities can be used for the communication between tools. There are, however, many disadvantages with this approach such as difficulty in expansion, duplication of role and effort in tools, manual co-operation between tools rather than assistance in a team effort, and loss of relationships between design data.

The second level is that of *data integration*. A set of data structures is agreed by all tools within an environment. A meta-schema is agreed upon by all tools before any development of these tools commences. Any future expansion will need to conform to this meta-schema. The advantage of this approach is that most of the actions necessary for analysing, validating, and converting data structures are no longer required within each tool. The disadvantage is that the way that the tools are used is not constrained or guided in any way. This can only be achieved by agreeing not only on the data structures but also

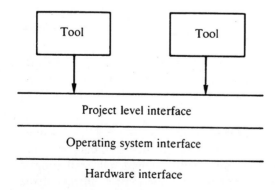

Project level interface

Operating system interface

Hardware interface

Figure 6.2 Tool integration.

on the *process* within which the tools will be used. The interest lies only in the management of information as a consistent whole and not how parts of the information are transformed or operated upon.

The third level is that of *method integration*. A set of data structures and the process model are agreed by all tools, which then interact effectively in support of a defined process.

Data integration and method integration imply that the tools communicate by interacting at a level of abstraction higher than the operating system, i.e. there is a project level interface which provides facilities and services for controlling the requirements specification process.

6.6 RESEARCH CASE FOR REQUIREMENTS ENGINEERING

6.6.1 Introduction

In contrast to commercial CASE, research tools for requirements engineering do not fall easily into predefined categories. Generally, CASE research prototypes do not attempt to provide complete or integrated support to the tasks of requirements engineering, focusing instead on specific problems such as acquisition, specification, validation, etc. Such tools have already been discussed in Chapters 3 and 6.

Research prototypes are usually concerned with proving the validity, feasibility, or applicability of a certain paradigm for practising requirements engineering. A paradigm, in general, is a specific way of doing things (solving problems) and as such it cannot easily be proved true or false. Research paradigms for requirements engineering often materialize as 'tools' or 'environments' which are exclusively used in controlled experiments rather than real-life applications. Eventually, some of the research ideas find their way to real life practice by being incorporated in commercial tools and methodologies.

In recent years, the paradigm that has received the most attention in requirements engineering research has been *knowledge-based requirements engineering*. The rationale behind viewing requirements engineering as a knowledge-based process has been discussed on many different occasions in previous chapters of this book. Viewing requirements engineering as a process which relies to a large extent on the availability of knowledge of various sorts, invokes a number of research issues:

- What types of knowledge are used in requirements engineering?
- How can such knowledge be formalized and represented within computers?
- How can the availability of this knowledge improve and sometimes automate the practising of requirements engineering?

Research addressing the above questions has produced tools which can represent and store knowledge about the domain the software application belongs to (*domain knowledge*). This knowledge is used for purposes such as completing and validating the requirements model. Reusable requirements knowledge speeds up the overall process (since less interaction with the users is required) and also improves the quality of the requirements model. Problems that still have to be overcome in this approach are related to the difficulty of identifying suitable sources of reusable requirements knowledge and the cost of eliciting and formalizing reusable requirements models.

Another source of knowledge which some research tools are based upon is method knowledge. It is fairly easy to automate the steps of a requirements method defined in an algorithmic way, which has well-defined inputs and outputs. Structured methodologies fall into this category, i.e. some of their steps and deliverables can be applied mechanistically and are therefore suitable candidates for automation. Unfortunately, this cannot be said for the more unstructured processes such as elicitation and validation. Tools which attempt to (even partially) automate such processes, therefore, are equipped with knowledge and methods of reasoning which mimics human knowledge and reasoning. Such tools are frequently called *intelligent requirements assistants* (Anderson and Fickas, 1989; Reubenstein and Waters, 1991). Again, before such tools can become commercially viable, a number of important issues related to their ability to stand up to real-life software systems requirements must be resolved. Figure 6.3 shows a generic architecture for an 'intelligent' requirements engineering CASE tool.

6.6.2 Intelligent CASE in requirements analysis and specification

In general, these tools can be distinguished along two dimensions. The first dimension is concerned with tools supporting *building of the specification*, whereas the second dimension is concerned with those supporting the *management of the specification and the building of the application out of a given system specification*.

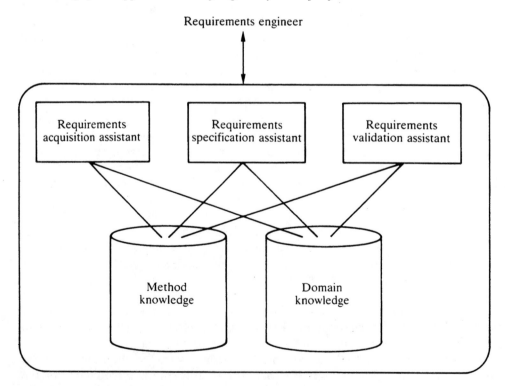

Figure 6.3 Architecture of an 'intelligent' requirements engineering tool.

The requirements for the next generation methods and CASE environments that are discussed in this section revolve around the activities of requirements capture and analysis, validation, and management of the captured knowledge. These issues give rise to two lines of investigation regarding the requirements for the next generation of development methods and CASE environments:

- Improved tools and techniques for assisting the process of deriving a conceptual specification of an enterprise.
- Improved tools and techniques for managing a conceptual specification and the building of the application out of a given system specification once such a specification has been developed.

These requirements give rise to a number of research issues discussed in the following sections that aim at providing intelligent support facilities during the process of conceptual specification design, conceptual specification management, and the generation of the application itself.

6.6.3 CASE for conceptual specification design

During the last decade, an intensive effort has been made by the industrial community as well as the research community to develop conceptual modelling formalisms that allow one to describe information systems (IS) in high-level terms, the so-called conceptual schema, and to reason about this description. However, little effort has been paid to model the process by which one can obtain a conceptual schema of a planned information system. In other words, there exists a plethora of formalisms for the representation of the requirements engineering product, whereas the number of techniques which deal with the requirements engineering process is very small (see also Chapter 2). As a consequence, CASE tools only concentrate on supporting the *population* of the repository in that they assist the requirements engineer to (i) enter the requirements engineering product in a diagrammatic form, (ii) store its contents in a repository, and (iii) document it. They do not help the requirements engineer in *constructing* the requirements product itself by supporting the transition process from an informal requirements description to a formal information system specification.

The upperCASE strand of research is strongly influenced by the application of artificial intelligence (AI) techniques. The purpose of applying AI techniques is better to understand and consequently, formalize the conceptualization process. In contrast with the lower-CASE approach, emphasis is placed on the way that requirements are acquired and the way that these are transformed to populate the conceptual schema of the business and the information system.

The system development process is characterized as non-deterministic because of the difficulties in identifying the limits of the problem area, the scope, and the goals of the information system and the approach to conceptual schema definition. However, from a management point of view, developers wish to control the development process through the use of formal techniques and experimental knowledge.

Taking these two dimensions of the information system development process into account, it is clear that its automation cannot be based solely, on a pure algorithmic solution. This has been recognized by some researchers who developed CASE prototype toolsets based on an expert system approach (SECSI: Bouzeghoub, 1985; OICSI: Rolland and Proix, 1986; Cauvet *et al.*, 1988). In such an approach, both experimental and formal knowledge are represented in the knowledge base, whereas the application domain knowledge is stored within the fact base. The development process is viewed as a knowledge-based process which, progressively, through the application of the knowledge base rules to elements of the fact base, transforms the initial requirements into the final information system conceptual schema.

Some approaches to process modelling attempt to employ meta-modelling formalisms and toolsets to represent explicitly the knowledge about the development method as well as the development product. The SOCRATES project (Wijers *et al.*, 1991) follows this approach in that it aims at offering automated support of the information-modelling processes by representing and manipulating the experienced practitioners' information-modelling knowledge. This approach advocates a model-independent architecture where the designer will be able to describe his or her method and the underlying modelling process using a number of formal languages.

Other approaches attempt to acquire automatically the knowledge used in the analysis process. Whereas in most of the approaches the development process knowledge is provided by human experts, here it is deduced using automatic learning techniques. For instance, the INTRES tool (Pernici *et al.*, 1989) uses explanation-based generalization for specifying static properties of elements of well-understood applications, based on examples of documents. In Mannino and Tseng (1988) the approach is based on the strategy of learning from examples employed in a form definition system. The tool automatically induces the form properties and some functional dependencies. This work has been extended further in Talldal and Wangler (1990) where the learning algorithms are optimized and the induced conceptual schema is expressed in an extended engineering requirements formalism.

6.7 SUMMARY

This chapter has been concerned with computer-aided software engineering technology as applied to the requirements engineering phase. The last two decades have witnessed a changing role of CASE in requirements engineering from simple clerical task handling to automating essential activities such as formal specification and validation.

Today's state-of-the-art CASE tool acts as an editor and repository for the various models created during requirements engineering (discussed in Chapter 4) as well as an interface between requirements engineering and other software development phases. CASE technology particularly suits those requirements engineering methodologies which rely on graphical models, mainly because such models can be quickly drawn, manipulated, and communicated (using techniques such as prototyping, animation, etc.) to the users.

The application of CASE technology to requirements engineering has been less effective when dealing with 'harder' problems such as requirements elicitation and formal validation. However, research into intelligent CASE has attempted to overcome the limitations of today's tools by utilizing expert system technology as well as our improved understanding of the processes involved in requirements engineering.

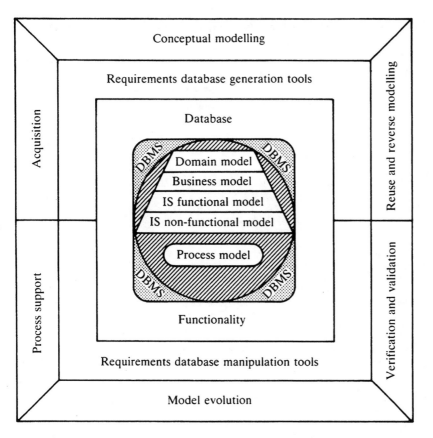

Figure 6.4 An architecture for the next generation of CASE tools.

An architecture for a requirements engineering CASE tool of the future is presented in Fig. 6.4. Such a tool will be capable of performing tasks which are currently the responsibility of the human engineer. These will include the following:

- Automatically completing the requirements model by utilizing pre-existing reusable requirements knowledge.
- Advising and supporting the human requirements engineer using domain and method-dependent knowledge and rules.
- Validating the requirements model using techniques such as natural language paraphrasing, symbolic execution, etc.
- Generating test cases directly from the requirements.

Such tools might be expected to lead to the CASE environments of the future that will support a very wide range of (if not almost all) stages in systems development with special attention paid to the specification of requirements. A CASE environment will then deal with the following functionality at the requirements engineering level:

- *Editing*—inserting new information in the corporate knowledge base.
- *Browsing*—viewing objects and sets of objects at various levels of detail.

- *Querying*—editing and executing queries pertaining to the stored corporate knowledge base.
- *Reporting facilities*—the reporting facilities range from simple access to data to more elaborated results used in decision support activities.
- *Analysis facilities*—analysis facilities will include scenario building and evaluation using different approaches including visualization techniques.

REFERENCES

Alderson A. (1993) *Meta-CASE Technology*. IPSYS Software, Macclesfield, UK.

Anderson J. and Fickas S. A. (1989) Proposed perspective shift: viewing specification design as a planning problem. In *Proc. 5th International Workshop on Software Specification and Design*, IEEE. Pittsburgh, PA.

Boudier G., Gallo F., Minot R. and Thomas M. J. (1988) An overview of PCTE and PCTE +. In *Proc. 3rd ACM Symposium on Software Development Environments*.

Bouzeghoub M., Gardarin G. and Metais E. (1985) Database design tool: an expert system approach. *Proc. 11th VLDB Conference*, Stockolm.

Bruce T. A., Fuller J. and Moriarty T. (1989) So you want a repository. *Database Programming and Design*, May.

Burkhard D. L. (1989) Implementing CASE tools. *Journal of Systems Management*, March.

Cauvet C., Rolland C. and Proix C. (1988) Information systems design: an expert system approach. In *Proc. International Conference on Extending Database Technology*, Venice.

Fuggetta A. (1993) A classification of CASE technology, *IEEE Computer*, **26**(12), 25–38.

Gibson M. L., Snyder C. A. and Carr H. H. (1989) *CASE:* clarifying common misconceptions. *Journal of Information Systems Management*, **7**(3).

Jackson M. A. (1983) *System Development*. Prentice Hall, Englewood Cliffs, NJ.

Macdonald I. G. (1986) Information engineering: an improved, automated methodology for the design of data sharing systems. In Olle, T. W *et al.* (Eds) *Information Systems Design Methodologies: Improving the Practice*. North-Holland, Amsterdam.

Mannino M. V. and Tseng V. P. (1988) Inferring database requirements from examples in forms. *Seventh International Conference on Entity–Relationship Approach*. Rome, Italy, pp. 1–25.

Martin J. (1989a) *Information Engineering*, Vol. 1. Prentice Hall, Englewood Cliffs, NJ.

Martin J. (1989b) I-CASE encyclopedia brings consistency to IS. *PC Week*, January.

McClure C. (1988) *CASE is Software Automation*. Prentice Hall, Englewood Cliffs, NJ.

NCC (1990) *SSADM Version 4 Manual*. National Computing Centre, Manchester.

Pernici B., Vaccari G. and Villa R. (1989) INTRES: INTelligent REquirements Specification. *Proc. IJCAI'89 Workshop on Automatic Software Design*, Detroit.

Reubenstein H. B. and Waters R. C. (1991) The requirements apprentice: automated assistance for requirements acquisition. *IEEE Transactions on Software Engineering*, **17**(3).

Rolland C. and Proix C. (1986) An expert system approach to information system design. In *IFIP World Congress '86*, Dublin.

Talldal B. and Wangler B. (1990) Extracting a conceptual model from examples of filled in forms. In Prakash N. (Ed.) *Proc. International Conference COMAD*. New Delhi, pp. 327–350.

Wijers G. M., der Hofstede A. H. M. and van Oosterom N. E. (1991) Representation of information modelling knowledge. *Proc. 2nd Workshop on the Next Generation of CASE Tools*, Trondheim.

Yourdon E. (1989) *Modern Structured Analysis*. Prentice Hall, Englewood Cliffs, NJ.

INDEX